READING

RESOURCE

BOOK

Particular contributors to the *Reading: Resource Book* include:
- Diana Rees, Education Department of Western Australia
- Glenda Raison, Education Department of Western Australia
- Dr Bruce Shortland-Jones, Curtin University
- Caroline Barratt-Pugh, Edith Cowan University
- Anna Sinclair, Education Department of Western Australia
- Alison Dewsbury, Education Department of Western Australia
- Sue Lambert, Catholic Education Office of Western Australia

First Steps was developed by the Education Department of Western Australia under the direction of Alison Dewsbury.

HEINEMANN
Portsmouth, NH

Heinemann
A Division of Reed Elsevier Inc.
361 Hanover Street
Portsmouth, NH 03801-3912

Offices and agents throughout the world

First published 1994 by
Addison Wesley Longman Australia
on behalf of the Education Department of Western Australia

Library of Congress Cataloging-in-Publication Data
CIP is on file with the Library of Congress.
ISBN 0-435-07255-2

Printed in the United States of America on acid-free paper
02   RRD   7 8 9

Contents

Chapter 6: Supporting Diversity Through Reading, Writing and Spelling (recognising the importance of home language and supporting English as a second language)

Chapter 1:

First Steps Reading in the Classroom

Introduction

The foundations of literacy are laid in the years before children come to school. Teachers, therefore, plan programs that build on children's existing knowledge and extend the natural learning process. Children come to school having learned to talk. Some can read and write a little. It is up to teachers to provide contexts for learning that will enable children to develop control over written language and enjoy using it, so that they can interact effectively in a literate society. It is crucial that children are encouraged and allowed to be critical thinkers who can 'read between the lines' and make independent judgements which they can defend. They need opportunities to construct meaning from a range of viewpoints. A successful language program is one in which reading, writing, speaking and listening are integrated in a supportive and stimulating environment in which independent and reflective critical thinking is fostered.

To help children learn, teachers need to plan programs to ensure that:

- P • Learners are encouraged to use a wide range of strategies to solve a problem (Problem Solving)
- E • Problems/challenges are set in a context that makes sense to the learner (Embeddedness)
- W • Students are not asked to do too many things at once (Working Memory)
- I • Students are provided with new opportunities to *interact* and use the new information
- T • There is sufficient *time* to practise the new skills/understandings as well as time to come to terms with the new information

The First Steps *Reading: Resource Book* complements the *Reading: Developmental Continuum* and aims to provide teachers with additional ideas for teaching students about reading. Many of the ideas suggested can be modified for use with children at different developmental phases.

Throughout this book there is a strong emphasis on the integration of spoken and written language, the need to encourage students to take control of their reading, the need for students to reflect on their reading and to use and be aware of strategies for reading.

The Role of the Teacher

There are many things teachers can do to help children construct meaning from text.

Read to Children Every Day

It is essential that teachers read to children every day. Exposure to a variety of fiction and non-fiction material will enable children to hear the rhythm of written language and build understanding of nuances of meaning. Reading to children can also assist their comprehension process by raising certain expectations of print and enabling them to see that reading is pleasurable and rewarding.

During reading sessions, teachers can model the strategies they wish children to use by talking about what is happening as they read, e.g. making, confirming or changing predictions; re-reading if meaning is unclear or using context to try and work out a difficult word. Teachers can also share with children times when they challenge a text, identifying stereotypes and exposing authorial bias. This helps children to see what efficient readers do.

Teachers:

- provide a good model for oral reading
- foster a love of reading
- model how they comprehend by thinking aloud about text
- demonstrate how to construct questions and find answers from text
- use oral cloze so that children see that they can predict words that make sense even if they don't choose the author's words
- encourage open and forthright discussion, relating what has been read to the life experiences of the reader and demonstrating that readers may construct meaning in different ways

Reading to children should be seen as a worthwhile activity, a shared pleasure and a springboard for creative and critical thinking.

Create a Supportive Language Environment

Children's attitudes to reading largely depend on what has happened to them during previous reading encounters and on the attitude to reading of important people in their lives.

Teachers:

- convey a positive attitude to children's learning and expect that all children will read
- provide an environment in which children are encouraged to take risks as they endeavour to make meaning from print. They see comprehension as an active process of predicting and verifying, or changing predictions to make meaning not as a 'right or wrong' exercise
- ensure that children have the opportunity to work collaboratively in different groups and are not always placed with children of like ability. This gives children the opportunity to share and compare interpretations of text and to see how others construct meaning
- are careful not to impose their own perspectives on readers, so that children are free to contribute their own constructs, offering insights from a range of socio-cultural perspectives

- encourage discussion so that children are given the opportunity to compare and justify their views and refine or clarify understandings about text
- plan language events to give children experiences (from books or life) so that they can build general knowledge and use their knowledge to interpret new reading material
- value time each day for all readers to read materials of their own choice
- provide a physical environment that is conducive to reading, i.e. variety of reading material, comfortable reading areas, tape recorders, organised routines for using equipment and storage areas for books being read

Readers should be engaged in the process of reading in a supportive environment.

Make Available Quality Reading Materials

Reading material can assist or impede children's comprehension.

Texts that assist the comprehension process of early readers are written in fluent natural language, are structured according to the conventions of a form of text and are of interest to children.

Texts that lack fluency, are poorly structured or are about topics that are of little interest or relevance to children will deprive the readers of some elements that help them construct meaning.

Reading material can affect comprehension positively or negatively.

Teachers of early readers:
- provide a range of fiction and non-fiction reading material, including topical and well structured informational texts
- make use of books that feature rhyme, rhythm, repetition and predictable language patterns to build children's confidence in their ability to read
- make available books in which the illustrations enhance and support the text
- allow children freedom to choose which books to read, providing guidance if required
- provide interesting stories written in fluent natural language, involving believable characters in well structured plots

If comprehension is all about thinking while reading, then reading material must make sense. In the past, books used to 'teach' reading often had controlled phonic-based words strung together in a series of meaningless phrases. These books encouraged children to 'bark at the print' but precluded the use of their background knowledge of life and language structure to help comprehension.

Clarify the Purpose Of, and For, Reading

Children learn how language works when they are able to use it for purposes that are clear to them. They need to know that the purpose of reading is to make meaning. Some children believe that 'getting words right' is the sole purpose of reading. These children are unlikely to be effective readers.

Teachers:
- share their own reading experiences with children
- talk with children about why we read
- allow children time to read for their own purposes

- make sure that children see the relevance of teacher-defined purposes for reading
- help children select appropriate reading strategies depending on the purpose for reading, e.g. skimming for a general impression or scanning to find specific detail

Children need to understand what they are reading and why they are reading.

Classroom Organisation

To ensure that the needs of all children are met, teachers build into their program times when they work with the whole class and times when they work with small groups and individuals.

There is no *one* organisational model that will meet the needs of all teachers and groups of children. It is therefore important for teachers to examine different suggestions for organising groups during the language program, and then through trial and error develop an organisational structure that meets their particular needs.

Grouping Children

It is important that grouping is flexible and that all children are exposed to different language models, interests of other children and varied social situations.

Special focus grouping occurs when the teacher recognises a group of children with a common need, whether for reinforcement, consolidation or enrichment.

Social grouping occurs on the basis of (a) children's choice, stemming from the desire to work together; or (b) the teacher's choice, which usually arises out of the wish that certain children team up or cooperate on the basis of work habits or behaviour.

Interest grouping arises from a common interest expressed by a group of children.

Selecting Strategies and Activities

To ensure that group work is effective, it is important that the teacher is able to work with one small group without being interrupted and that the remaining children are able to work independently.

The activity or activities given to the children who are not working with the teacher should be carefully planned and cater for their levels of skill development. The *Reading: Developmental Continuum* identifies appropriate strategies for different phases of development. The children need to be clear about the purpose of the activity and the expected outcome. They also need to know that they will be praised for working independently and cooperatively while the teacher is busy helping another group.

Whole-class Reading Experiences

Content area reading
Read and retell
Language experience
Shared Book experience
Modelling reading to children

Small-group Reading Experiences

Read and retell
Supported reading
Guided instructional reading
Request procedure (QAR)

Individualised Reading

Interest reading
Supported reading
DEAR (Drop Everything and Read)
USSR (Uninterrupted Sustained Silent Reading)

Suggested Organisational Structures

Example 1

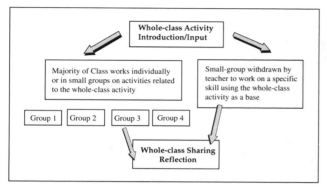

Belanger. C. *The T-Shirt Song*, Rigby Education, 1988

Whole-class Experience

Step 1 Introduce the big book *The T-Shirt Song* (Belanger 1988, Rigby Education) to the class. Children are asked to look at the cover and make predictions. Some of the children's predictions are recorded on the chalkboard. Children identify the author, the illustrator, Sing-a-long logo, title page information.

Step 2 Play the tape and turn the pages so the children can follow the text.

Step 3 Return to the children's predictions and encourage them to discuss these, confirming or rejecting their original ideas.

Step 4 Play the tape a number of times, setting a purpose for listening and encouraging the children to sing along.

Step 5 Set a task for the whole class; for example:
    (a) Children can search for rhyming words and record these.
    (b) Children write slogans for some new T-shirts they are designing.
    (c) Individual reading.

Small-group Experience

Step 6 Teacher works with a small group of children experiencing difficulty with some aspects of reading. See boxed text at top of page 8.

Step 7 Special-focus group returns to seats and goes on with the set class activity.

Individualised Experience

Step 8 Teacher works with individuals in the class.

(a) Focus the children's attention on the lines of print. Frame the following:

I have a T-shirt, I have a T-shirt.
And I love it so
I wear my T-shirt, I wear my T-shirt
Everywhere I go.

(b) • Provide practice in recognising lines of print; for example: Say the line aloud – then ask – 'what does this line say?' Repeat for each line.
  • Provide practice in identifying lines from the text; for example: With the same sentences as above, ask ... What does it say? Children identify the lines.
  • Write these lines onto cards:
    - do lots of oral activities to recognise/identify the lines of print
    - sequence the lines
    - read and draw
    - read, sequence the lines, draw – share

• Cut lines into parts
  [I have] [a T-shirt]
  Repeat activities for recognising, identifying and sequencing text.
  Introduce cloze activities (use a pocket chart); for example:

I have a [ ]	I have a [ ]
And I [ ] it so	
I wear my [ ]	I wear my [ ]
Everywhere I [ ]	

• Cut the lines into words:
  [I] [wear][my] [T-shirt]
  - children identify words in text
  - sequence words to make lines
  - introduce simple cloze activities
  [I] [ ] [my] [T-shirt]

• Provide opportunities to read and reread lines/parts of lines/words.

• Put individual words from the text into an envelope. Children sort/arrange into the correct order.

Special-focus group activities (see Step 6 page 7)

Whole-class Experience

Step 9   Children share the work they have done. They are encouraged to reflect on the learning and receive feedback about different aspects of the session.

Some more activities that could be used in this session:

Whole-class/Small-group Activities

• Children write their own T-shirt slogans.
• Children create a design for their own T-shirts, incorporating their slogans.
• Display the finished shirts with captions suggesting where the children might like to wear them.
• Children innovate on the text by substituting a word for T-shirt.
• Discuss the common poetry format in the text for this song and use of capital letter at the beginning of each line of verse. (Look for other examples of poems and other songs using this format.)
• Children identify contractions used in the song. (Discuss and add to the *contraction chart*.)
• Children identify rhyming words.
• Focus on the word for the day 'comfortable'. Play *What Comes Next?* (see First Steps *Spelling: Resource Book* page 54). See how many smaller words the children can find in the larger word.
• Make use of the text of the song to further develop the children's graphophonic knowledge; for example:

sh<u>ir</u>t	<u>goo</u>d	j<u>ea</u>ns	m<u>e</u>
zipp<u>er</u>	sch<u>oo</u>l	r<u>ea</u>ding	<u>e</u>ven
			agr<u>ee</u>

• Identify action words and add to the class chart, e.g. playing, running, reading.

- Focus on homonyms such as:

  some/sum
  wear/where
  their/there

- Involve the children in *Charting and Chanting activities*.

Red T-shirts	Small T-shirts
Black T-shirts	Comfortable T-shirts
Big T-shirts	I love T-shirts

- Prepare a cloze activity from the text by deleting rhyming words.
- Children prepare a list of the clothes they would take if they were going away for the weekend.

Specific Activities for Readers Experiencing Difficulty:

(See also Chapter 5 of this book)

- Cloze activities
  - Cloze activities can be incorporated into the reading of 'Big Books'.
  - Games of cloze:
  Each child in the group has a board.
  Turn a pack of word cards face down.
  Each player has a turn to turn up a word card, read it and see if it will 'cloze' a sentence on the board. First board completed is the winner.

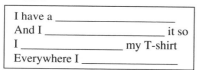

Board

```
I have a _____
And I _____ it so
I _____ my T-shirt
Everywhere I _____
```

Word cards

```
go
T-shirt
love
wear
```

- Frame sentences

I have a	Children write words on cards to complete sentences
I like my ...	Children chant the sentences
Some people like ...	Sentences can be photocopied and glued into a book

- Supported reading
  NIMBLE approach. Child listens to taped song and follows the lines of print in the book with eyes and finger.
  Repeat as many times as possible at school and at home.
  Child chooses the time when she/he wants to read the book to the teacher.
- Peer Reading
  Choral reading of song in pairs or groups
  Pairs helping each other read
  Pairs reading alternate pages

Example 2

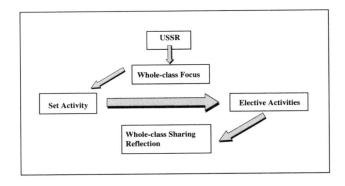

Whole-class Experience

Step 1 Introduce the big book *The Balloon Tree* by Phoebe Gilman, Scholastic. Children read the title, look at the cover and make predictions, e.g. fairytale, princess, king, queen, evil character, problem, resolution, happily ever after, etc.

Step 2 Read *The Balloon Tree* and then return to children's predictions.

Step 3 Re-read the story and then brainstorm to find the main events, listing them in order. Rate the excitement of each event, then plot onto a grid producing a plot profile. (See page 102 in Chapter 2 of this book.)

Set Activity

Step 4 Explain the whole-class activity and the elective activities. The children are to read *The Paperbag Princess* by Robert N. Munsch, Ashton Scholastic, and then, working in small groups, complete a plot profile on the story.

Step 5 Children work on elective activities.

Small-group Experience (Special Focus Group)

Step 6 Teacher works with small group of children, focusing on comprehension strategies.

Step 7 Involve the children in retelling the story of *The Balloon Tree* and then have them sequence chunks of text and justify their order.

Step 8 The group of children then work with the teacher to produce a 'Story Grammar' of *The Balloon Tree*. (See page 100 in Chapter 2 of this book.)

Step 9 The children return to their seats and continue working on the elective activities.

Individual Experiences

Step 10 Teacher works with individuals in the class.

Whole-class Sharing and Reflection

Step 11 Children share the work they have done; they are encouraged to reflect on their learning. They receive feedback about different aspects of the session.

Elective Activities

Choose a partner and work together to write a Readers Theatre script for 'The Balloon Tree'.

Retell the story to a friend and then write your retell for others in the class to read.

Work with a partner and compare this story with 'The Paper Bag Princess' Compare : - Illustrations — Characters - Setting

Select a character from the story. Find the pages with your character on it. Think about what your character might be saying. Choose a part to draw. Write a speech bubble to match.

Activities for Readers Experiencing Difficulty

(See also Chapter 5 of this book)

- Cloze activity — children predict the words and then discuss their choices.
- The children work with the teacher to develop a story map.
- Children ask the teacher questions about the story.
- Children substantiate answers to teacher questions by reading the appropriate section from the book.
- Children work with the teacher to develop an 'Interesting Words Chart'. (See page 67 in Chapter 2 of this book.)
- Children select another fairytale to read individually.
- Children read another fairytale in a 'directed silent reading' lesson with the teacher.

Example 3

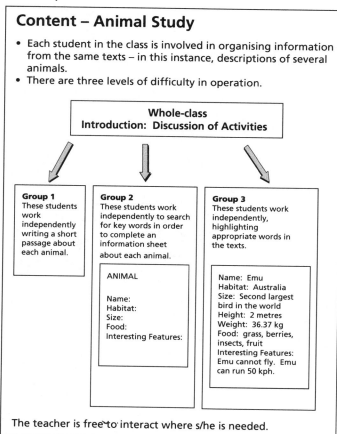

Content – Animal Study

- Each student in the class is involved in organising information from the same texts – in this instance, descriptions of several animals.
- There are three levels of difficulty in operation.

Whole-class Introduction: Discussion of Activities

Group 1
These students work independently writing a short passage about each animal.

Group 2
These students work independently to search for key words in order to complete an information sheet about each animal.

ANIMAL

Name:
Habitat:
Size:
Food:
Interesting Features:

Group 3
These students work independently, highlighting appropriate words in the texts.

Name: Emu
Habitat: Australia
Size: Second largest bird in the world
Height: 2 metres
Weight: 36.37 kg
Food: grass, berries, insects, fruit
Interesting Features: Emu cannot fly. Emu can run 50 kph.

The teacher is free to interact where s/he is needed.

Example 4

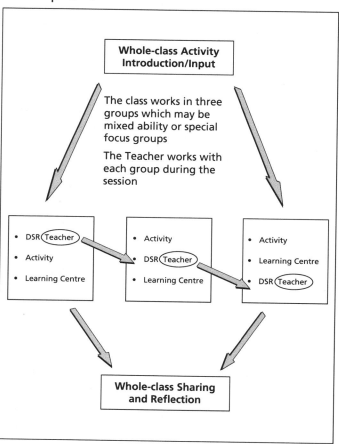

Whole-class Activity Introduction/Input

The class works in three groups which may be mixed ability or special focus groups

The Teacher works with each group during the session

- DSR (Teacher)
- Activity
- Learning Centre

- Activity
- DSR (Teacher)
- Learning Centre

- Activity
- Learning Centre
- DSR (Teacher)

Whole-class Sharing and Reflection

Teaching Children Reading Strategies

To foster reading development, teachers need to help children learn how to use reading strategies and to foster their awareness of the strategies they are using intuitively.

The following framework suggests how teachers can plan purposefully. It focuses on both teaching strategies and meaning-making strategies that can be employed in order to achieve the suggested student outcomes.

Strategies for Making Meaning

Prediction
- Questioning
- Directing the students to look at the pictures
- Use of key words
- Stopping at a part of a story and having children predict what will happen next
- Predicting the ending
- Predicting what the character will say
- Predicting character traits
- Predicting sequence of events

Self-Correction
- Reading for sense
- Reading to confirm
- Using:
  - meaning
  - sentence structure
  - letter details to self correct
- Reading on (to confirm)
- Using positive and negative miscues
- Reading back to make sense

Word Identification
- Looking for little words in big words
- Syllabification
- Using
  - root words
  - prefixes
  - suffixes
  - common letter clusters
- Using and understanding graphophonic relationships
  - identifying words with the same sounds
  - identifying words with the same letter patterns
- Recognising compound words
- Understanding the structure of singular and plural words

Student Outcomes

The student is a risk taker, i.e. willing to have a go at using new skills, guessing what will happen next, and predicting what the book/text is about.

The student is responsible for self-correcting and monitoring accuracy when reading independently.

The student is able to use a variety of strategies to attack unfamiliar words with confidence—the student is a risk-taker

- Breaking words into syllables
- Using knowledge of word derivations and root words
- Using knowledge of common letter clusters

Conventions of Print
- Punctuation
  - attending to punctuation when
  - attending to punctuation when writing
- Reading to show the left-right direction
- Turning pages conventionally
- Knowing starting, ending points, spaces, top to bottom

The student is able to see connections between reading and writing.

The student is able to reflect an understanding of punctuation in written work.

The student is aware of the conventions of the English language. ESL children may need additional help in this area.

The Three Cueing Systems
- Modelling correct usage
- Questioning
- Attending to environmental print
- Creating text innovation
- Using knowledge of syntax to make meaning
- Using knowledge of context to make meaning
- Using graphophonic knowledge to confirm meaning
- Using knowledge of graphophonics to make meaning
- Integrating the three system

The student is aware of the gramatical features of the English language.

The student begins to acquire a language for talking about language.

The student used the 'three cueing system' to make meaning.

Questioning
- Ensuring that all levels of comprehension are being adequately covered, i.e.
  - Literal
  - Inferential
  - Evaluative
  - Critical/Creative
- Eliciting the main ideas with supporting detail
- Ensuring questions are asked at appropriate intervals, not just at the end

The student is able to respond to and reflect meanings he/she has constructed of the text.
The student is able to ask and answer questions.
The student is able to demonstrate an understanding of the text at various levels.

Comprehension
- Using Before, During and After Strategies (see pages 56-109 of this book)

The student is able to demonstrate an understanding of a text at various levels.

Reflection and Critical Thinking
- Reflecting on own interpretation of a text
- Reflecting on perception of author's intended meanings
- Reflecting on possible impact of text and the language that has been used on others

The student is aware of the meanings that he/she has created and is able to extend them and compare them critically with those perceived by others.
The student is able to infer the stance of the author and identify how language has been used to convey that stance.

Planning Classroom Procedures and Activities

It is important to provide a balanced literacy program using a variety of procedures and materials.

Most teachers will adapt and change procedures according to the children's needs, their own level of comfort, their school organisation and the availability of resources.

An eclectic approach to teaching reading could include the following classroom procedures:

- Shared Reading
- Reading to Children
- Guided Reading
- Independent Reading
- Language Experience—speaking, reading and writing
- Modelled and Shared Writing

In this section the procedures are presented separately for the sake of clarity and, although they are called reading procedures, they integrate the four language modes (speaking, listening, reading and writing).

Shared Reading
(Also called Shared Book Experience)

Shared Reading demonstrates that reading is a worthwhile experience available to all. It is not only reading to children. It is a strategy that can help children as they learn to read. It involves a teacher and students in reading and re-reading from a large print text in a positive, supportive and interactive environment. It capitalises on the familiar and enjoyable home reading experiences and is especially worthwhile for children 'at risk' in reading, or for those for whom English is a second language. It is essential that Shared Reading is seen as an enjoyable experience that focuses on making meaning from print. Children will learn what they are ready to learn from Shared Reading.

In Shared Reading sessions the teacher and children sit together around a big book, so that all can see the print and the illustrations. The teacher (or a child) may point to the print and children join in, reading at their own level of expertise. All approximations are accepted positively.

Traditionally, Shared Reading has been valued as a procedure for use with younger children. Now, there are large print books available for use with all children. There are non-fiction books suitable for use in curriculum areas such as Science, Social Studies and Health. There are also novels, stories, plays, biographies, poems, rhymes and songs that enable the teacher to demonstrate different forms of text. Books can be grouped according to topic, language features, text structure or conventions of texts. The books become a basis for developing reading, writing, speaking and listening skills across the curriculum.

While all children will learn from Shared Reading experiences, they also will need further explicit information and independent practice to develop reading skills. Standard versions of the books should be made available for children to read independently after sharing sessions.

Purpose

Shared Reading is a procedure that is used to help students see how reading is 'done'. It enables them to participate in real reading with guaranteed success.

Outcomes

Shared Reading helps develop positive attitudes because it:

- is fun
- helps children to develop and share their knowledge of book and text conventions
- exposes children to a variety of text forms
- allows children to practise being readers in an environment that is non-threatening
- provides opportunities for teachers to model fluent, expressive reading
- stimulates and inspires students to be actively involved in reading
- stimulates imagination and generates new ideas for talking and writing
- stimulates and fosters critical and reflective thinking
- provides text models that can be used in children's own writing (both fiction and non-fiction)
- allows teachers to demonstrate skills in a context that makes sense to the reader
- enables teachers to focus on discussions and demonstrations of strategies that can be used to make meaning from print
- enables teachers to demonstrate the use and integration of semantic and syntactic cues to 'work out' unfamiliar words and the use of graphophonic cues to confirm or change predictions made
- encourages children to interact with the text at their own level
- allows children to enjoy reading together in a 'community of readers' where the less able are encouraged to join in because they feel that their mistakes are not noticed
- allows children to experience success and satisfaction as they become familiar with the material
- provides a common starting point for further research

Points to Remember

- Shared Reading is pleasurable because it promotes involvement in reading in a meaningful, supportive environment
- The repeated sharing of a particular text should only continue as long as children's interest is maintained. The temptation to work a text to death should be resisted.
- The number of focuses for each reading should not detract from the enjoyment of Shared Reading sessions
- Children need time to apply and practise new understandings on their own and they need access to the shared-reading material
- Shared Reading is a strategy for helping children develop reading skills and understandings—it is not the only strategy needed to teach children to read

Before Reading

- Teachers decide:
  - what is to be read
  - why it is to be read
- Choose three or four big books so that children have a store of books with which they become familiar
- Decide on the objective for the session. The focus may be on the contents of the book or on the strategies that are used to read the book.
  The focus could be to introduce:
  - a story
  - a topic
  - a theme
  - an author or illustrator
  - a genre
  - language conventions or literary devices used for a specific purpose in different text types
  - a particular reading strategy

If teaching is to be focused on the **contents** of books, Shared Reading may be used:
  - to enable students to enjoy a story
  - to teach about the characteristics of books—fiction and non-fiction
  - to teach about conventions of print, e.g. left to right directionality
  - to introduce a model for text innovation
  - to introduce a new or familiar author, topic, genre or theme
  - to help children approach a text critically, reflectively and with confidence in their own perceptions
  - to develop a basic sight vocabulary of high-frequency words
  - to introduce a new sound or letter pattern
  - to consolidate a known pattern

If teaching is to be focused on the **processes and strategies** involved in reading, Shared Reading can be used to:
  - show how real readers use semantic and syntactic cues to predict and then confirm or change their guesses using graphophonic cues
  - encourage students to predict from the context by using oral cloze, that is, pausing during reading and allowing children to fill in an appropriate word
  - encourage students to bring their own understandings to bear on the text as they construct meaning
  - observe which of the children's reading behaviours are established and those that need to be practised

- Decide what is to be read, e.g. an extract, a chapter, or the whole text
- Encourage children to:
  - **Look**
  - **Talk**
  - **Share**
  - **Predict**
- Display the book on an easel or stand so that all can see it. Use a pointer so that children can see what is being read.

If children have not read the text before:

- show the cover and read and discuss the cover illustration and title

- brainstorm to find and activate any background knowledge that will help children relate to the book
- ask children to predict what the text may be about
- ask general questions such as:
  Why do you think there is a person's name in the title?
  What do you think will happen?
  Who do you think is the main character?
- encourage predictions about:
  - the text type likely to be encountered (Fantasy? Informational Text? Autobiography?)
  - the format or layout
  - the content (real things or make-believe?)
  - the type of language which might be used
  - the likely purpose of the reading
- provide any essential knowledge that will assist children's understanding of the new material
- prediction sessions should be short and stimulating so that children are keen to listen to the reading that follows

If children have read the text before:
- brainstorm to activate any background knowledge children have retained from their previous reading of the text, e.g. characters, plot, setting, illustrations, rhymes, refrains, dialogue, 'hard' words, text features, type of text or publishing conventions
- discuss the contents and ask children to retell parts of the text that they enjoyed
- tell children the purpose for re-reading the text, e.g.
  Today we are reading:
  - so that we can look for rhyming words
  - because it was such a funny story
  - to find out more about frogs for our projects...

During Reading
- Read the text as naturally as possible with few stops
- Encourage children to:
  Join in
  Take risks
  Predict
  Use picture cues
  Use semantic, syntactic and graphophonic cues
  Look for information

Note: If students are looking for particular information from a non-fiction book, it may be advantageous to check the Table of Contents and only read the relevant section of the text in one session. This will help children to develop the understanding that reading is used for different purposes.

Teachers should show how they react to a text as they read. By modelling surprise, curiosity, excitement, sadness, happiness and interest in language or illustrations, teachers can demonstrate their enjoyment of reading.

It is important to realise how great an impact a teacher's interpretation of a text can have on children. The position taken by the teacher in relation to a text profoundly influences the way in which children construct meaning. Sometimes children feel that the reason for comment and question is to satisfy the teacher's expectations rather than to construct meaning for themselves. Every person, including the teacher, creates their own meaning and brings their own perceptions to bear on a text. It is crucial that this is acknowledged and that alternative readings of a text are elicited, valued and given equal status to that of the teacher. It is only when this is understood by all participants that children will focus on their own constructs rather than those of the teacher. Questions and answers will then cease to be part of a game of 'guess what's in the teacher's mind' and will constitute a genuine search for meaning.

- Encourage children to participate and predict as the reading proceeds
  What will ......do?
  How will this end?
  How do you think ..... would feel?
  What do you see in your mind?
- Re-read the text
- Encourage children to participate in the reading and predict the text to come. Ask:
  What is the next word?
  What is the next letter?
- Encourage children to observe and demonstrate reading strategies. Ask:
  Does it make sense?
  How can we work out this tricky word?
- Encourage children to recognise, use and demonstrate understanding of language conventions
  What do we do when we see a full-stop?
  Why is this word written this way?
- Address the chosen focus using the context of the book to help make the teaching point explicit. For example, if the focus was to look for rhyming words, these could be chosen from the text by the children.
  Let's find all the words that rhyme with 'me'
  Words could be written on the board and then discussed. Children sort and group the words according to similar letter patterns to help them understand that different letter combinations make the same sounds.

  | *monkey* | *funny* | *see* | *me* |
  | *money* | *silly* | *tree* | *he* |

  Return to the text and look for more words in context
- If the language of the text shows gender or cultural bias, or if gender, role or age stereotypes are presented, discuss this openly with the children and decide how it could be changed. Sometimes texts that present such bias can be used with great effect to heighten the need for reflective and critical thinking (see the comment on 'Cinderella' on page 3 of the *Reading: Developmental Continuum*).

After Reading

- Make available standard versions of the big book so that children can re-read these. Taped stories also encourage children to re-read the text. (Stories can be read onto tape by older children).
- Reflect on, and respond to, reading
  Encourage children to:
  Talk
  Think
  Share
  Compare
  Substantiate

Extend beyond the text
Challenge the text if neccessary
Reflect on and analyse the content

There are many ways that children can respond to text and extend their understanding of what has been read. Not every text requires a written response. Children may be encouraged to follow Shared Reading by:
– independent reading
– discussion with a partner, group or whole class
– writing
  – a text innovation to make a class big book
  – a retelling, either from the original text or with variations (change the point of view, change the form, change the character, change the ending)
  – individual or group cloze activities
  – project work
– construction of story maps, summaries, plot profiles, literary letters, reports, etc.
– research into a related topic
– choral reading for an audience
– drama and Reader's Theatre
– listening to audio cassette of the text
– making choices from a Learning Centre where there is a range of activities related to the shared book

• Sharing Time:
  – provides a real audience for responses and encourages a high standard of presentation
  – gives practice in the use of acceptable social skills expected by presenters and audiences
  – gives students practice in listening and speaking skills
  – provides a forum for critical thinking

After some training, children can be encouraged to conduct their own sharing sessions, independently or with a minimum of teacher intervention.

Materials

It is helpful if books are available in two sizes—big books for class sharing and standard books for Independent Reading.

Big books are ideal for Shared Reading as the print and illustrations are large enough for a whole class of children to see. There should also be multiple copies of the matching small books for students to read independently. Audio cassettes for read-along activities are sometimes available commercially and are valuable for follow-up reading. If these are not available they can be made by older children for use by others.

Shared Reading is most likely to be successful if the material chosen has at least some of the following features:

Fiction
• A recognisable storyline
• Attractive, relevant illustrations that support and enhance the text
• Predictable text that features rhyme, rhythm and repetition

- Stories and rhymes with cumulative structure, e.g. *The Musicians of Bremen, There Was An Old Lady Who Swallowed a Fly, The House That Jack Built*
- Stories with repetitive structure or rhyming episodes, e.g. *Five Little Ducks Went Out One Day, The Three Billy Goats Gruff*
- Never ending, or circle stories and rhymes, e.g. *There's a Hole in the Bucket*

Non-fiction
- A recognisable format which is appropriate to the form of writing
- Standard text conventions such as headings, sub-headings, table of contents, index and bibliography
- Diagrams, tables, graphs, photographs and illustrations that support the text

The aim is to involve the children and entice them to read the book. The emphasis should be on reading for meaning.

Grouping

Shared Reading is suitable for groups or whole classes. Children learn from seeing and hearing how others read. Language learners need to collaborate and share. Mixed ability groups work best as children can participate at their own level.

Talking with Parents

Parents need to be given information about the use of Shared Reading in the classroom. They should be told how it is used to help children read and why the teacher has chosen to use it as part of the class program.

It may be useful to introduce parents to the strategy by inviting them to see a Shared Reading session in the classroom. This could be followed by a discussion about what the children were learning and what processes children were using to read.

Text Innovation

This is a particularly appropriate follow-up activity when a story has a predictable text that features rhyme, rhythm or repetition. Children enjoy writing their own books and are encouraged to use the author's underlying pattern to create their own text. When they come to read their books they are already familiar with the pattern so are able to read them more easily.

Reference: Marshall V. and Tester B.,
Bernard was a Bikie, Stage 5, Bookshelf Publishing, 1988

Materials required:
Paper for draft writing
Large sheets of blank paper (40 cm x 30 cm)
Coloured pencils or felt pens

Procedure:
Read the original text several times until children are familiar with the language patterns.

Discuss how their text is going to be different from the original, e.g. a different character with a different plot, *Bernard was a Bikie* (Bookshelf Publishing) could become *Susan was a Singer*; *The T-Shirt Song*, (Rigby) could become *The Blue Jeans Song*.

Children then work co-operatively with teacher in small groups or individually to write allocated pages that follow the language pattern, but include the different character or plot.

When writers are satisfied with the page, class and teacher come together to edit and revise, referring to the original text to verify pattern if necessary. (Use overhead projector or make multiple copies for children to edit.)

Children assemble draft pages in order and check.

Copy text onto large paper and have children illustrate pages they have composed.

Assemble pages in order and add cover, authors' names, page numbers and other necessary conventions.

Re-read the books frequently and leave for children to read.

Make available extra copies in standard-size books for class library.

Making Class Big Books

Class-made big books often become favourites. There are many different activities that can lead to the construction of these books. The activities require students to discuss, write, retell in correct sequence and demonstrate understanding of the original text. They are also required to extend their knowledge beyond the text as they generalise or synthesise information to create a new text.

Language experience

Recording events in the classroom provides opportunities to produce big books that can become favourites during Independent Reading time. Texts can be supported by photographs or drawings. The forms of text should be dictated by the purpose for which the book is written, e.g.

- Recounts of an excursion
- Procedures used in a recipe, a science experiment or
- to solve a maths problem
- Reports on animals or insects being studied

Materials:

- Paper for draft writing
- Large sheets of blank paper (40 cm x 30 cm)
- Coloured pencils or felt pens
- Photographs (if required)

Procedure:

- Teacher and children discuss the language event, decide how it is to be recorded and jointly construct text.
- Revise and edit together. Teacher writes text on large pages and children illustrate or add photographs where appropriate.
- Display pages, in sequence, as wall charts or murals to be used as shared reading until children become familiar with text.
- To make the book, assemble pages in order and add cover, authors' names, page numbers and other necessary conventions.
- Re-read the books frequently and leave for children to read.
- Make available extra copies in standard size books for class library.

Informational texts

After children have read a non-fiction text and noted the different language structures and publishing conventions used, they can jointly construct big books using the same format.

Materials:

- Paper for draft writing
- Large sheets of blank paper (40 cm x 30 cm)
- Coloured pencils or felt pens
- Photographs (if required)

Procedure:

- Re-read the text that is being used as a model.
- Discuss and chart the conventions observed by children, e.g. contents page, index, headings, bibliography, etc.
- Check the contents page and use this as a guide for the construction of a big book about a similar topic, e.g. *An Introduction to Australian Spiders* (Bookshelf — Ashton Scholastic) uses the following headings that could be easily adapted to other creatures:

  What spiders look like
  Where spiders live
  What spiders do with silk
  How spiders feed
  Spiders and people

Could become

  What bees look like
  Where bees live
  What bees do with pollen
  How bees feed
  Bees and people

- Children carry out research to find information for each section.
- Teacher and children jointly construct text using information from children's research. Revise and edit.
- Transfer information onto large pages using suggested headings. Children illustrate to match text.
- Display as a series of wall charts. Read frequently and talk about the language used in informational texts.
- Assemble pages and construct big book together. Discuss the placement, form and function of the various publishing conventions.
- Leave for children to use as a reference for content headings while they do research about other creatures and construct their own books.

Other big books

There are many different ideas for making big books that children choose to read together or individually.

- News books
  Teacher scribes news from one student each day. Newsgiver illustrates. Class reads news for the day and selections from past news.
- Recipe books
  Teacher writes recipes from cooking time. Class reads to remember ingredients or method used.
- Limerick books
  Children learn the format and rhyme patterns required for limericks and write their own. Teachers write the best limericks into large book. All read them and add any new ones produced.
- Song and poem books
  On the contents page write the names of songs or poems learned in class. Read the list to select songs to be sung or poems to be recited. Favourite verses may be written in a book for children to follow.
- 'Beginnings' books
  As children read they look for introductory paragraphs that interest, intrigue or excite them. These are written in large print, discussed and read frequently to show how real authors use language to attract readers.
- Favourite phrases books
  As for 'Beginnings' books but children select phrases or sentences that they like.
- Riddle and joke books
- Class journals
  Take five minutes to reflect on the events of the day and record information in a big book. Entries may include:
  What we learned today
  How we felt about …
  The good things today …
  The bad things today …
  The funny things today …
  The sad things today …

Reading to Children

Reading to children is a valuable and worthwhile activity that should have an important place in the daily program. Students of all ages will benefit from having books read to them in a warm, supportive environment. Teachers are free to choose any books that appeal to them and that they feel the children will enjoy. The books need not be 'Big Books' that are well illustrated, with bold print, but can be chosen for their content alone. Children often enjoy having 'old fashioned' books or newsprint read to them. The focus of reading to children is on the sharing of a text for pleasure or for another specific purpose, not for teaching reading strategies or for overt teaching about language structures.

Purpose

Reading aloud provides opportunities for teachers to demonstrate their love of reading and to immerse children in the patterns of language in narrative, poetry or informational text.

Teachers can offer children the opportunity to immerse themselves in a story, knowing that the reading of the text will not be interrupted by comment, question or instruction. It is when teacher and children alike are lost in the magic of literature that attitudes and understandings are most positively shaped. Children also enjoy listening to newspaper articles, reviews or any other text that is topical and informative. When teachers read to children they are often surprised at the depth of understanding that is generated. For instance, children are often able to deal with issues or to relate to satire or subtle humour much more readily when read to than if they were reading by themselves.

Outcomes

Reading to children will help students develop positive attitudes by:

- stimulating and inspiring them to read
- stimulating imagination and generating new ideas for talking and writing
- demonstrating that reading provides pleasure

It will enable teachers to develop children's understandings about literacy by:

- modelling good oral reading
- introducing new vocabulary and language patterns in context
- presenting quality literature that children may find difficult to read on their own
- introducing children to a wide range of different forms of writing, both fiction and non-fiction
- exposing children to a range of authors and their literary styles
- introducing new books and authors

Before Reading

- Tell children why you have chosen the text

During Reading

- Enjoy it
- Don't interrupt the flow unless it is clear that a child or children have a need that must be met

After Reading

- Reflect on and respond to the reading if this seems appropriate.
  Encourage children to:
  - **Talk**
  - **Think**
  - **Share**
  - **Compare**
  - **Substantiate**
  - **Extend beyond the text, discussing implications and perceptions**
  - **Reflect on and analyse the content**

  Allow time for children to discuss what they have heard. Discussions should not always be teacher directed, or question and answer sessions. They should provide opportunities for students to extend their perception of what they have experienced and help them connect prior knowledge to newly acquired information. Journal writing also provides excellent opportunities for children to respond to what they have heard. Children should be encouraged to discuss the author's intentions, to match the view of the world presented in the text with their own and to detect bias and stereotyping.

- Return to the text.
- Make available texts that have been read so children can explore them independently. Be prepared to re-read texts which have been enjoyed by students.

Materials

Conduct a survey to ascertain students' reading habits and preferences to help select material that they will find relevant and enjoyable. It is important for teachers to read stories to students that they themselves find enjoyable, because this will best communicate the feelings of excitement and pleasure that can be derived from reading.

Introduce children to a wide range of reading material, including:

- poems
- rhymes
- short stories
- stories that have accompanying audio tapes
- novels
- traditional tales and fantasy
- realistic, historical or science fiction
- newspaper or magazine articles

Parent Information

Parents should be encouraged to continue reading to their children after the children start school. They can read favourite stories, jokes, magazine articles, newspaper reports or any material of general interest. This reading activity can involve the whole family in an enjoyable exchange of information (without the television!). Parents can also show how they use reading in their lives. Children will model their reading habits on those they see around them.

Guided Reading

Guided reading is a procedure that enables teachers to observe a small group of children (no more than ten) as they develop understanding of reading processes and practise their literacy skills. The group reads books assigned by the teacher. The teacher facilitates discussion and guides or directs the readers. Groups are sometimes, but not always, ability groups. They are formed according to children's needs and the purpose of the session.

Purpose

- To explore with children the questions, feelings and ideas arising from the text
- To develop children's confidence in making predictions
- To reinforce that meaning is the end result of reading
- To facilitate discussion that will help children refine their understanding as they read
- For teachers to assess children's levels of understanding
- To use real contexts for the teaching and learning of specific skills and reading strategies needed by children

Outcomes

Guided, or Directed, Reading sessions enable teachers to:
- observe strategies used by children
- help children see reading as purposeful
- demonstrate that reading is a thinking process by discussing what happens 'inside our heads' when we read
- help children reflect on how they read
- demonstrate how to link prior knowledge and new information to construct meaning
- demonstrate how to frame questions to direct reading
- demonstrate the different levels of understanding required, e.g. literal, inferential, evaluative
- motivate children to read independently
- demonstrate strategies used by readers, e.g. prediction, use of semantic or syntactic cues to work out unknown words, re-reading, self-correcting using graphophonic cues
- explore children's reactions to text
- help children move beyond the text and attempt to identify the world view of the author, comparing it with their own
- provide a model of critical and reflective reading

Before Reading

- Teachers decide:
  - what is to be read
  - why it is to be read
- Decide on the composition of the group.
  Small groups can be formed for different purposes and selection of group members may be guided by: particular needs, ability, interest, friendship or specific tasks which need to be completed. All group work should involve a high degree of collaborative learning and teachers should be seen as facilitators within the group.
- Decide on the objective for the lesson.

28

The focus could be to introduce, or develop further understanding of:
- a story
- a topic
- a theme
- an author or illustrator
- a new genre or form of text
- language conventions or literary devices used for specific purpose in different text types
- a particular reading strategy which needs to be practised

- Select suitable reading material.
- Discuss the purpose for reading. Give each child a copy of the text to be read.
- Discuss the cover and read and discuss the cover illustration and title.
- Encourage children to:
  Look
  Talk
  Share
  Predict
- Encourage predictions about:
  - the text type likely to be encountered (Fantasy? Informational Text? Autobiography?)
  - the format or layout
  - the content (real things or make-believe?)
  - the type of language that might be used
  - the likely purpose of the reading

  Prediction sessions should be short and stimulating so that children are keen to read the text for themselves.
- Brainstorm to find and activate any background knowledge children may have that will help them relate to the book.
- Provide any essential knowledge which will assist their understanding of the new material. This could include unfamiliar vocabulary or concepts.

During Reading

- Read the text.

  The way the Guided Reading is conducted depends on the objectives for the lesson. Teachers should direct their questions and children's discussion to achieve the outcomes required.

  Encourage children to:
  Read for meaning
  Monitor understanding. Ask: *Does this make sense? Does it sound right?*
  Adjust reading rate if necessary
  Select a reading style to suit purpose
  Read on or read back to retain meaning
  Predict
  Take risks (have-a-go at unknown words)
  Imagine
  Share understandings
- Set a focus question and ask students to read a section of the text silently in order to find the answer. Early finishers can be asked to set other questions as they think about the text.

- Discuss the passage by first answering the focus question. Allow students to ask some of their own questions. Talk about children's different interpretations of the text.
- Talk about strategies used to gain understanding, e.g. *How did you work out that bit?*
- Discuss how children felt about the text.
- Re-read the text.
  Children need to have the opportunity to return to a text to enhance their understanding and substantiate their answers.
  Before reading the text:
  - pose questions which will invite readers to return to the text to justify, dispute or substantiate answers
  - encourage children to reflect on the predictions made before the first reading
  - encourage children within the group to discuss anything from the text that they feel is important
  - encourage children to talk about and demonstrate reading strategies that they used to complete reading
  - encourage children to go back to words which were difficult and try to find their meaning and pronunciation

After Reading

- Reflect on, and respond to, reading.
  There are many ways that children can respond to text and extend their understanding of what has been read. Not every text requires a written response.
- Encourage children to:

  Talk
  Think
  Share
  Compare
  Substantiate
  Discuss their perceptions of the author's intentions
  Extend beyond the text
  Generalise
  Reflect on and criticise content

Activities which require children to return to the text should follow Guided Reading. Children should be encouraged to suggest and choose their activities. The following list is meant as a guide only:
- Independent reading
- Discussion with a partner or group member
- Writing
  - entering details of the text in a Reading Log
  - writing in Reading Journal
  - constructing story maps, summaries, plot profiles, literary letters, reports, etc.
  - retelling, either from the original text or with variations (e.g. change the point of view, change the form, change a character, change the ending)
  - individual or group cloze activities
  - project work
  - research into a related topic

- making choices from a Learning Centre where there is a range of activities related to the book
- – Choral reading for an audience
- – Drama
- – Listening to audio cassette of the text
- • Sharing Time

Sharing responses with class or group can provide opportunities to extend understanding.

Sharing:

- – provides a real audience for responses and encourages a high standard of presentation
- – gives practice in the use of acceptable social skills expected by presenters and audiences
- – gives students practice in listening and speaking skills

After some training, children can be encouraged to conduct their own sharing sessions with a minimum of teacher intervention.

Materials

Books to be used in Guided Reading sessions should be selected to match the readers' abilities and interests. They should provide a challenge without being so difficult that readers become discouraged. Texts should be 'real' books.

Talking with Parents

Parents need to be given information about the use of Guided Reading in the classroom. They should be told about reasons for grouping children and assured that groups are flexible and varied. Parents need to understand how Guided Reading is used to help children read, and why the teacher has chosen to use it as part of the class program.

Independent Reading

Children learn to read by reading and by seeing others read. The ultimate aim of any reading program must be to produce independent readers. All children, therefore, even the very young, need to be given daily opportunities to read independently.

Purpose

By allocating time for children's independent reading, teachers are able to reinforce the idea that reading is a valued and worthwhile pastime and to encourage children to engage in real reading.

Children are able to:

- practise, reinforce and gain confidence in what they currently know about reading
- experiment with, and evaluate their methods of reading and learn from their mistakes
- focus on things that they still need to practise

Outcomes

Time for Independent Reading ensures that readers:

- have time to choose books and enjoy reading for pleasure
- realise that the teacher values reading
- have the opportunity to return to familiar texts that they have read during shared reading or guided reading sessions
- can pursue favourite authors or types of books
- can learn to select texts that match their interests and ability

Suggestions for Teachers

Independent Reading will only occur if students have a desire or purpose for reading. As attitudes to reading are formed on the basis of previous reading encounters, teachers may need to spend some time establishing positive attitudes to reading. Good books on their own will not guarantee that children will read independently. Time must be allocated within the school program. Some independent reading may be inspired by a children's television serial or a current craze such as dinosaurs. Although it is important that children immerse themselves in good literature, it is equally important that they are 'turned on' to reading, which might mean that comics and joke books are the entree of the reading feast.

Maybe more time should be spent allowing children to *learn* to read and less time given to *teaching* them.

Before Reading

- Students decide:
  - what is to be read
  - why it is to be read
- The teacher's role:
  - set aside time each day for Independent Reading. (This may be Sustained Silent Reading or an adaptation of it.) It may be difficult for children to remain 'silent' during reading. Some classrooms run extremely successful interactive reading sessions. It is important that everyone is engaged in reading and that positive behaviour is rewarded.
  - ensure the supply or a range of suitable reading material
  - give students time to select material
  - establish a routine
- Encourage children to:
  Look
  Think
  Predict
  Decide how to read

During Reading

- Read the text
  Encourage children to:
  Read on
  Read back
  Predict
  Clarify
  Have-a-go at unknown words
  Make mental pictures
  Use all cueing systems
- Let children see that teachers read
- Everyone read

After Reading

- Reflect on and respond to text either informally by talking about it or by choosing to engage in a written activity that involves returning to the text.
- Sharing

  It may be appropriate after Independent Reading to spend some time sharing what has been happening. Children may wish to respond to what they have read, or perhaps promote their book to others. Sharing helps to widen the range of books children know about in their class.

  Initially some time may be spent reviewing the routine and discussing any problems that have arisen.

Materials

There should be a range of reading material available for Independent Reading. Class books can be supplemented by books brought from home and bulk loans from the library. All forms of text should be available with a range of difficulty.

Provide access to books read to children and those used in Guided Reading sessions so that children can return to the texts as often as desired.

Class-made books or students' own writing provide popular choices for students' Independent Reading.

Some teachers like to store books they have read with the children in a separate book box so that children know where to find their favourite books. If big books have been shared with children, it is sensible to have multiple copies in standard format because these titles will be sought by children for Independent Reading.

Notes for Parents

Parents should be encouraged to value time for children to read independently.

They can:

- talk about, and let children see, the enjoyment they get from reading
- allow children to read independently without interference
- praise and encourage children's reading efforts and spend time discussing material being read (not quizzing children to see if they can answer questions about the content)
- give books for presents
- encourage children to:
  - follow favourite authors or topics
  - visit the library regularly
  - to read quietly in bed before going to sleep
  - ask questions about books they are reading

Language Experience—Speaking, Reading, Writing

The most meaningful words for children are likely to be those they use in their own written or oral language. Language Experience is a method of teaching that draws on students' experiences to generate oral and written language. In the classroom, teachers can plan activities that provide learning experiences and capitalise on any unplanned events that offer interesting opportunities for children to expand their knowledge of language and the world.

The teacher records language from the children. Then teacher and children co-operatively revise and edit the text. The final text is to be used for shared or individual reading.

Purpose

Language Experience activities provide opportunities for children to talk and write about events in which they have all participated. By broadening children's experiences, teachers are able to provide contexts for enriching their language.

Outcomes

Language Experience sessions:

- show the interrelationship of written and oral language
- provide a meaningful common context for children of different abilities as all participants feel they 'own' the text
- provide opportunities for vocabulary enrichment
- motivate children to read because they understand and have ownership of the text
- demonstrate the use of language for different purposes
- provide opportunities for teachers to model the writing process and draw attention to various language features

Suggestions for Teachers

Language experience events may be planned or may simply 'happen'. Planned events could include cooking, class camps, picnics, visits to the zoo, shops, parks or other places, talks from guest speakers, watching films, reading books, art or craft activities or visits from touring entertainers.

Events which just 'happen' include any incident which captures children's interest. These incidents could include a bogged sand truck outside the school fence, a stormy day, a new building under construction or any unexpected event.

Before Reading

- Choose the experience.
- Plan the event with children so that they have the opportunity to share the planning, excitement and anticipation. Where appropriate, discuss things which need to be done and then allow children to be involved in the organisation of such items as transport, helpers, bookings, food supplies and invitations.
- Gather any relevant items (books, charts, ingredients, utensils, information brochures).
- Talk informally about children's expectations. Help children pose questions that they would like to answer.

- Divide a large sheet of paper into two columns with headings *Before* and *After*. Record background information that children already know about the topic under the *Before* heading. After the experience, complete the *After* section. Compare the two.
- Provide the experience allowing children to be as involved as possible. Take photographs throughout. Ask questions to guide discussion as children participate. Children should be able to react spontaneously using their natural language to express their feelings, opinions and thoughts.
  Encourage children to:

  Look
  Talk
  Share
  Predict
  Question
- When it is time to record the experience, scribe for children. With the children, read and re-read to revise and edit text until it is ready to publish.
- Publish the text in a big book, including photographs, drawings and significant artefacts to illustrate the text.
- Use the big book in shared reading time. Make it available for independent reading. If possible. reproduce copies of the book for children to keep.
- Encourage children to write about the experience and to engage in related purposeful writing activities, e.g. thank you letters, assembly reports, newspaper articles. Individual writing can be collated into a book for the class library, e.g. Our Thoughts About Camp.

After Reading

- Encourage children to:

  Talk
  Think
  Share
  Compare
  Generalise
  Substantiate
  Find out more about the topic on their own
- Complete the *Before* and *After* chart.
- Keep class books as a record of experiences. These books are often the most sought after by class members. Re-read books in shared reading time.

Talking with Parents

Parents use opportunities to build language into everyday experiences for their children. They can be encouraged to listen to children and assist them to retell the events of the day. They can talk about what is happening and ask questions that require children to think about events. Parents can also provide support and encouragement for children to attempt their own written accounts of exciting things in their lives. Sometimes it may be appropriate for parents to encourage children to write a thank-you letter or to write about an important event. Parents can be encouraged to display children's writing.

Dear Grandma,

We went to Mandurah for a holiday. Can you come and have a holiday with me.

Love from Emma.

xxo xxo

Modelled and Shared Writing

Reading and writing are closely linked and each provides support for the development of the other. Children should be encouraged to 'read as writers' and to 'write as readers'.

Modelled and Shared Writing provide opportunities for students to see a proficient writer in action.

Teachers can plan short, writing workshop sessions each day to demonstrate processes and skills involved in writing. These sessions may involve the whole class or a small group of children who need more exposure to a particular area of writing. Children should always be involved in these sessions and should be invited to read and re-read the text with the teacher as the writing takes shape. Contributions, ideas and questions are encouraged so that interest is maintained. In addition, there are many opportunities for incidental demonstrations of writing to occur throughout the day.

Questions Teachers Ask

What about basal readers?

There are many different 'basal reader' series. Some are good; others dull and boring. Some are designed solely to 'teach' reading but bear little resemblance to real books. Others provide a selection of different relevant material that stimulate children of different ability and interests. When children start to read, they try to make sense of what they are reading. Consequently, the type of material selected is important, as it can help or hinder the process of learning to read.

No-one would suggest that reading schemes should be abolished, rather that they should be appraised critically and used selectively to serve the needs of readers. In the past, teachers have tried valiantly to make children fit reading schemes and felt guilty when children failed to read all books at the prescribed level and to complete the activities within a prescribed time. The guilt prevailed even when the reading scheme was poorly written or inappropriate for children learning to read.

We want children to choose to read independently and to see that reading provides pleasure and is purposeful. Some basal series provide opportunities for readers to choose, others do not. Some invite readers to read them, others do not. It is interesting to note that many 'basal-fed' children see reading as something you do for the teacher and never choose to read from their basal text during independent reading sessions. Surely this is a message for teachers! Choosing books is an important part of reading.

So What Can Teachers Do?
Understand how children learn to read

If teachers understand how children learn to read they can provide an environment (including reading material) that will enhance reading experiences.

Points to Remember

Children learn to read by reading. Reading is all about making meaning from a piece of text. Children learn best when they:

- are actively involved in their learning
- see that their learning has purpose and meaning
- combine their existing knowledge gained from past experiences with information from text to construct meaning. (Background information is an important part of reading as it provides a familiar context.)
- use the three cueing systems as they read. The graphophonic, syntactic and semantic systems are used interactively by efficient readers.
- are risk-takers and problem-solvers. They predict, confirm, modify or change predictions as they read. They monitor understanding and adjust their reading as they seek to make sense of print.
- have the opportunity to work individually, in small groups and as part of the whole class
- are given time to practise a skill or process

We know that language-learners will be well on the way to becoming confident readers if they:

- have stories read to them

- have clear expectations about what they will find as they read
- see that reading is relevant to them
- have an intention to read
- see a purpose for reading
- see reading modelled as a pleasurable activity

Reading material that is interesting and relevant will be read many times, giving children valuable practice. This means that the necessary high frequency words are encountered often, without the added complication of new character names or content words. Success in reading will lead to growing confidence.

To give early readers every opportunity to succeed at reading, materials must be whole texts that are predictable, interesting, meaningful and relevant. They must have all the characteristics of real books that serve real functions. No materials that divert attention away from comprehension should be acceptable.

Look critically at the books
In the past the authenticity of reading books was not considered to be nearly as important as the way they were structured. There was a pre-occupation with teaching the mechanics of reading words in the hope that children would later make meaning from, and see the purpose for, reading.

The publication of two main types of 'reading books' emerged reflecting differing views of teaching reading. The first group relied mainly on a phonic approach where children were taught sound units and encouraged to 'sound out' words in order to decode them. Books that relied on this approach had to make the sound-symbol relationship consistent and construct books in which only certain word families appeared. This led to nonsensical texts similar to:

The pig sat in the gig.

Jig, jig, big pig.

A big pig is in the gig.

Children could 'sound-out' words but probably couldn't understand why anyone would want to read for pleasure or to gather information. They were also unable to use their contextual and linguistic understandings to help them to read.

The second group of books was based on a controlled and gradual building of vocabulary where words appeared approximately four times in the first book and were repeated in the second along with new words and so on. Separate books were designed for each year level. Before any book-reading took place, the words were often presented in isolation and 'drilled' so that children would recognise them when they were eventually given the book. Some children waited months to get a book because they couldn't recognise the words without a context. Children must have been building some strange understandings of reading!

The books had such texts as:

Look.

Look.

Look Jim.

Look Jane.

Look. Look.

Jim look at Jane.

Jane look at Jim.

Jim and Jane look.

See Jane look.

See Jim look.

See Jane and Jim look.

These books also led to interesting misconceptions about written language. Many had sentences exactly one line long, so children deduced that full stops should appear at the end of every line. This soon showed up in children's own writing much to the dismay of teachers.

In their efforts to simplify text, book publishers had made reading more difficult for early readers who could be excused for believing that reading was about getting words right, not about making meaning. Readers were denied the use of semantic cues (meaning) and sometimes, because of the unfamiliar sentence patterns, syntactic cues were useless. The pleasure, and purpose, of reading was lost because it was just too hard.

Children's expectations of print, developed from birth, were not met by these 'reading books'. Some of the books had no discernible storyline and made just as much sense if the last page was read first and then the second last page and so on. Children must have had great difficulty seeing any purpose for reading. If basal readers are from either of these two categories, teachers may have to decide whether the material is helping children learn to read.

Teachers must, therefore, look critically at reading material. Reading material must be authentic and relevant to the readers.

Recognise quality reading material

The main aim in selecting books is to choose those that children can read and want to read. With the wide range of books available today, teachers can select a variety of enjoyable and interesting material, some of which may come from reading series, some from published children's books and some from other sources.

When considering a reading series, there are some characteristics that are important.

Teachers can ask:
- Are the books like the books that children would choose to read?
- Is there a range of books to suit different ability levels and interests of the readers?

- Is the text written using natural language patterns that will assist readers to use semantic and syntactic cues to predict as they read?
- Are some books predictable because of familiar content or repetitive language patterns?
- Do some books feature rhyme, rhythm and repetition?
- Would the text make sense to children?
- Does the text follow conventions and forms that children could expect to find in other reading materials?
- Is there a range of authors and illustrators who employ different styles?
- Do the illustrations, diagrams or photos enhance and extend the text?
- Is there a wide range of forms of text?
- Do the stories have recognisable plots that involve believable characters?
- Does the expository text present authentic information that is clearly written?
- Is the expository text organised with appropriate features, such as a table of contents, index and bibliography?

If we believe that children learn language when pursuing purposes that are important to them, then we need to examine the reading material carefully. A complete literacy program should have books of literary quality, be functional and relevant to the learner and teacher. If reading series meet these requirements, then there seems to be no problem. If reading schemes are inadequate, material from other sources should be made available and future book purchases planned carefully.

Be Selective
The selection of reading material should be guided by the needs and interests of students, not by a desire to 'get through' a set of books at a predetermined level. Children should not be forced to read every book at every level. If the contents are unsuitable the book should be left and a more suitable text chosen. This is what happens to real readers. The ability to select suitable books is an essential part of reading that should be encouraged.

It may also be desirable to use books from different levels for purposes such as reading to children, looking for specific information or making comparisons. Teachers should be flexible in their use of books from reading schemes.

Always remember the purpose of reading. Reading to complete a reading scheme is a superficial purpose that probably does more harm than good. Reading schemes are part of a reading program, not the totality.

Encourage children to choose their own reading material.

What about the blackline masters that go with my reading scheme? I feel guilty if the children don't use them all.

Many reading series provide additional components for the program. They offer student workbooks and blackline master activity sheets to be completed after reading.

If teachers believe that reading is a thinking process, then the activities that follow reading should stimulate children to reflect on their reading and encourage them to return to the text to clarify their understandings. In many cases, talking about what is to be, and has been read, is of more value than 'doing a sheet'. If we learn to read by reading, and to write by writing, then maybe the time saved by avoiding meaningless tasks could be used to do more reading and writing.

Teachers need to use their professional judgement to determine whether so-called activity sheets will involve children in active, authentic reading and writing tasks, or whether the activities are just time-wasting, colouring and cutting exercises that distract children from real reading and writing and may lead them to conclude that the purpose of reading is to 'do a sheet'.

What about permanent ability groups?

In our school children are placed in ability groups after they have done a standardised test to assess their reading age. The bottom kids go to the remedial reading teacher for 40 minutes each day.

The above statement (or a similar one) has often been heard in the past. Children have been labelled, grouped and will be 'fixed-up' by someone else.

Permanent ability groups soon make children believe that some are 'dumb', some are 'average' and some are 'clever'. They also discover that these perceptions never change. Groups can be called 'Dogs', 'Cats' and 'Birds' or 'Comets', Rockets' and 'Satellites'. The group names don't fool anyone but we know that a year 1 Snail, often is still a Snail in year 7. By then (if not before) the Snails group has become a difficult, disinterested bunch who expect nothing of themselves and seldom have the desire to complete school tasks. They prefer to concentrate on disrupting others. They have been harmed, not helped, by ability grouping.

Often the groups are also given quite different tasks to do and are taught differently. The top group of children is allowed to read independently and choose books, while bottom group members only get teacher chosen 'easy books' and spend time doing read and draw, or cut and colour activities that require little reading or thinking. Traditionally the bottom group spends less time engaged in reading than other groups and are asked to do the most difficult tasks. These children are often required to read aloud to the teacher, i.e. to read fluently, with expression and to get the words right or risk correction in public. This is a difficult task. They spend more time drilling words in isolation than other groups. They are expected to remember words without the help of context clues. These practices defy logic if we believe that children learn to read by reading.

Ability grouping has been tried many times. If it worked, surely there would be fewer educational problems in the upper grades. The problems, however, remain. Perhaps permanent ability groups are partially to blame for the problem. Confidence in the ability to succeed is vital if children are to succeed.

At risk readers need to remain within the classroom where their contributions are valued. They may need more time to develop skills but they still need to read (and be read to) to develop their reading and to write (and see others writing) to develop writing.

Language is not a set of isolated subskills arranged hierarchically and shouldn't be taught that way. At risk learners (more than others) need to see connections. They must be given the opportunity to see that reading is a thinking process; not merely 'barking at print'.

Do I have to hear my kids read every day?

Listening to reading has been accepted as part of the role of both teacher and parent. This practice takes a lot of time so we must be very clear about why we listen to children read aloud.

Listening to children read aloud should be an important teaching time. It is a time when teachers monitor a student's use of effective reading strategies and assess the impact of the class program on student's progress. It should not be a time of pressure to get the words right, rather a time to observe the processes being used. These observations can then guide the teacher's program planning. Not all children need to read aloud every day. Some who are progressing well may only need to be heard once or twice a week. Others may need more individual or small group time with the teacher.

If the purpose of hearing children read aloud is to monitor the use of reading strategies and to help teachers plan, we need to ask if it is fair or profitable to ask parents to 'hear' reading. Parents who wish to help their child to read may be better advised to read along with the child, read the book to the child, talk about the book after the child has read it and support the child's reading, rather than insisting that the child read aloud.

Books taken home should be able to be read independently by children.

Teachers must think about the purpose for hearing children read. Then make sound professional judgements about who should listen and how often.

How can I start planning?

To implement and manage a balanced literacy program, it is important to:

- allocate blocks of time
- vary the grouping of students according to the purpose of the learning experience
- organise space to facilitate children's movement, interaction, group work, whole-class activities and individual tasks
- have a sound knowledge of resources available and
- incorporate the teaching of language into all subject areas

Chapter 2:

Reading Comprehension

Introduction

What is Comprehension?

Comprehension can be described as an active process that involves the reader in making meaning from visual information (e.g. print, punctuation, illustrations) and non-visual information (e.g. background knowledge based on past experiences with language and the world).

If this definition is accepted, it is the reader's background knowledge that will shape the understanding and interpretation of text.

In class, every time reading occurs, teachers deal with 30 children who use different background knowledge to construct meaning from the same text. This may help to explain why comprehension seems so difficult to teach. It is evident, therefore, that the more non-visual, or background information that a reader can bring to the text, the more likely it is that sensible, coherent meaning will be made. Students' prior knowledge prepares them for reading. There is often no one 'right answer' as different meanings can be made from the same text. It is important that different interpretations of text are acknowledged and valued, and that children are encouraged to provide evidence that supports their interpretations.

Readers bring a range of background information to any text. Consider the various meanings that could be constructed from the following text depending upon the reader's previous experiences:

saw four on the floor. (These words could mean gear configuration, or people dancing, blocks on the floor or something else.)

Making Connections

As readers process text, they make connections or inferences using a variety of information from different sources. They use:

- **Socio-cultural information** (this is what readers know about the world in which they live).
- **Semantic information** (this is what readers know about the words in the world in which they live).
- **Syntactic information** (this is what readers know about the grammar or structure of their language).

- **Graphophonic information** (this is what readers know about written symbols of language that help them to decode).

This information is used concurrently and interactively to construct meaning.

Using and Controlling Strategies

Comprehension also depends on the readers' ability to use and control strategies that help make meaning or recognise when meaning is lost and adjust the reading process accordingly.

Construction of meaning cannot be a passive or receptive activity. Readers are required to predict, confirm, think and reflect on information as they read. Comprehension is not a static activity. Readers often construct deeper and more extensive understandings of a text over a considerable period of time.

Explicit teaching of strategies will help children become efficient readers.

Good readers	Weaker readers
• monitor their comprehension well	• are not able to judge how well they understand
• select, apply and adjust strategies	• use fewer strategies and are unable to adjust them
• integrate the use of graphophonic, syntactic and semantic cues with their world knowledge	• often rely only on one cueing system
• understand the purpose of reading	• have little understanding of the purpose of reading
• understand that purpose drives the process of reading	• may not understand that reading has many purposes
• reflect and self-question to see if they have effectively achieved their purpose	• do not have the strategies to reflect on their reading
• are able to correct errors that are semantically or syntactically inappropriate	• are less able to correct inappropriate syntactic or semantic errors
• understand how to apply their background knowledge to create new meaning	• do not connect their background knowledge to new knowledge contained in print

Teaching Comprehension

The teacher's role is to help readers use, extend and integrate their:

- knowledge of the language of written texts
- topic knowledge
- cultural (world) knowledge
- knowledge of strategies or procedures for use in understanding and monitoring reading for meaning

Teachers can teach comprehension, not just test it.

There must be:

- motivation
- interest in material read
- knowledge of the purpose for reading
- ability to attend to what is important in the text
- ability to reflect critically on what has been read

If reading material is authentic, interesting and relevant to the reader, comprehension is greatly enhanced.

Helping Children Construct Meaning From Text

Ensure That Children Have a Reasonable Sight Vocabulary of Words Commonly Seen In Books

Although the essential focus of reading is the message rather than individual words, it is essential for children to have access to a bank of words that they can instantly recognise. If they do not have sufficient sight words, they struggle to retain meaning while puzzling out many unknown words. The best way to introduce common words is in context.

Teachers

- provide opportunities for children to meet the same words in different contexts to help build their bank of familiar, high-frequency words
- read to children and allow children time to read so that they hear and see words many times in meaningful contexts ensuring that the words become part of their receptive vocabulary (reading and listening)
- allow children to write frequently and share their writing so that common words become part of their expressive vocabulary (speaking and writing)

Children need to read new words many times before they become part of a sight vocabulary. Some children may need additional activities using the words in context in order to recognise them instantly.

There is a high correlation between the extent of knowledge of common sight words, and comprehension.

Select Appropriate Activities

The comprehending process requires readers to use comprehension strategies that enable them to combine prior knowledge with new knowledge to make meaning. Activities selected to complement this process should not be regarded simply as time-fillers. They should be chosen to enable readers to practise using strategies and to transfer the use of those strategies to different situations. Activities should make readers aware of how they process print, and help them see connections between the strategies they use and the purposes for which they use them.

Teachers:

- have a clear understanding of the objectives to be achieved by using an activity
- provide activities where the purpose is clear to the children
- provide opportunities to discuss why particular strategies might be used to complete an activity
- give prior instruction to ensure that children succeed
- choose activities that allow children to interpret text and justify their interpretation
- allow children to choose activities that they enjoy and in which they make some of the decisions about how to proceed
- provide opportunities for children to share their responses with the whole class as this develops speaking and listening skills

It is not necessary to follow reading with a written response or activity. It may be more appropriate to discuss the material and re-read to clarify any areas of doubt.

Activities should help readers reflect on their reading.

Make Careful Use of Questioning

Comprehension takes on true meaning when readers are involved in thinking about and comparing their interpretation of text with that of others. Teachers can nurture this process by careful questioning. For example, a question such as

How tall was the dinosaur?

has only one possible answer and once answered there is no opportunity for further discussion. However, if the teacher asks questions such as

The story says the dinosaur was six metres tall. How tall is six metres?

Every child can participate in a discussion that will clarify personal meanings. Everyone will be encouraged to think, interpret and infer. All will be truly 'comprehending', i.e. bringing background knowledge to new information to make meaning.

Teachers:

- ask questions that stimulate thoughtful discussions
- ask questions that invite children to relate all they know to new information so they can organise new meanings
- ask questions that invite children to question their own meanings
- ask questions that relate to the author's (or illustrator's) technique of composing the text or picture

Open-ended questions can put children in touch with their thoughts and feelings generated by reading. It is important that if children are asked questions involving values, perceptions or views of the world, their opinions are listened to, respected, valued and given equal status with those of the teacher.

Teach Comprehension Strategies

A comprehension strategy is a plan of action that can be applied generally to assist the reading process. Efficient readers use many strategies to make meaning from what they read. They use their linguistic knowledge and their background experience to predict, test, confirm, reject and correct as they actively respond to text. They use these strategies interactively and continuously through the reading process. Some readers need to be taught specific strategies, i.e. have explicit lessons in meaningful contexts, followed by practice activities that allow application of their new knowledge in other contexts. **Teachers need to teach strategies.**

Teachers:

- teach strategies for improving comprehension
  - decide what strategies to teach
  - decide how to teach strategies
  - decide when to use particular strategies
- help children understand what they should be doing as they read
- help readers maintain use of strategies
- develop readers' ability to decide where and when to use strategies

49

- develop the reader's ability to apply and integrate comprehension strategies in a variety of situations
- teach readers how to monitor their use of strategies
- teach readers to recognise whether or not strategies they are using are efficient.

Effective readers understand how they are reading and how they monitor their understanding.

Teaching Children Comprehension Strategies

How Can Comprehension Strategies Be Taught?

Comprehension strategies are best taught in a **meaningful context** and in **conjunction with comprehension skills.**

Comprehension instruction should involve **word level, sentence level** and **whole-text level** of comprehension.

Comprehension instruction should **integrate existing oral and written language knowledge with new knowledge.**

Comprehension instruction should assist **the process of comprehension, a process that occurs before, during and after reading.**

Strategies can be grouped into awareness, monitoring and adjusting strategies.

Awareness Strategies

- topic or background knowledge which may help comprehension
- level of comprehension required
- purpose for reading
- different reading styles for different purposes
- text organisation
- text inaccuracies or ambiguities
- differences in explicit and implicit information

Monitoring Strategies

- checking understanding by
  - summarising information
  - paraphrasing information
  - synthesising information
- integrating prior knowledge with new text information
- evaluating information
  - confirming predictions and hypotheses
  - evaluating consistency of main ideas and details
  - critically considering information

Adjusting Strategies

- re-reading
- backward-forward searching
- self-questioning
- locating point of mis-comprehension
- substantiating information from the text

Teaching the Strategies

- teach **awareness, monitoring and adjusting** strategies to help children make meaning or to recognise and adjust when the meaning is unclear
- model the use of strategies before, during and after reading, and allow children to practise them in context
- spend time encouraging children to predict what will happen, and then to confirm or change their predictions as they read
- focus more on talk, so that children can clarify their understandings

A Cycle for Teaching a New Strategy

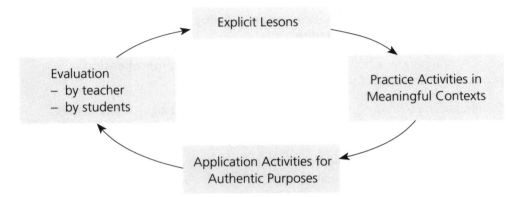

- Children need at least four opportunities to implement the plan when learning a new strategy
- Children learn best when they can use a strategy in a variety of different contexts

Teaching Sequence

1 Identify purpose
(e.g. to find the main idea of a text)
Q *What am I trying to do?*
A *Oh yes, find the important information or main idea.*

2 Apply background knowledge
Q *How do we usually find the main idea?*

3 Plan a strategy
Plan:
    Read text
    Underline and list key words
    Compare key words with a partner
    Discuss differences
    Discuss what we think is the main idea

4 Rehearse the Plan

Talk with a partner about what you plan to do

5 Try the Strategy

Text: Spiders

There are <u>many</u> varieties of <u>spiders</u> in <u>Australia</u>. Spiders belong to the group called anthropods. They have <u>two</u> <u>body parts</u> (a cephalo thorax and abdomen). They also have <u>eight legs</u> which end in claws. The legs are attached to the cephalo thorax. Spiders also have fangs which are used to seize prey. <u>Some</u> spiders are <u>poisonous</u>.

List of key words:

   many
   spiders
   Australia
   two body parts
   eight legs
   some
   poisonous

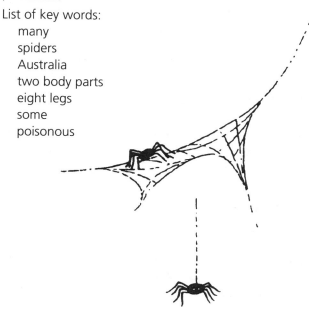

6 Solve the Problem

Many types of spiders live in Australia. They have two body parts and eight legs. Some are poisonous.

7 Evaluate

Compare summaries with others in the group

Two Sample Applications of Teaching Sequence

This lesson plan can be applied to the teaching of a variety of strategies. Children need to have the plan modelled and they should practise the application of the plan at least four times for each new strategy.

Focus	Application Explicit Lesson Example 1	Child's Response
Identify Purpose	To review or clarify vocabulary	To work out word meanings
Apply Background Knowledge	How do I usually work out new vocabulary?	I usually stop and ask someone
Plan a Strategy	Read the text. Note the new vocabulary and the page number. Make an Interesting Words Chart and fill in all possible details	Find the word Read around it Try and work out the meaning by thinking about it
Rehearse Plan	Discuss above plan with partner	Repeat to partner
Implement Plan with Text	Use plan on piece of text	
Solve	Complete Interesting Words Chart with words and explanations	
Reflect	Do I understand the meaning of the new vocabulary?	I managed to work out most words I used the dictionary for one

Sample application using suggested teaching sequence

Focus	Application Explicit Lesson Example 2	Child's Response
Identify Purpose	To activate background knowledge	I need to think about what I know to help me understand
Apply Background Knowledge	What do I usually do before I read?	I like brainstorming because you get lots of information
Plan a Strategy	Read title (topic) Brainstorm—write down everything I know Categorise information in a skeleton outline Skim text, add information	I'll work with a group to get more information
Rehearse Plan	Discuss above plan	Repeat to partner
Implement Plan with Text	Skim read to activate any further knowledge and add to overview	
Solve	Produce skeleton outline that shows existing knowledge in categories	
Reflect	Did this help me recall useful information before I read the text?	I didn't realise that I knew much about …

When To Use Comprehension Strategies

Before Reading

Aim: To prepare for reading.
Preparation involves much discussion and sharing of ideas.

Reading is an active process so:

- readers must have a clear understanding of *why* they are reading, *what* they are expected to gain from reading and *how* they are going to use the information
- understanding is more likely to occur if readers are interested and motivated to read (they must perceive reading as relevant to them)
- readers need to be aware of suitable reading methods they can choose to use before they read the text
- readers should realise that the reading strategies they choose will depend upon whether the reading is for
  - pleasure
  - to gain information
  - to get general meaning
  - to find particular details
- readers need to see processes modelled demonstrating how competent readers construct meaning
- by activating background knowledge readers are made aware of the extent of their existing knowledge and realise that this may be used to help the process of comprehending new information

  Assist readers to use strategies to:

  - promote enthusiasm for reading
  - activate background knowledge
  - recognise and clarify purpose for reading
  - select a suitable reading style
  - link existing knowledge to new information
  - review and clarify new vocabulary
  - analyse text organisation
  - raise awareness of the processes involved in reading

During Reading

Aim: To self-monitor reading and recognise point of miscomprehension.
To focus on details or concepts that are relevant to the purpose for reading.

Reading is an active process so:

- readers need to see processes modelled so that they see how competent readers construct meaning and respond to text
- readers need to be able to employ specific strategies to identify and substantiate important information, e.g. the main idea
- readers need to be aware of the different levels of comprehension so that they will be able to understand how to comprehend (i.e. they need to go beyond the author's literal statements to draw inferences and make judgements in order to gain full understanding)

- readers need to be able to monitor and evaluate their understanding so that they can recognise the point of miscomprehension and adjust their strategies
- readers need specific word identification strategies to enable them to independently read unfamiliar words
- readers should be aware of organisational patterns of text
- readers must recognise when purposes have been accomplished

Assist readers to use strategies to:

- identify important information
- monitor understanding
- raise awareness of processes involved in reading
- recognise and process text at different levels of understanding
- adjust reading style
- identify words

After Reading

Aim: To reflect on, and respond to, text.
To select, organise and use relevant information for a specific purpose.

Reading is an active process so:

- readers need to see processes modelled so that they see how competent readers construct meaning and respond to text
- readers need strategies that enable them to substantiate understandings or information they derive from their reading of a text
- readers need to have strategies that help them to draw conclusions and make generalisations
- readers need to be able to extract and organise important information from a text
- readers need to be able to detect authorial bias and language that attempts to position the reader socially, culturally or intellectually
- readers need to be able to make comparisons with other texts
- readers need to recognise that the purpose for reading has been achieved

Assist readers to use strategies to:

- identify and extract important information
- substantiate information from within the text or by inference
- summarise text structure
- recognise when purpose has been accomplished
- draw conclusions, make judgements and generalisations

Adapting Strategies

In a balanced literacy program students need to interact with a variety of forms of text.

Within each form there are particular conventions followed by the writer. Effective readers learn to anticipate the use of conventions and the more a reader knows about them, the easier the text is to read. As readers become more experienced with each form they are more easily able to:

- make predictions about what is to be found in a text
- construct meaning or comprehend the text
- write using conventions appropriate to the form of text

Readers adapt strategies according to the type of text being read.

Different forms of text serve different purposes, necessitating different responses from readers. For convenience, the activities have been divided into two sections.

- **Activities suitable for informational texts** (those that inform, explain, report, etc)
- **Activities for use with narrative texts** (those that entertain or amuse)

It should be noted that some activities can be adapted for use with both types of text. All activities are designed so that children can practise the use and transfer of suitable reading strategies in a meaningful context. The strategies are basically the same but are practised in different contexts.

The activities are further divided into before, during and after reading activities. Once again it is important to note that some activities do not fit neatly into this arrangement. They may be started before reading and be completed after reading.

The strategies and activities need to be modelled many times before children are asked to use them independently.

It should be noted that:

- most strategies suggested are suitable for a range of ages and abilities
- strategies need to be taught
- most strategies will be more successful if readers are able to discuss the task and share ideas before, during and after activities

Teaching Strategies Using Informational Texts

In recent years, there has been an increased awareness of the need to introduce non-fiction material to young readers. The following strategies can help children to understand how to approach these texts and to give them help to make them competent and discerning readers of non-fiction or informational texts.

The strategies are organised into before, during and after reading categories but can be adapted by teachers, e.g. some strategies can be used before reading to direct the reader and then completed after information has been selected from the text (e.g. Skeleton Outline).

Plan Your Reading Trip

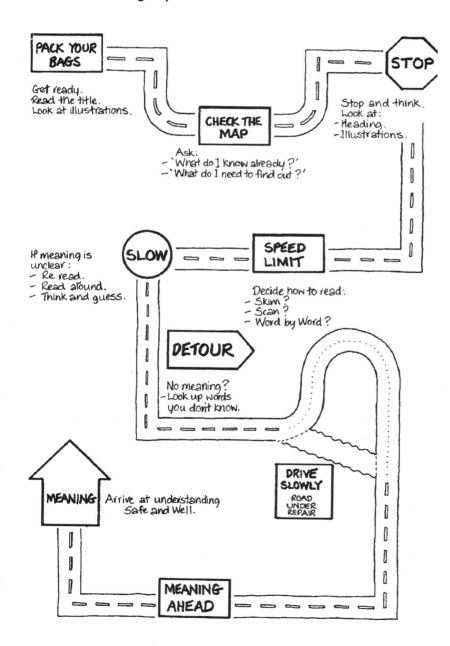

Adapted from Paris, S. 1989, *Reading and Thinking Strategy Kits*, Collamore Educational Publishing, D.C. Heath and Company, Lexington.

Before Reading

Aim: To prepare for reading

Assist readers to use strategies to:

- promote enthusiasm for active reading
- activate background knowledge
- recognise and clarify purpose for reading
- select a suitable reading style
- link existing knowledge to new information
- review and clarify new vocabulary
- analyse text organisation
- raise awareness of the processes involved in reading

Make Predictions About:

- text structure and setting out
- publishing conventions
- information likely to be found
- language style that will be used
- vocabulary likely to be encountered

Try these activities:

Brainstorm and Categorise
Before and After Charts
Prediction
Think Sheet
Ask Questions
Set a Purpose
Select a Reading Style
Interesting Words Chart
Graphic Outline
Signal Words

Brainstorm and Categorise

When teachers draw attention to the background information that is drawn upon in reading, children begin to understand its importance to comprehension. It promotes active reading as students set out to find information that is important to them.

Procedure:

Before children begin to read a piece of text, ask:

What do you already know about this topic?

Record all responses on cards.

After initial brainstorm session, work with children to categorise or classify information into some sort of logical structure.

This information could be used as a Skeleton Outline to be completed after reading.

Example: (Year 3 class)

What do you know about insects?

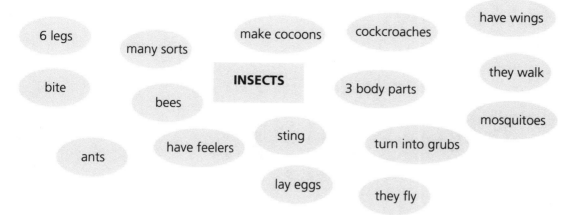

Now classify and group related information.

INSECTS

TYPES OF INSECTS	BODY PARTS	LIFE CYCLE	MOVEMENT	OTHER FEATURES
bees	6 legs	lay eggs	fly	sting
mosquitoes	feelers	turn into	walk	bite
ants	3 body parts	grubs		
butterflies	some have wings	cocoons		
cockroaches				

Then ask:

What do you want to find out?

Children discuss or write one or two things they wish to know, e.g.

What do insects eat?

How do they bite or sting?

Children read to find information.

There are many ways of representing information within a logical framework

```
                              Food
         ┌───────────────────┬───────────────────┐
     Imported              Exported          Consumed locally
    ┌────┼────┐          ┌────┼────┐        ┌────┼────┐
 canned fresh dried   canned fresh dried  canned fresh dried
```

```
                    Rubber
                    tyres
                    seals

    Metal                          Plastic
  body chassis                  instrument panel
                                     trims
                    Material
                   used in cars

                                   Glass
                                  windows
                                  mirrors
```

Before and After Charts

This strategy is suitable for individuals or groups of children. It reminds children what they already know and helps them to link this to new information. It also clarifies the purpose for reading.

Procedure:
Before reading, students list all they know about a topic to be studied.

After reading they write all they have learned.

They compare the two lists and then write questions they still need to answer.

What I know about snails	
Before reading	**After reading**
have shells	are called gastropods
slimy	some live in water
have feelers	have a head at the front and a foot underneath; the rest of the body is inside the shell
eat plants	have a rough tongue like a rasp for scraping and tearing food
lay eggs	lay eggs through its head
like damp places	put down slime to help them move

Prediction

It is vital for all children to be involved in prediction activities because efficient readers are constantly making and revising predictions as they seek to make sense of text.

Prediction activities will help to:
- identify important information
- activate background knowledge
- motivate interest and enthusiasm for reading
- assist readers to focus on the strategies they use for reading
- recognise and clarify purpose for reading
- recognise different levels of comprehension

Invite children to predict from:
- the title
- the cover
- the table of contents
- pictures, photographs, diagrams

Ask children to make predictions about:
- information they might find in the text
- vocabulary and language style likely to be used
- text structure, e.g. problem/solution list, cause/effect
- publishing conventions and layout, e.g. table of contents, headings, index

Prediction activities should be short and stimulating.

Think Sheet

This strategy directs students to set a purpose for their reading when they are trying to gain information from the text. Chapter titles, headings and subheadings are used to predict what information may be in a passage.

Procedure:
Use a specific chapter or section of a textbook.

List all the headings and subheadings (if no subheadings are provided, list key phrases from the first sentence of each paragraph—usually the topic sentence).

Students work with partners to think about what information might be included in each section. Discuss and record predictions (in pencil).

Students read text to assess accuracy of predictions.

Students substantiate or revise predictions from the text.

Meet with original partner to revise information and record any changes or additional information.

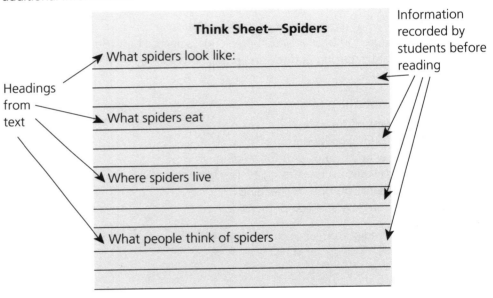

Adapted from Raphael, Taffy E., 'Question-Answer Strategies for Children', *The Reading Teacher*, November 1982, pp. 186–90. © The International Reading Association.

Ask Questions

Before reading teach children to formulate questions so that they then read to find solutions or answers to their own questions.

Procedure:
What do I know?
Talk about what children already know about the topic.

What do I want to find out?
Children formulate their own questions using guiding words such as: Who? Where? What? Why? How?

Make a chart to display.

Set a Purpose

Procedure:

- Discuss the material and establish why the text is being read so that readers can select a suitable reading style and recognise when the purpose has been accomplished.
- Students should ask:
  Why am I reading this text?, e.g.
  - for enjoyment
  - to retell (orally or in writing)
  - to answer questions
  - to make comparisons
  - to get the main idea
  - to gather information
- Successful readers vary the way they read depending on their:
  - purpose for reading
  - topic understanding
  - knowledge of text structure
  - perception of the difficulty of the text
- Students should ask:
  How shall I read this text?
- Readers need to select their reading approach according to the type of text and the purpose for reading.
- Encourage students to make a deliberate choice about the way they will read, e.g. skim (to get an overall picture), scan (for specific information), read and re-read (to remember details, etc.) depending on the purpose for reading.
- Reading instruction should include strategies for different types of reading.

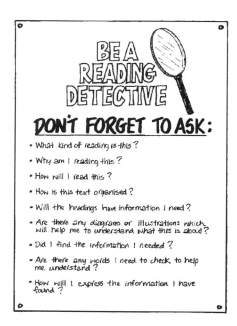

- Jointly constructed charts can be displayed to remind readers of procedures.

Select a Reading Style

Students need to be aware of which reading strategies to use to increase their reading efficiency. Two useful strategies are skimming and scanning.

Skimming

Skimming involves glancing through material to gain a general impression or overview of the content.

Procedure:

- Children work with a partner or in groups. All have a copy of the same text. Texts with headings and subheadings are suitable starting points as they give children a focus to begin.
- All quickly skim text, write predictions for each section. Compare predictions with group members.
- Read text.
- Discuss outcomes to see how well predictions matched contents.

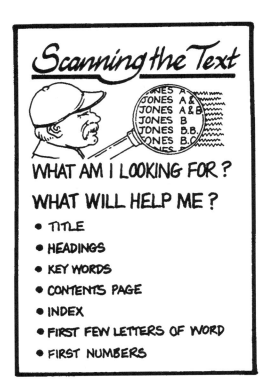

Adapted from Paris, S., 1989, *Reading and Thinking Strategy Kits.*

Scanning

Scanning involves glancing through material to locate a specific detail such as a name, date or place.

Procedure:

- Children work with a partner or in groups. All have a copy of the same text and a list of questions which can be answered directly from the text.
- Students read the question and identify the key word. They then quickly scan the text to locate the key word and answer the question orally in groups.
- Children can work independently or in groups to complete the page.

Interesting Words Chart

These charts can be used to review and clarify vocabulary that will be within a text and also to help students use context clues to work out word meanings. (Students may need considerable help to determine whether context clues are available.) The activity also requires students to paraphrase, which is useful for note-taking and summarising. The strategy should be modelled until students are able to recognise and use context clues successfully.

Some teachers prefer to use Interesting Words Charts *after* reading.

Adapted from Morris, A. and Stewart-Dore, N. 1984, *Learning to Learn from Text. Effective Reading in the Content Area,* Addison-Wesley, p.93. (Adapted by Peter Short)

Graphic Outline

Some reading materials that include pictures, diagrams, tables, graphs, photographs to support text are not easy to follow. The text may be split into columns or placed alongside unrelated graphics in a way which hinders comprehension. Knowledge of text layout can assist children's ability to comprehend texts.

Construction of a Graphic Outline will provide students with a clear diagram of information located in the text and help readers become familiar with typical text organisation. It can also be used as a framework for note taking or summarising information. It is not necessary to use a Graphic Outline for each text. Graphic Outlines help weaker readers look for 'signposts' which facilitate understanding.

Procedure:

- Look through the text and list the sequence of the features as they occur, i.e. main headings, subheadings, diagrams, maps, etc.
- List each of these features on the left-hand side of the page.
- Write details on the right-hand side of the chart and draw boxes around information.
- Make box sizes that show comparative importance of information where practical.
- Give clues as to how many ideas or points may be included under a heading (where no subheadings are provided).
- Students use a Graphic Outline to pick out the features in the text BEFORE READING IT.

Graphic Outline
(Analysing Text Organisation)

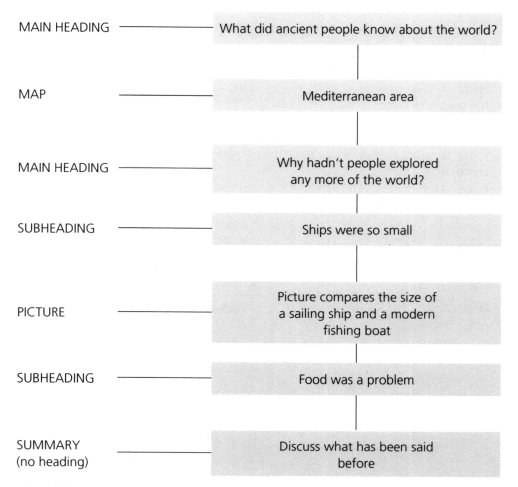

MAIN HEADING	What did ancient people know about the world?
MAP	Mediterranean area
MAIN HEADING	Why hadn't people explored any more of the world?
SUBHEADING	Ships were so small
PICTURE	Picture compares the size of a sailing ship and a modern fishing boat
SUBHEADING	Food was a problem
SUMMARY (no heading)	Discuss what has been said before

Adapted from Morris, A. and Stewart-Dore, N. 1984, *Learning to Learn from Text. Effective Reading in the Content Area*, Addison-Wesley, p.59. (Adapted by Peter Short)

Signal Words

Authors use different organisational patterns in text. If students are to use these patterns to help process information effectively, they need to have practice in identifying particular patterns and selecting appropriate methods of summarising the information.

Procedure:

- Introduce class or group to a particular type of text organisation in a text being read.
- Discuss signal words to look for in text.
- Discuss ways of recording information using diagrams which suit the organisational pattern of the text.
- When students are familiar with identifying and using one pattern, introduce another.
- Build up reference charts recording the organisational pattern, the signal words and ways to record information.

Text patterns	Signal words to look for	Recording information
Cause and effect	makes, causes, leads to, results in, forms, creates, because, results in, so, consequently, so that, if, then	Paragraph 1 Cause Effect: 1 　　　　2 　　　　3
Compare and contrast	although, whereas, yet, however, compared with, unlike, like, different, similar	Retrieval chart
Time order	as well, in addition to, besides, furthermore, finally, after, next, before	Flow charts Time lines
Explanation	because, for, is made up of, composed of	Skeleton outlines, pyramids

Retrieval chart:

	No. of players	Ball shape	No. of umpires
Football Netball Soccer Rugby			

During Reading

Aim: To self-monitor reading and recognise point of miscomprehension

To raise awareness of processes involved in reading

To involve students in reflecting and thinking about information and ideas as they read

To identify important information

To monitor understanding

To recognise and process text at different levels of understanding

To adjust reading style

To identify words

Try these activities

Word Identification Strategies
Stop and Think
Check the Text
Directed Silent Reading
Read, Write, Read
Ask the Teacher
Analyse the Question
Find the Main Idea

Adapted from Paris, S. 1989, *Reading and Thinking Strategy Kits.*

71

Word Identification Strategies

Children need many strategies to deal with unknown words. They need to use their knowledge of syntax, semantics and graphophonics to help them work out unfamiliar words.

Teachers should introduce these strategies one at a time and work with students to gradually build up a reference chart. The strategies should be modelled incidentally and explicitly until children are using them automatically.

What to do if I don't know a word?

- Stop, think about the meaning and make a guess which retains meaning.
- Check the first letters of the word to help confirm guess.
- Leave the word out and read on to the end of the sentence.
- If meaning is lost, stop and ask for help.
- Make a note of new words (write page numbers).

Stop and Think

Students should be encouraged to monitor their understanding as they read and understand how to adjust reading if meaning is lost. The following activity provides opportunities to practise the strategy.

Procedure:

Encourage students to pause after reading a paragraph and ask themselves ...

- Do I understand what that was about?
- Were there any parts I do not understand?
- Could I explain what I've read to someone else?
- What might the next paragraph be about?
- Are there any questions I need to have answered?

Repeat this procedure each day using a variety of texts to familiarise students with the procedure.

Check the Text

This strategy is useful for individuals or mixed ability groups working collaboratively. It encourages readers to interpret illustrations and diagrams when reading.

Procedure:

- Cover text so that children can examine diagram or picture.
- Allow time for children to discuss the picture.
- Children then write text to match the pictures.
- Uncover the text and compare children's version with the text.

Directed Silent Reading (DSR)

DSR gives students practice in identifying important information and raises their awareness of the processes involved in reading for meaning. They are also encouraged to monitor their understanding by sharing responses with other group members.

Each student needs a copy of the text. DSR lessons should be short (10 minutes.) DSR is not a written comprehension exercise. Questions are designed to be answered orally and discussed using text as reference. This strategy is useful for small group work.

Procedure:

- Discuss pictures and title with students—make predictions about content.
- Set a focus question to give purpose to the reading.
- Group reads silently.
- Early finishers can be asked to set the group another question.
- Discuss the passage by first answering the focus question.
- Allow students to ask some of their own questions.
- Probe students' understanding by asking questions that require different levels of comprehension.

Read, Write, Read

This is a useful activity to help children read for meaning and to focus on important information.

All participants require a copy of the same text.

Procedure:

- Children all read a paragraph or page of the text silently after having been told to read to remember as much as they can.
- After reading, close books.
- Children brainstorm.
- Teacher records everything without questioning or commenting.
- When finished, delete repetitions.
- Return to text to check or substantiate responses if necessary. Categorise information.
- Repeat the procedure with next section of text. Continue until text is complete. Summarise the information from the brainstorm sessions.

Ask the Teacher

This strategy improves students' comprehension by teaching them how to formulate questions independently and monitor their comprehension.

Procedure:

- Students and teacher silently read the first sentence, paragraph or chapter of the text. Teacher closes book and students ask as many questions as they can.
- When students finish asking questions, teacher asks questions that will add to students' understanding of text.
- Different types of questions can be modelled by teacher, e.g. *What do you think…? Would the author agree that…?* Continue this procedure with next part of the text.

Analyse the Question

This strategy assists students to use texts to answer different types of questions. It also reinforces the understanding that comprehension depends on the reader's ability to integrate new information with existing background knowledge.

Procedure:

- All read a short paragraph of text.
- Ask students literal questions that can be answered directly from the text. Discuss these as 'Right There' questions.

- Ask questions that require students to make inferences from information in the text. Discuss these questions as 'Read and Think' questions.
- Ask questions that require students to evaluate or judge information from text. These are 'On My Own' questions.

Adapted from Raphael, Taffy E., 'Question-Answer Strategies for Children', *The Reading Teacher*, November 1982, pp 186-190. © The International Reading Association.

Find the Main Idea

Students are often asked to read a piece of text and find the main idea or ideas. The main idea may be stated in a topic sentence and require literal translation. It may be implied and require the reader to connect information and make inferences. Sometimes text has no main idea, simply enumeration of detail. Efficient readers need to be able to recognise facts and details that are important to achieve their purpose. The following activities are suggested as starting points.

Classifying

Write words from topic onto cards and work with students to classify them according to common features. Give each category a heading. Have students work in groups to practise classifying. To vary the activity, sometimes specify the categories and sometimes allow students to study the words to see relationships and devise appropriate categories.

Making Generalisations

All students read a paragraph. Teacher offers a selection of statements about the text. Students select one that summarises or makes a generalisation about the text. Discuss why particular statements are more suitable than others.

Visual Models

Use a visual model to explain how a main idea relates to details that support it, e.g.

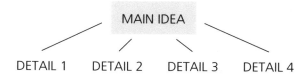

Group Summaries

Students read first paragraph silently. Then, as a group, summarise the paragraph by producing a single phrase or sentence. They repeat the procedure for each paragraph. When all paragraphs have been treated in this way, they examine the phrases and decide whether the final results have captured the meaning.

Previewing

Students look closely at the title, headings or sub-headings in the text. They change these statements into questions. Previewing will help readers establish what is important in the text. This activity should be done with the whole class until students can set their own questions and see the relevance of setting a purpose for reading.

Adapted from Paris, S. 1989, *Reading and Thinking Strategy Kits*

75

After Reading

Aim: To reflect on and respond to text
To select, organise and use relevant information
for a specific purpose

Assist readers to use strategies to:

- Identify and extract important information.
- Substantiate information from within the text or by inference.
- Summarise text structure.
- Recognise when purpose has been accomplished.
- Draw conclusions, make judgements and generalisations.

Try these activities:

| Key Words |
| Notemaking |
| Cloze |
| Student Quiz |
| Change the Form |
| Skeleton Outlines |
| Pyramids |
| Semantic Grids |
| Flow Charts |
| Retrieval Charts |
| Three Level Guide |

Think About the Text

1 Was it interesting?
2 Was it clear?
3 Was it believable?
4 Was it fact or fiction?
5 Why did the author write it?
6 Did it meet your needs?
   – did it answer questions?
   – did you enjoy it?
7 Did the author do a good job?

Key Words

Key words, usually nouns or verbs, are the important words that provide the key to understanding the ideas in a text.

Whatever notemaking strategies are used, success depends on the ability to select appropriate key words.

Procedure:

- Work with whole class initially and discuss the function of key words. (They generally tell who, what, when, where, how or why.)
- Begin with a single sentence and have all students underline key words.
- In pairs or groups, students compare and justify their choice of key words.
- Gradually increase length and complexity of sentences.
- Stress that effective key words:
  – must be specific enough to be meaningful
  – must trigger the memory to allow for recall of extra details

Notemaking

Students need strategies to identify and extract important information from texts. Notemaking skills must be taught explicitly.

Materials used for notemaking should be:

- relevant to current class work
- appropriate to the notemaking method used
- easy to read

Students need to understand the purpose for which the notes are to be made, including:

- help in understanding content
- organising and summarising content
- recording information for an assignment

Students need:

- reading, viewing and listening skills to successfully make notes.
- to be able to identify main ideas, supporting details and keywords in the text.
- to read the material in detail before making notes.
- to understand that particular notemaking methods are appropriate to particular questions or types of information.
- to make notes from a variety of resources including books, videos and tapes.
- to practise notemaking methods.

Teachers should:

- initially use the same material for the whole class when introducing a model of notemaking.
- initially model notemaking methods

See page 78 for suggestions.

Very young children can begin to make notes from texts.

The following sequence could be implemented over a period of time, allowing children to practise each strategy until they are confident to proceed to the next.

DEVELOP NOTEMAKING SKILLS:

1. Begin notemaking using discussion about a picture.

Discuss the picture.
Write one word about the picture.
Write a sentence which indicates
something about the picture.
– Include the key word.

2. Extend the activity.
Discuss the picture.
Write 4 or 5 key words.
Remove picture.
Put each word into a sentence
about the topic.

3. Extend to writing.
All read a short passage
on a topic which is
familiar and interesting.
Circle key words.
List key words.
Write them in sentences without
referring to the original text.

N.B. Not everyone will have the
same key words, but they
should have mainly nouns
. or verbs.

4. Answering own questions:
Decide: "What do I want
to know?"
Skim read to find the answer.
Write key words.
Write sentence to answer the
question.

5. Short Answer/
Long Answer.

TOPIC: Spiders	
QUESTION: What do spiders look like?	
SHORT ANSWER	LONG ANSWER
many types 2 body parts 8 legs compound eyes	There are many types of spiders. They vary in colour, size and shape. Spiders have two body parts . . .

Rule the page as shown above.
Read relevant text and write
short answer notes.
Remove text and compose long
answers.

6. Evaluate.
Children work in small
groups, and share and
compare summaries.

Cloze

Cloze procedure originated as a testing technique but is now widely accepted as a teaching technique. It allows readers to practise effective reading strategies.

Cloze activities can be designed to enable students to practise specific strategies.

1 To encourage students to focus on use of syntactic cues when reading, construct cloze activities deleting particular parts of speech, e.g. verbs, pronouns, adjectives.
2 To encourage students to focus on semantic cues, delete a key word that encourages students to read around the word to gain information.
3 To encourage students to confirm predictions using graphophonics, leave initial or final letters or letter clusters and delete the rest of the word.

Procedure:

- Teacher produces text in which some words have been deleted.
- Students read the passage and insert suitable words. Words should be chosen after students ask:
  Does it make sense?
  Does it sound right?
- When starting to use written cloze, it may assist students if they are given two or three words to choose from for each deletion.
- The cloze procedure works well when students work in groups and debate their choice of words. They are forced to read

Student Quiz

This activity is an effective way of assessing children's understanding of the content of the text.

Procedure:

- Students compile a set of quiz questions based on the information they have gained from reading the text.
- The questions may be written on a card and placed in an envelope for use by other readers.

Change the Form

By writing information in a different form, students will see the need to use different conventions to suit the form. They will need to identify important information and monitor their understanding of the text and make inferences that can be substantiated.

Procedure:

- After reading, students are asked to present the information in a different form. For example:
  – a diary may be presented as a timeline
  – a recipe may be presented as a flow chart
  – a diagram may be presented as a written or oral explanation

Skeleton Outline
Procedure:

- Identify vocabulary that is essential for understanding the concepts and supporting detail of text.
- Arrange these words into a pattern that shows their relationship.

Skeleton Outlines can be used before, during or after reading to form an overview of a topic. They help readers to link new information with existing knowledge in a logical framework.

Skeleton Outlines can be used as a basis for making notes. They assist students to extract and organise important information.

Discussion plays an important part in this strategy as students need to substantiate, make judgements and deal with new information so that meaning is made.

Skeleton Outlines

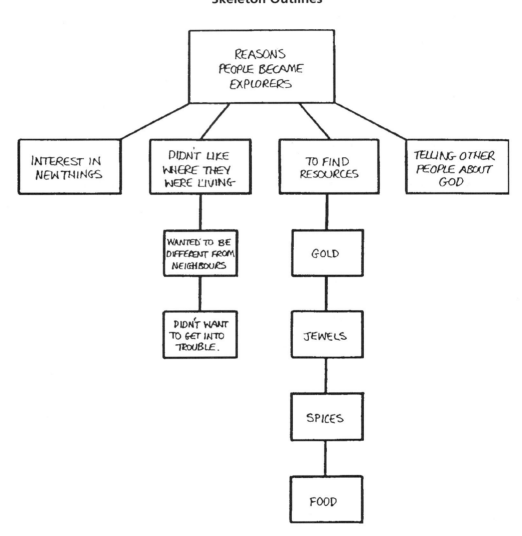

Adapted from Morris, A. and Stewart-Dore, N. 1984, *Learning to Learn from Text, Effective Reading in the Content Area*, Addison-Wesley, p.54 (Adapted by Peter Short).

Pyramids

This strategy can be used to record and organise important information according to main headings, sub-headings and supporting details. Students will also practise drawing conclusions, making judgements and generalising from the text. They will be required to substantiate information from within the text or by inference.

Procedure:

- Students read a chapter, section or short article.
- Students read aloud facts from the passage, teacher writes each fact on a card.
- Teacher displays cards.
- Students sort detailed cards into groups—form the base blocks of the pyramid.
- Teacher asks for suitable headings for the baseline groups (sub-headings).
- Students are then asked to discuss all the information in the pyramid.
- Main idea of passage is derived by asking the question, 'What is the author saying about the subject?' which is written into top block of pyramid.

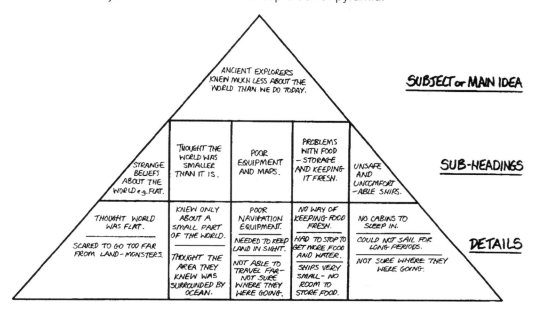

Semantic Grids

Semantic Grids require students to match a set of attributes with particular concepts.

Procedure:

- Draw up a grid with concepts on one axis and a list of adjectives or attributes that could apply to this list on the other axis.
- Students complete grid by:
  - marking off pairs that match
  - marking in page number that substantiates information

Example: Year 3 'Choose a Pet' project after reading:

Semantic Grid

	Expensive to feed	Need to be exercised	Need grooming	Need home to be cleaned	Need affection
Dogs	✓ p. 6	✓ p. 6	✓ p. 6		✓ p. 6
Cats			✓ p. 7		✓ p. 8
Goldfish				✓ p. 7	
Canaries				✓ p. 9	✓ p. 9
Horses	✓ p. 5	✓ p. 5	✓ p. 5	✓ p. 5	✓ p. 5

The chart provides a graphic display that enables easy identification of details and comparison of properties of qualities.

Flow Charts

A flow chart is an excellent replacement for notes.

To construct a Flow Chart, students need to identify and extract important information. They need to draw conclusions and make judgements about what is important. In order to complete the activity, students often need to return to the text many times.

Procedure:

- Use arrows to link important steps or information.
- Students may use pictures, words or a combination of both, in a flow chart.

FLOW CHART

① Sift 1 cup plain flour and 1 pinch salt into bowl.

② Add 1 egg and work flour in from sides.

③ Add ½ pint milk a little at a time. Beat well.

④ Stand for 1 hour.

⑤ Heat pan. Grease lightly.

⑥ Pour some batter into pan and cook slowly on both sides.

⑦ Remove from pan and sprinkle with lemon juice and sugar.

⑧ Roll up and serve.

Retrieval Charts

A Retrieval Chart is one on which information about a number of categories or topics is organised so that comparisons can be made. Students need to be able to extract important information and make generalisations.

Procedure:

- Teacher constructs the headings and asks students to complete retrieval chart.
- Students enter information onto a grid after reading.

Retrieval Charts

Resources	Where Found	Processing Involved	Finished Products
timber	SW of WA	mills	furniture, houses
oil	Barrow Island	refinery	petrol, oil, plastic
alumina	Pinjarra	smelter-refinery	utensils, houses
iron ore	Pilbara	smelter	cars, machinery

Problem	In the Kalahari Desert	In Your Community
How do people shelter?		
Where does food come from?		
From whom do people learn?		
How is a message passed on?		

Three Level Guides

Three Level Guides are based on the question–answer relationships described by Raphael (1984) and Morris and Stewart Dore (1984). They are designed to improve students' literal, inferential and applied comprehension.

Level 1 statements require readers to locate relevant information directly from the text. The wording of the statements may not always be exactly the same as in the text but the meaning is similar. This requires literal level comprehension.
(Reading on the lines—Right there—The author said it.)

Level 2 statements require readers to reflect on literal information and see relationships between statements. They require students to think and search for answers. This is interpretive level comprehension.
(Reading between the lines—Think and search—The author meant it.)

Level 3 statements require readers to apply and evaluate information by relating it to their own background knowledge. This is applied level comprehension.
(Reading beyond the lines—On my own—The author would agree with it.)

Use of Three Level Guides encourages the participation of students of different reading ability in a non-threatening situation.

Procedure:
Students work in small groups. They read and re-read the text and discuss the relevance of each statement on the Three Level Guide. Statements are ticked when consensus is reached.

To construct a Three Level Guide:
Determine content objectives—What do you want students to get from this text?

Write applied level statements first (Level 3). These should be based on the content objectives—the main idea, major concepts and generalisations beyond the text.

Write literal level statements next (Level 1). These should contain information on which the applied level statements are based.

Finally, write interpretive level statements (Level 2). These should help students draw inferences from the information in the text.

Construct and display a chart similar to the one below. Refer to it when discussing reading.

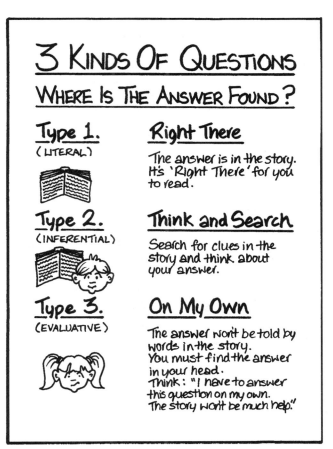

Adapted from Raphael, Taffy E., *'Question-Answer Strategies for Children'*.
The Reading Teacher, November 1982, pp. 185–90. © The International Reading Association.

Three Level Guide

Read text and complete the Three Level Guide

Level 1: **The Author Said It—Right There**

Tick the statements that say what the author actually said.

_____ 1   People once thought the earth was flat.
_____ 2   Sailors went for days without seeing land in ancient times.
_____ 3   There was little room to store food on sailing ships.
_____ 4   Fresh food was easy to get on ancient boats.

Level 2: **The Author Meant It—Think and Search**

Tick the statements which you think the author meant.

_____ 1   Early explorers knew a lot about the world.
_____ 2   'Headlanding' kept the sailors from becoming scared.
_____ 3   It was difficult to sleep on old ships.
_____ 4   Early explorers were lucky to have survived.

Level 3: **The Author Would Agree With It—On My Own**

Tick the statements which you think the author meant.

_____ 1   Early explorers probably were sick many times.
_____ 2   Seaports would have been close together in ancient times.
_____ 3   It would have been fun to be a sailor in ancient times.
_____ 4   Early explorers would be surprised how far ships travel today.

Discuss your choices with a partner.
Work in your group and compare your responses. See if you can ALL agree on statements that should be ticked.

Literal level
– select important information

Interpretive level
– draw inferences

Applied level
– address major content objectives

Adapted from Morris, A. and Stewart-Dore, N. 1984, *Learning to Learn from Text, Effective Reading in the Content Area*, Addison-Wesley, pp. 103–105. (Adapted by Peter Short)

Strategies for Informational Texts

Teachers can use these charts to help them identify the skills and knowledge they wish their students to develop (see horizontal axis). They can then scan the vertical axis to determine which activities they would like to implement. The dots indicate activities for before, during and after reading that relate to each area.

Activities	Before Reading						During Reading					After Reading				
	to promote enthusiasm for active reading	to recognise and clarify purpose for readings	to select reading styles to suit purpose	to link existing knowledge to new information	to activate background knowledge	to review and clarify vocabulary	to identify important information	to help students identify how they comprehend	to recognise different levels of comprehension	to identify the organisational pattern of text	to monitor construction of meaning and to recognise the point of miscomprehension	to substantiate information from within the text or by inference	to identify and extract important information	to summarise text structure	to recognise when purpose has been accomplished	to draw conclusions, make judgements and generalisations
Brainstorm and Categorise	●	●	●	●	●	●										
Before and After Charts	●	●	●	●	●	●						●	●	●	●	●
Prediction	●	●	●	●	●	●	●	●	●	●	●					
Think Sheet	●	●	●	●	●	●						●	●	●	●	●
Ask Questions	●	●	●	●	●	●										
Set a Purpose	●	●	●	●	●	●										
Select the Reading Style	●	●	●	●	●	●										
Interesting Words Chart	●	●	●	●	●	●										
Graphic Outline	●	●	●	●	●	●										
Signal Words	●	●	●	●	●	●	●		●	●	●					
Word Identification Strategies							●	●	●	●						
Stop and Think							●	●	●	●	●					
Check the Text							●	●	●	●						
Directed Silent Reading	●	●	●	●	●	●	●	●	●	●	●					
Read, Write, Read							●	●	●	●	●	●	●	●	●	●

Strategies for Informational Texts

Activities	Before Reading						During Reading					After Reading				
	to promote enthusiasm for active reading	to recognise and clarify purpose for readings	to select reading styles to suit purpose	to link existing knowledge to new information	to activate background knowledge	to review and clarify vocabulary	to identify important information	to help students identify how they comprehend	to recognise different levels of comprehension	to identify the organisational pattern of text	to monitor construction of meaning and to recognise the point of miscomprehension	to substantiate information from within the text or by inference	to identify and extract important information	to summarise text structure	to recognise when purpose has been accomplished	to draw conclusions, make judgements and generalisations
Ask the Teacher							●	●	●	●	●					
Analyse the Question							●	●	●	●	●					
Find the Main Idea							●	●	●	●	●					
Key Words							●	●	●	●	●	●	●	●	●	●
Notemaking												●	●	●	●	●
Cloze								●	●	●	●	●	●	●	●	●
Student Quiz												●	●	●	●	●
Change the Form												●	●	●	●	●
Skeleton Outlines	●	●	●	●	●	●	●	●	●	●	●	●	●	●	●	●
Pyramids												●	●	●	●	●
Semantic Grids												●	●	●		●
Flow Charts												●	●	●	●	●
Retrieval Charts												●	●	●	●	●
Three Level Guides							●	●	●	●	●	●	●	●	●	●

Teaching Strategies Using Narrative Texts

The following strategies are presented as ideas that will help readers become familiar with the whole text structure, language features, setting and characterisation found in narrative texts.

The ideas are organised to help teachers focus on different areas before, during and after reading.

Before Reading

Aim: To prepare for reading

Assist readers to use strategies to:

- promote enthusiasm for active reading
- activate background knowledge
- recognise and clarify purpose for reading
- select a suitable reading style
- link existing knowledge to new information
- review and clarify new vocabulary
- analyse text organisation
- raise awareness of the processes involved in reading

Try these activities:

> Prediction
> Picture Flick
> Book Features
> Set the Scene
> Brainstorming
> Written Predictions

Prediction occurs when the reader brings previous knowledge to new material.

Prediction

Predictions are not wild guesses. They occur when the reader previews the new material (visual information) and eliminates unlikely alternatives using prior knowledge (non-visual information).

Prior knowledge consists of:

- knowledge of world experiences (semantic information)
- understanding of language patterns (syntactic information)
- understanding of written symbols of language (graphophonic information)
- the meaning already generated by what has been read

By encouraging children to be involved in prediction activities, teachers can:

- motivate interest and enthusiasm for reading
- show how purpose guides the process of reading
- assist readers to select reading styles to suit purpose
- activate background knowledge
- help readers to focus on strategies they use to construct meaning

Prediction activities help readers to understand that reading is an active process about constructing meaning, using what they know and combining this information with new material from the text. They also set a purpose for reading and promote active involvement in the reading process.

Prediction activities should be brief and lively and should encourage children to become active readers.

Picture Flick

This activity is a more formal version of what children and adults do before they read a book that includes illustrations. Big books with obvious storylines are ideal for this.

Procedure:

- Show the front cover of the book and invite comments.
- Open the book and display it page by page.
- Encourage children to look at the pictures but not to comment.
- Allow children to form small groups and 'tell the story'.
- Return to whole group and read the story to the children.
- Make available small books for students to read independently.

Book Features

Because different forms of text have different conventions, it is important that children build up understandings about texts they encounter.

Procedure:

- Show the book.
- Discuss the layout, e.g. title, author, illustrator, blurb, chapters, contents, captions, dust jacket.
- Ensure that children hear the correct terms and apply them when they discuss books.

Set the Scene

Getting ready to read should involve building expectations of the text to be read. It should be a short, sharp activity.

Any discussion that helps to activate background knowledge will assist comprehension.

Procedure:

- Discuss the title, the illustrations and the author.
- Help children to recall any previous stories that have the same author or illustrator.
- Discuss the type of story, e.g. myth, and ask children to suggest anything they know about myths.

Brainstorming

This activity is suitable for mixed ability groups or whole class. It provides opportunities to link new knowledge to existing knowledge and promote enthusiasm for active reading.

Procedure:

- Talk about the story structure, e.g. fable — The Ant and the Grasshopper.
- Ask the children such questions as,
  What do you know about fables?
- Record all answers and refer to them after reading. The following answers were given by year three children who had read and discussed several fables:
  They usually have animals that act like people
  There's a lesson at the end
  They're usually short stories
  They teach us a lesson
  The bad animal gets punished
- Talk about the theme...
  Relate children's experience to the theme or topic, e.g. *Sometimes people are very lazy ... Can you tell us about a time when you have been lazy? ... The story today is about a lazy grasshopper. What do you think happens?* Teacher records all responses.
- Talk about the language ...
  What sort of words or phrases might you expect to find in this fable?
  Children's responses:
  tricked, clever, stupid, smart, busy, idle, bully, scared, planned, greedy, lazy, serves you right, punished.
- After the fable has been read, children reflect on their responses and make comparisons with the text.

Written Predictions

Written predictions form a basis for discussion that will help children gain insight into the factors that influence their comprehension, i.e. background knowledge of topic, text structure, word meanings, cultural influences, historical knowledge, etc.

Procedure:

- After writing initial predictions, children read a section of text. They then think about their first prediction and change or confirm their prediction. They continue to read the passage part by part, stopping to refer to their previous prediction and making changes when necessary.

During Reading

Aim: To self-monitor and recognise point of miscomprehension.
       To involve students in reflecting and thinking about information and ideas as they read.

Assist readers to use strategies to:

- identify important information
- monitor understanding
- raise awareness of processes involved in reading
- recognise and process text at different levels of understanding
- adjust reading style
- identify words

Try these activities:

> Readers' Circle
> Oral Summaries
> See the Picture
> Read and Think

Adapted from Paris, S. 1989, *Reading and Thinking Strategy Kits*

Readers' Circle

This activity is suitable for all readers from beginning to independent. It works best with a heterogeneous group of six or more. It should be repeated frequently so that readers begin to reflect automatically as they read. By teaching readers to reflect on what happens when they read, we are empowering them to take responsibility for the strategies they use when reading and raising their awareness of processes involved in reading.

Procedure:

- Each participant requires the same material. The material should be written in natural language and should be predictable. Participants sit in a circle with the teacher.

  Teachers may:
  - read to children
  - read aloud with children
  - have children read aloud with a partner (or take turns)
  - have everyone read silently
- Read the title and ask for predictions. Encourage children to use key words from the title or any other information in order to make predictions. While accepting all predictions without judgement, seek clarification if necessary. Ask questions such as:

  If you were the author, what would you make happen in this story?
  Who might the characters be?
  Who do you think the main character is?
  What sort of characters do you imagine might be in this story?
  Do you think the characters in this story are like real life people?
  Where could the story take place?
  When do you think the story could have happened?
- After children have had time to make their predictions, they return to the text to confirm their ideas.
- As predictions are substantiated or rejected, ask children to make further predictions and then continue with another section of the text.
- The reading is interrupted to ask questions such as:

  Why do you think the author is telling us that? Where does it fit into the story?
  How important do you think that information will be to the outcome?
  What is the author doing to make us want to read on?
  What is happening inside your head as you read (or listen) to that part?
  Do you think that's what the author wanted you to think? How did the author manage to make you think that way? Do you agree with her/him?
- When the reading is finished, readers can retell the story from pictures and a Story Grammar Chart (see page 100).

Oral Summaries

This activity helps children to monitor their comprehension and invites them to substantiate answers from the text.

Procedure:

* Each participant has the same text. All read a section of text. Each person then summarises what has happened so far in the story. Discussion and substantiation are encouraged.

See the Picture

This strategy helps children move from word-by-word reading to whole text reading. It also allows for interpretation of text and justification from the text or from outside.

Procedure:

* Children read a section of text and imagine the character, setting or action. They then tell a partner what they are imagining and why they have created that image. They return to skim or scan the text and substantiate or change their image.

Read and Think

Although reading is all about making meaning from print, some poor readers see reading as the chore of decoding symbols, governed by an incomprehensible set of rules that nobody has taught them. The following strategy will help them focus on processes involved in making meaning from text.

Reading material should be chosen because it is of interest to children and is well written. Children do not need a copy of the text for the first reading but it should be available for them to read later if they choose.

Procedure:

- Read the first paragraph of the text to the children. Stop.
- Discuss such questions as:
  Do you like the story so far? Why?
  Teachers should not expect all children to like every story. Children should be encouraged to express an opinion, even if it differs from that held by the teacher.
  What was happening inside your head while you were listening?
  This question will evoke many different responses, all of which should be valued and discussed.
  What do you think will happen next?
  All suggestions should be accepted. No-one is 'right' or 'wrong'.
  What questions are you asking in your head?
  Share all responses.
- Ask readers to think – *What is it that I am bringing to this story that causes me to think in this way?*
  This question helps make readers conscious of the sort of background knowledge they bring to reading. It may be knowledge of topic, text structure, word meanings or historical and cultural knowledge associated with the text. Readers are also encouraged to reflect upon their own values.
- Continue to read the text, stopping at intervals to repeat the procedure outlined. Make the reading material available to children.

After Reading

Aim: To reflect on and respond to text.
        To select, organise and use relevant information for a specific purpose.

Assist readers to use strategies to:

- identify and extract important information
- substantiate information from within the text or by inference
- summarise text structure
- recognise when purpose has been accomplished
- draw conclusions, make judgements and generalisations

Try these activities:

Reflection Sessions	Character Interviews
Retelling	Change the Point of View
Map a Story	Character Diaries
Change the Form	Character Self Portrait
Story Grammar	Character Ratings
Cause and Effect	Literary Letters
Jumbled Stories	Report Card
Time Line	Police Report Form
Plot Profile	Wanted Poster
Newspaper Report	

Think About Your Reading

- What's the **title**?
- Who are the **characters**?
- What is the **action**, the **outcome**, the **setting**?
- Ask yourself **who, what, where, when** questions.
- Say it in your **own words**.
- Make a **summary**.

Story Structure

By reflecting on story language and story structure, readers will gradually build expectations of how stories are constructed. This knowledge will support the development of speaking, listening, reading and writing.

Knowledge of how stories work will assist comprehension. As children are exposed to a variety of narrative texts, they will come to expect that, in most stories, the main character will be confronted with a major problem. They predict that episodes will follow until the problem is resolved. Once the problem is solved, readers do not expect that the story will continue. They know that the story is finished. Within this story structure, episodes may be repetitive (*The Three Billy Goats Gruff*), cumulative (*There was an Old Lady Who Swallowed a Fly*), interlocking (*Epaminondas*) or chronological (*Solomon Grundy*), or a combination of these. Readers need to know that stories do have a basic structure and also have structures within. This information will assist readers to recognise and predict events and their consequences.

By discussing story structure and using the following activities, teachers can help children to:

- predict the plot
- activate background knowledge of similar written forms
- identify and extract important information
- identify the organisational pattern of the text
- draw conclusions and make judgements or generalisations
- substantiate information from within the text or by inference

It is important for readers to understand how a story unfolds as this information helps vocabulary development and also reinforces the understanding that reading is for making meaning.

Reflection Sessions

Sessions are conducted after a group of children have read a text independently. Group talks should be directed by children. They are not meant to be teacher-directed question and answer sessions.

Teachers need to model the sorts of questions that require participants to think about the text, formulate opinions and express feelings.

Procedure:

- Ask questions to stimulate discussion, e.g.
  What did you expect the story to be about?
  Did it turn out that way?
  What characters did you like (or dislike)? Why?
  Could you understand how a particular character felt because something similar happened to you?
  What was your experience?
  Would you recommend this story to others? Why?
  Did you think that ....was a fair way of describing ..?
  What did the story tell you about the author and her/his way of looking at life?
  Is that the way you think about ..?

Retelling

Retelling can be used to teach and/or test comprehension and it involves students in all modes of language, i.e. reading, writing, speaking and listening. It enhances comprehension at word, sentence and whole text levels and requires readers to recall, select, organise and summarise information. Retelling also provides meaningful practice in the use of a range of oral or written conventions. Different types of retelling can be developed to suit a range of reading and writing abilities.

The Retelling procedure described here has been developed by Brian Cambourne and Hazel Brown in the book *Read and Retell,* (Nelson, Aust. 1987). Their research in this area has provided teachers with an insight into the value of using the procedure with a variety of texts for many purposes. The contribution of the authors is gratefully acknowledged. There are different ways in which retelling may occur:

Oral-to-oral retelling is suitable for non-readers and non-writers.

Teacher tells story and children retell:

- to a partner
- onto a tape
- in groups taking turns
- using pictures as a guide

Oral-to-written or drawing retelling is suitable for immature and mature readers/writers.

Teachers tell the story and students retell:

- individually in writing
- in groups writing collaboratively
- using drawings with a minimum of writing
- using drawings only

Written-to-oral retelling is suitable for reluctant or immature writers.

Students read the text and then retell it orally:

- to a partner
- onto a tape
- in groups taking turns

Written-to-written retelling is suitable for students who have some control over reading and writing.

Procedure:
- Students read title and write a sentence to explain what the text will be about.
- Share predictions from volunteers.
- Students write a few words that they expect to find in the text. Discuss words obtained from volunteers.
- Students read text silently and think about their predictions.
- Students then read the text as many times as they wish until they feel they understand it. They are encouraged to read for understanding, not to memorise chunks of text.
- Students then put the text away and write their interpretation of the text for someone else who has not read it. Students are told not to look back at the text or to worry about neatness or spelling, but to write as quickly as they can.
- After 10–15 minutes students read their recounts to a partner and spend time comparing their versions. Encourage students to discuss any number of aspects of their retells and ask questions such as:
  Why did you include/exclude this part?
  Is there any part of the retell that was unclear?
  Is there any part of the retell you would like to borrow?
- After discussion, the whole class meets and volunteers to share their writing.

Written-to-drawing retelling is suitable for students who can read but are unable or reluctant to write.

The procedure is similar to that described above, but students respond by drawing (perhaps with labelling). Drawings are then compared and discussed.

Variations

- If the text is very lengthy or complex, ask students to picture a particular part of the text and retell from that part.
- Retell the story changing the ending.
- Retell adding a character.
- Retell deleting a character.

Reference: Brown, H. and Cambourne, B. 1987, *Read and Retell*, Thomas Nelson Australia, 102 Dodds St South Melbourne 3205.

Map a Story

Drawing a map that captures events in a story is a useful way of summarising information. Some stories lend themselves to this strategy more than others. Children require several demonstrations of the process before being asked to complete the task independently.

Map events in the story.

Maps should show important parts of the setting and trace the movement of the main characters. Children can retell the story from their map.

Change the Form

Students work in pairs or small groups to re-write the story in a different form, e.g. a play, a journal, a comic strip, a picture book.

Story Grammar

Teachers and students brainstorm to compile headings that suit the story being read. Children select details from the story and place them under appropriate headings. (See photocopiable sheet on page 217.)

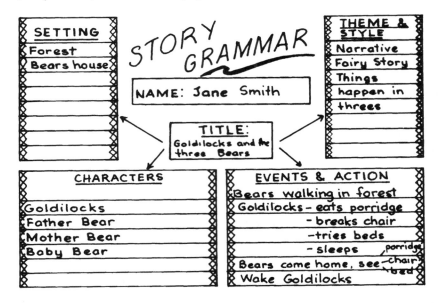

Cause and Effect

Discuss the story. Record main events (or episodes) and show how actions lead to the reactions as the plot develops.

Setting	Episode 1	Episode 2	Episode 3, etc.
Who	Goldilocks	Goldilocks	Goldilocks & bears
Where	Bears' house	Bears' house	Bears' house
When			
What	went in	sat on	went to sleep
Initiating event or problem	ate porridge	sat on chairs	bears angry
Reaction	didn't like father's or mother's porridge	didn't like father's or mother's chair	bears angry
Resolution or outcome	ate baby's porridge	broke baby bear's chair	chased Goldilocks

Jumbled Stories

Students work in pairs and each completes a written retell of the story they have read. The retells are then cut into paragraphs and the partner attempts to reassemble the story correctly.

A Time Line		About:	
Time	**Notes**	**Illustrations**	

Time Line

Students construct a Time Line that indicates the events of the story in sequence. (See photocopiable sheet on page 219.)

101

Plot Profile

After reading the story several times, brainstorm to find the main events. List these in order. Rate the excitement of each event, then plot onto the grid.

Teachers should work through the process several times and then encourage the children to work in small groups to complete a plot profile of a well known story.

After several profiles have been completed, there should be discussion about the similarities and differences in the various profiles produced. (See photocopiable sheet on page 216.)

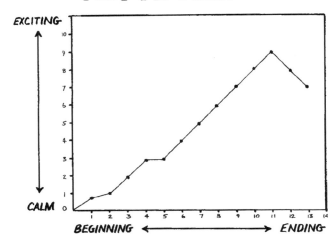

PLOT PROFILE

LIST MAIN EVENTS IN ORDER :

1. Bears go for a walk.
2. Goldilocks goes into bears' house.
3. Goldilocks eats porridge.
4. Goldilocks breaks chair.
5. Goldilocks goes to sleep.
6. Bears come home.
7. Bears see that porridge has been eaten.
8. Bears see broken chair.
9. Bears go up to bedroom.
10. Bears wake Goldilocks.
11. Goldilocks screams.
12. Goldilocks jumps out of the window.
13. Goldilocks runs home.
14.

Adapted from Johnson, Terry D. and Louis, Daphne R. 1985, *Literacy Through Literature,* Thomas Nelson Australia, 102 Dodds St South Melbourne 3205.

Newspaper Report

Report the whole story or an important incident as though it were an event being reported in a newspaper.

The following characteristics should be included:

- headline—to capture attention
- date and place
- lead sentence — to encourage the reader to read on (similar to headline but with more detail)
- details: who, what, why, how and when
  (It may also include quotes from eye-witnesses)
- conclusion

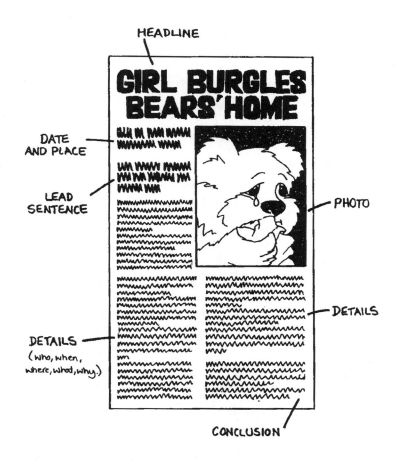

Adapted from Johnson, Terry D. and Louis, Daphne R. 1985, *Literacy Through Literature*, Thomas Nelson Australia, 102 Dodds St South Melbourne 3205.

Characterisation

By examining the actions and reactions of characters in a story, readers gradually build understandings of how characters help the story to unfold. They also begin to understand how and why authors build characters into stories.

In order to build understanding about characters, children:

- make inferences about characters based on their actions
- interpret and evaluate information
- make judgements
- see the relationship between cause and effect
- consider the point of view from which the story is written

Characters in stories range from naive and simple to sophisticated and complex, so it is important to enable children to discuss and reflect upon characters in a variety of stories. The following activities help readers to understand how characters' actions and reactions form an integral part of the plot of a story.

Note:

- all activities should be preceded by time for discussion
- collaborative learning should be encouraged
- most of the activities can be applied to different narrative texts. Teachers however need to select or modify activities to suit their students' needs

Character Interviews

Children work in groups of about six. After everyone has heard or read the story, choose one person to be a character from the story. Group members then discuss the sorts of questions which would be appropriate. (Teachers may need to model questions.) Group members take turns to ask questions.

Optional follow-up: group composes a newspaper article about the character.

Change the Point of View

Read the story.
Discuss how the story would change if it was written by the villain. Write the story from the villain's viewpoint.

> Once upon a time there was an unkind family of goats. Their name was Gruff. The goats always had to outsmart other animals.

Character Diaries

Group members discuss what it would be like to be a character from the story. They then write an account of a day in the life of that character.

> MONDAY.
> What a day! I should have chased the small billy goat. He thinks he's so clever...

Character Self Portrait

Children assume the personality of a character from the story and write details under the heading on the 'All About Me' form. (See photocopiable sheet on page 215.)

All About Me

I am:	a Troll.
I live:	under a bridge.
I eat:	billy goats.
I have:	eyes as big as saucers.
I like:	frightening things.
I hate:	fighting.
I wish:	billy goats were not so smart.

Character Ratings

Children rate a story character along a continuum and then justify their rating. The criteria used may be selected by the teacher or children and may change according to the character being rated. (See photocopiable sheet on page 000.)

The Troll

	VERY	QUITE	NEITHER/BOTH NO INFORMATION	QUITE	VERY	
BRAVE		✓				COWARDLY
COMMENTS : I think it was brave to fight the big goat.						
QUIET				✓		NOISY
COMMENTS : He shouted a lot.						
KIND					✓	MEAN
COMMENTS : He shouldn't scare goats.						
IMAGINATIVE					✓	DULL
COMMENTS : He lives on his own in dark places.						
CHEERFUL					✓	SAD
COMMENTS : He must be lonely.						

Adapted from Johnson, Terry D. and Louis, Daphne R. 1985, *Literacy Through Literature*, Thomas Nelson Australia, 102 Dodds St South Melbourne 3205.

Literary Letters

This activity can be introduced by the teacher composing a letter to one of the characters. The children then respond appropriately, writing a reply as that character.

Under the Bridge
16th May.

Dear Billy Goats,
        I wish to apologise for my unforgivable behaviour last month. I wish that the whole incident had never happened . . .

Adapted from Johnson, Terry D. and Louis, Daphne R. 1985, *Literacy Through Literature*, Thomas Nelson Australia, 102 Dodds St South Melbourne 3205.

Reports on Fictional Characters

Read the story and choose one character. Discuss the character's actions and reactions in the story. Decide what information will be needed to complete the activity. (See photocopiable sheets on pages 214, 220–1.)

At first, teachers should model the procedure and direct the discussion to enable children to select appropriate information.

SCHOOL: Bridge Primary. STUDENT'S NAME: C. Troll. YEAR: Senior TEACHER'S NAME: B. Smith			GRADES: A – VERY GOOD B – GOOD C – NEEDS TO IMPROVE

REPORT CARD

SUBJECTS	GRADE	COMMENTS
Kindness	D	Cornelius finds it difficult to relate to others.
Bravery	A	Cornelius was willing to fight the biggest goat.
Common Sense	C	He could have attacked the small goat instead.
Happiness	D	Cornelius seemed to be a sad, lonely animal.

REPORT CARD

POLICE REPORT FORM

WANTED

SUSPECT'S NAME: Troll.

CRIME: Aggravated assault.
    Suspect attacked a gentle goat.
DESCRIPTION OF SUSPECT:
    Skin colour – green.
    Height – 2.00 metres.
    Wrinkled skin, long hair.
DISTINGUISHING FEATURES:
    Very large eyes.
    Long narrow nose.
DESCRIPTION OF CRIME: Unprovoked attack on goat walking across bridge at 2pm. Saturday, 14th May.
PAST CRIMES: Suspect has often approached and harassed small goats.   Known vagrant.

POLICE REPORT FORM

WANTED

NAME: Cornelius Troll.   AGE: Unknown.

LAST KNOWN ADDRESS: Under the
                        stone bridge.

PHYSICAL DESCRIPTION: Wrinkled green skin,
    Height – 2.00 m.   long hair.
    Weight – 200 kg.
SPECIAL FEATURES: Eyes as big as saucers.
    Nose as big as a poker.
        Bandages and plaster.
OTHER INFORMATION: Last seen limping along highway towards the ocean.

WANTED POSTER

Strategies for Narrative Texts

Teachers can use these charts to help them identify the skills and knowledge they wish their students to develop (see horizontal axis). They can then scan the vertical axis to determine which activities they would like to implement. The dots indicate activities for before, during and after reading that relate to each area.

Activities	Before Reading						During Reading					After Reading				
	to promote enthusiasm for active reading	to recognise and clarify purpose for readings	to select reading styles to suit purpose	to link existing knowledge to new information	to activate background knowledge	to review and clarify vocabulary	to identify important information	to help students identify how they comprehend	to recognise different levels of comprehension	to identify the organisational pattern of text	to monitor construction of meaning and to recognise the point of miscomprehension	to substantiate information from within the text or by inference	to identify and extract important information	to summarise text structure	to recognise when purpose has been accomplished	to draw conclusions, make judgements and generalisations
Prediction	●	●	●	●	●	●										
Picture Flick	●	●	●	●	●	●										
Book Features	●	●	●	●	●	●										
Set the Scene	●	●	●	●	●	●										
Brainstorming	●	●	●	●	●	●										
Written Predictions	●	●	●	●	●	●										
Readers' Circle	●	●	●	●	●	●	●	●	●	●	●					
Oral Summaries							●	●	●	●	●					
See the Picture							●	●	●	●	●					
Read and Think							●	●	●	●	●					
Reflection Sessions												●	●	●	●	●
Retelling	●	●	●	●	●	●	●	●	●	●	●	●	●	●	●	●
Map a Story							●			●		●	●	●	●	●
Change the Form												●	●	●	●	●
Story Grammar												●	●	●	●	●

Strategies for Narrative Texts

Activities	Before Reading						During Reading					After Reading				
	to promote enthusiasm for active reading	to recognise and clarify purpose for readings	to select reading styles to suit purpose	to link existing knowledge to new information	to activate background knowledge	to review and clarify vocabulary	to identify important information	to help students identify how they comprehend	to recognise different levels of comprehension	to identify the organisational pattern of text	to monitor construction of meaning and to recognise the point of miscomprehension	to substantiate information from within the text or by inference	to identify and extract important information	to summarise text structure	to recognise when purpose has been accomplished	to draw conclusions, make judgements and generalisations
Cause and Effect							●	●	●	●	●	●	●	●	●	●
Jumbled Stories												●	●	●	●	●
Time Line							●					●	●	●	●	●
Plot Profile												●	●	●	●	●
Newspaper Report												●	●	●	●	●
Character Interviews												●	●	●	●	●
Change the Point of View												●	●	●	●	●
Character Diaries												●	●	●	●	●
Character Self Portrait												●	●	●	●	●
Character Ratings												●	●	●	●	●
Literary Letters												●	●	●	●	●
Report Card												●	●	●	●	●
Police Report Form												●	●	●	●	●
Wanted Poster												●	●	●	●	●

Chapter 3:

Research Skills

Introduction

A mass of information is constantly being processed and stored in print, audio-visual and electronic media. School libraries offer a wealth of resources to students to assist them in their research. In order to succeed in school and in today's world, it is extremely important that students are able first to identify their informational needs and then to access the desired information quickly and efficiently.

A six-step inquiry process has been outlined to provide a guide for teachers and students wishing to develop skills in this area. The Inquiry Process framework represents the steps undertaken by students when completing a research task. The focus of this document is the first three steps of the process.

Six Step Inquiry Process

1	Identify and define the topic
2	Locate resources
3	Select and record information
4	Process and organise information
5	Create and share information
6	Evaluate

Teaching suggestions are offered that are suitable for the phases of reading development focusing on the primary school years. Most of the activities suggested are already embedded in the primary curriculum. For students to develop an understanding of the process of inquiry, the skills are best developed in the context of a topic or task for which they need information.

Teaching Suggestions for Steps 1 – 3 of the Inquiry Process

Identify and Define the Topic

- Develop the topic
  - develop the language base
  - brainstorm — explosion chart — concept map
  - identify and define keywords
- Formulate/Analyse the question
  - identify keywords in question
  - brainstorm — explosion chart — concept map

This stage builds a foundation for the remainder of the Inquiry. Students clarify their understanding of a task or topic to focus on the information they need to locate and for what purpose.

Role-Play and Experimental Reading Phase

- Key Events: encourage children to talk about, and draw, key events after listening to a story. As they gain confidence they can be encouraged to draw a sequence of key events.
- Topic Focus: encourage children to stay 'on topic' when speaking or writing. Sometimes help them to develop a framework that will provide guidance, e.g. a 'Newstelling' framework that includes When? Who? Where? What? and Why? (see section on Newstelling on page 61 of the First Steps *Oral Language: Resource Book*).
- Semantic Webs: children enjoy brainstorming words connected with a key word or idea that takes their fancy. Take a large sheet of butcher's paper and write the key word in the middle. Then write words anywhere on the paper as children call them out. When children run out of words, read them through together and draw pictures beside any word they can't remember. Children are then encouraged to make connections between words, using any criteria which make sense to them. Connected words are linked by lines, thus creating a web of words. This activity helps children to develop classification and sequencing skills, as well as increasing their vocabularies.

Early Reading Phase

- Topic Focus: encourage children to maintain topic focus when speaking or writing. Extend the use of frameworks for oral and written presentations.
- Semantic Webs: extend the use of semantic webs by creating alternative classifications and exploring the ways in which boundaries are crossed, leading to a beginning understanding of a Venn diagram.
- Brainstorming: encourage children to use brainstorming to generate preliminary notes and lists of ideas
- Text Maps: provide opportunities for children to participate in the generation of text maps (story maps and graphic outlines, see pages 99 and 68 of this book)

Transitional Reading Phase

- Regrouping information: teach children to regroup events, information and ideas into categories, then provide an appropriate heading for each category. Build on their previous experience with semantic webs
- Brainstorming: encourage children to use brainstorming to generate preliminary notes and lists of ideas. Use word sources, i.e. class dictionaries, word lists to extend the language base.
- Text Maps: provide opportunities for children to develop text maps to guide the structure of a range of texts, e.g. stories, descriptions, recounts and reports

Independent Reading Phase

- Asking questions
  - encourage students to ask questions about topic and purpose to focus on the central meaning of the text
  - teach children to reframe headings as questions and to focus on comprehension
- Regrouping information: teach children to regroup events, information and ideas into categories, then provide an appropriate heading for each category
- Brainstorming: encourage children to use brainstorming to generate preliminary notes and lists of ideas
- Text maps: provide opportunities for children to develop text maps to guide the structure of various texts

Locate Resources

- Use search strategy
  - subject index/catalogue and Dewey System
  - encyclopaedias and references sources
  - periodical indexes
  - vertical file
  - sources beyond school

Students develop the skills to locate and choose potential information for their needs and purposes. Key words are used and may be refined, combined and revised during a search. A wide range of sources of information need to be introduced at increasing levels of sophistication.

Role-Play and Experimental Phases

- The Alphabet
  - alphabet play: encourage children to play with alphabet blocks and magnetic letters
  - alphabetical-order: foster awareness of the order of letters of the alphabet through songs and play.
  - answer questions if they arise regarding the purpose of punctuation in different contexts
- Spine labels: talk about the function of a library book's spine label
- Fiction/non-fiction: develop awareness of the differences between fiction and non-fiction
- Dictionaries—function: develop an awareness of dictionaries and their functions, helping children to construct simple personal word lists
- Newspapers and Magazines
  - provide newspapers and magazines for children to 'read'
  - develop awareness of how magazines differ from newspapers and books, i.e. that magazines look different because of variations in colour, size and layout
- Information texts: read a variety of information texts with the children, using 'Big Books' in Shared Reading sessions. Expose children to a range of different formats.

Early Reading Phase

Developing an awareness of the organisation of the library resource centre.

- Alphabetical order
  - share with children how alphabetical ordering is used in an index
  - help children to explore the system of alphabetically ordering books on a shelf.
  - shelf order: introduce children to the non-fiction system of categorisation, using some familiar categories
  - fiction order: teach children that fiction in libraries is shelved in alphabetical order according to the first three letters of the author's surname
- Dictionaries
  - continue to develop an awareness of dictionaries and their functions
  - teach children to use a personal dictionary to record and check spelling
- Newspapers and Magazines
  - provide community newspapers for children to explore
  - draw attention to different parts of a newspaper, e.g. news, reports, entertainment, television guide, advertisements etc.

- develop an awareness of the layout of a newspaper i.e. headlines and columns
- provide a range of magazines for children to read
- develop an awareness of different types of magazines, e.g. children's comics, fishing and gardening magazines
- Collecting information: encourage children to collect information from a source other than own knowledge, e.g. other people, books, television programs, and to share it with the class

Transitional Reading Phase

- Alphabetical order
  - teach children to use alphabetical order to find and order simple indexes, reference lists etc.
  - teach children to place lists of words beginning with the same first few letters in alphabetical order
  - teach children to apply knowledge of alphabetical order to find words in indexes, commercial dictionaries, catalogues etc.
- Fiction location/catalogue: teach children how fiction is catalogued, and encourage them to find titles by particular authors
- Non-fiction book parts
  - develop understanding of the organisation and function of headings, sub-headings, indexes, reference lists, glossaries, and help children to apply this understanding when reading and writing non-fiction books
  - encourage children to provide indexes, tables of contents etc. in their written work where appropriate
  - using the catalogue: teach children how non-fiction books are catalogued, and help them to apply this understanding to find particular titles and books on a particular subject
- Newspapers and Magazines
  - provide newspapers for children to read
  - teach children how sections of the newspaper are organised, e.g. how classified advertisements are divided into vehicles, real estate, public notices etc.
  - teach children about the organisation of newspaper articles, e.g. bylines, headlines, dateline, introductory sentence, body of the article etc.
  - provide a range of magazines for children to read
  - develop the understanding that magazines are written for particular audiences and may be highly specialised
- Seek information: encourage children to seek further ideas or information through research or discussion with others

Independent Reading Phase

- Alphabetical order
  - teach children to use alphabetical order to find and prepare reference lists and bibliographies
  - teach children the conventions for ordering words like west — westerly, ANZAC — another and McKay-Moore etc
  - teach children the convention of cataloguing systems, e.g. The Snow Goose is listed under 'S'
- Indexes: teach children to use complex indexes
- Catalogue: provide opportunities for children to develop competency with non-fiction catalogues

- Dictionaries: teach children to use a commercial dictionary:
  - to check conventions regarding the addition of suffixes and prefixes
  - to find the entomology of words
- Thesaurus: teach children to use a thesaurus to select the most suitable word for the purpose, audience and subject
- Newspapers and Magazines
  - provide newspapers for children to read
  - teach children about special features and magazine sections in newspapers
  - teach children how various sections of the newspaper are organised, e.g. how classified advertisements are divided into vehicles, real estate, public notices etc
  - teach children about the organisation of newspaper articles, e.g. bylines, headlines, dateline, introductory sentence, body of the article etc.
  - develop the understanding that newspaper articles offer one version of an event and may be biased
  - discuss the way content, style and presentation of magazines are shaped for target audiences
  - discuss the way colour and flexible or innovative layout are designed to engage the audience
- Collecting information: teach children to collect information from a variety of sources including the use of on-line information sources

Select and Record Information

- Select resources
- Skim and scan to
  - find information
  - determine readability
  - select relevant information
- Make notes
- Summarise

Students develop strategies to select and record the information they need for a task from resources they have selected. They use techniques such as skimming, scanning and notemaking.

Role-Play and Experimental Reading Phases

- Pictures and diagrams: use and discuss pictures and simple diagrams, encouraging children to draw their own for recording purposes
- Book parts: develop the understandings that printed materials may have pages, covers, titles, authors, illustrators, publishers etc.
- Fiction orientation: read to children showing them:
  - the orientation of books — front, back, first page etc.
  - discuss the title, illustrator and author on the book's cover
- Non-fiction
  - show children the orientation of books, front, back, first page etc.
  - talk about the title, illustrator and author on the book's cover
  - develop the understanding that in using non-fiction a range of starting and end points can be chosen according to the reader's purpose and interest
  - develop awareness of the differences between fiction and non-fiction
  - refer to the functions of maps, atlases and globes, encourage children to draw maps where appropriate e.g. treasure maps during a pirate theme
- Notemaking
  - draw children's attention to simple sets of notes such as lists
  - encourage children to make simple lists using key words
- Graphs: teach children to arrange pictures and objects in graph form using simple captions
- Recalling facts: give children practice at orally recalling key ideas from texts
- Key events: encourage children to draw key events from oral or written texts

Early Reading Phase

- Simple figures: provide opportunities for children to use and record information from simple figures
- Maps
  - draw attention to simple uses of maps
  - encourage children to draw simple maps with legends, labels and titles
- Timetables
  - draw children's attention to simple timetables
  - develop the understanding that timetables indicate when events of the day are likely to occur
- Advertisements
  - discuss different types of advertisements
  - discuss advertisements that are aimed at children

- Evaluative comprehension: encourage children to make judgements regarding:
  - reality or fantasy
  - fact or opinion
  - validity
  - appropriateness
  - acceptability
- Notemaking
  - provide opportunities for children to make simple notes
  - teach children to group ideas under simple headings
  - teach children to paraphrase simple information
- Graphs
  - teach children to arrange pictures and objects in graph form using simple captions
  - teach children to draw picto-graphs and simple tallies
- Recalling facts: provide opportunities for children to recall significant information orally and in writing
- Grouping information: teach children to group ideas and information under headings provided by the teacher
- Text interpretations: share your enjoyment of literature with children and encourage them to talk about different interpretations of texts.

Transitional Reading Phase

- Illustrations, maps, diagrams
  - encourage children to get information from and draw diagrams to complement a text
  - develop an awareness of how illustrations, diagrams and accompanying captions can make the message clearer
  - develop understanding of how prominent features on a map are usually represented, e.g. to discern rivers from roads, land from sea etc.
  - provide opportunities for children to interpret and draw simple maps and legends
- Book parts: develop the understanding that printed materials may have:
  - contents
  - indexes
  - chapters
  - copyright statements
  - date of publication
  - information about the author
  - publisher's logos etc
- Fiction: teach children the function of cover design, 'about the author' section
- Non-fiction
  - teach children to use indexes
  - develop understandings of the factual nature of non-fiction, but that authorial bias can be detected as readily in non-fiction as in fiction
  - develop understandings of the organisation and function of a contents page and indexes
  - encourage the use of these understandings to decide what pages should be read
- Evaluative comprehension: encourage children to make judgements regarding:
  - reality or fantasy

- – fact or opinion
- – validity
- – appropriateness
- – acceptability
- Reading for information: develop the ability to skim through books to find topics of interest, then slow pace to read for detail and enjoyment.
- Summaries: provide opportunities for children to present oral and written summaries, developing the understanding that summaries paraphrase the key points and involve a deliberate selection of the information to include
- Notemaking
  - – teach children to note key words and main ideas when listening and reading
  - – teach children techniques for extracting and paraphrasing information
  - – teach children to collect information from two or three sources
  - – help children to construct semantic webs, graphic outlines, skeleton outlines, compare-contrast tables
  - – teach children to regroup events, information and ideas into categories, then provide an appropriate heading for each category

Independent Reading Phase

- Diagrams: teach children to get information from and draw diagrams to complement a text
- Develop the understanding that printed material may have introductions, prefaces, International Standard Book Numbers (ISBNs), bibliographies, cross referencing, footnotes, appendixes
- Non-fiction bibliographies: teach children about the organisation and function of bibliographies, and help children apply this understanding to seek further information
- Expect and encourage children to provide indexes, tables of contents, glossaries, reference lists, footnotes etc. in written work where appropriate
- Develop understandings of the organisation and function of headings, sub-headings, indexes, reference lists, glossaries, and help children to apply this understanding when reading and writing non-fiction books
- Encourage children to provide illustrations, diagrams, maps etc. in non-fiction writing
- Teach children to use a commercial dictionary:
  - – to check additional meanings
  - – to check usage
  - – to check spelling
- Teach children how various sections of the newspaper are organised, e.g. how classified advertisements are divided into vehicles, real estate, public notices etc.
- Teach children about the organisation of newspaper articles, e.g. bylines, headlines, dateline, introductory sentence, body of the article etc.
- Teach use of grid references and map legends
- Develop an awareness of different sorts of information that can be found in maps, e.g. natural and constructed features, population, vegetation, climate etc.
- Develop the ability to present, interpret and compare information in graphs and tables
- Develop the understanding that magazines are written for particular audiences and may be highly specialised
- Develop the understanding that advertisements may have different purposes, e.g. to sell, to educate, to inform, and may target different audiences

- Provide opportunities for children to analyse advertisements that are characterised by:
  - wording designed to enhance appeal and impact
  - succinct language
  - the provision of information
- Teach children to use headings and sub-headings to form a general idea of what the text is about and to make predictions about information that might be expected
- Develop an awareness of relevant and irrelevant information
- Help the children to identify ambiguities and inconsistencies in information
- Discuss the plausibility of answers to inferential and evaluative questions drawn from a text
- Skim and scan: develop the ability to match reading pace to purpose:
  - scan texts for headings and key words
  - skim to gain a general idea of what the text is about
  - read slowly when making notes and when reading for detailed information
- Develop the understanding that, depending upon the purpose and type of text, the sequence of ideas and information can be governed by:
  - priority order
  - chronological order
  - logical flow of ideas etc.
- Discuss the way content, style and presentation of magazines are shaped for target audiences
- Discuss the way colour and flexible or innovative layout are designed to engage the audience
- Develop the understanding of the persuasive intent and content of advertisements, and that advertisements are used:
  - to sell products
  - to alert the public to environmental, health and social issues, e.g. Quit Program
- Provide opportunities for children to analyse methods of appeal used in advertisements including humour, stereotypes, music, 'everyone does it, repetition, famous people, urgency, fantasy, patriotism, egotism, one-sidedness, emotionalism, oversimplification, snob appeal, innuendo, transference of feelings of beauty, youth, image, wealth
- Teach children to survey a text for headings, illustrations, captions, sub-headings, graphs etc. before reading
- Teach children to use headings and sub-headings to form a general idea of what the text is about and to make predictions about information that might be expected
- Teach children to reframe headings as questions to focus comprehension
- Develop an awareness of relevant and irrelevant information
- Develop and awareness of bias and prejudice
- Encourage children to make judgements about the authenticity and validity of a source of information
- Teach children that in summaries:
  - redundancies and repetitions should be eliminated
  - the text should be succinct
- Develop the understanding that summaries are designed to let the audience understand the essentials of the original text with minimal reading or listening
- Teach children to generate headings, main ideas and key points when listening and reading

- Teach children to collate, rearrange and paraphrase information from several sources
- Graphs: teach children to draw graphs such as pie graphs and scattergrams
- Maps
  - teach children to interpret and draw a variety of maps for different purposes
  - teach children to read maps and select and justify a preferred route from A to B, e.g. in orienteering
  - teach children to understand the function of and how to use grid references, e.g. in a street directory
- Diagrammatic notemaking: teach children to represent diagrammatically the relationship between events, ideas and issues, e.g. timelines, semantic webs, graphic outlines, hierarchical summaries etc
- Precis and summaries: give children opportunities to write precis and summaries of texts
- Regrouping information: teach children to regroup events, information and ideas into categories, then provide an appropriate heading for each category

Chapter 4:

Assessment and Evaluation of Reading

Introduction

Children learning to read must develop the following understandings about reading:

1 Reading is making meaning.
2 Good readers know the process they use.
3 Effective reading involves making predictions on the basis of semantic and syntactic information and then confirming or reflecting the prediction (often using graphophonic knowledge).
4 Good readers use a range of strategies to try and retain meaning.
5 Good readers use semantic, syntactic and graphophonic information interactively.
6 Effective readers are confident to take risks when reading.
7 Effective readers reflect on what they have read and make judgements about it based on their own values and experience of the world

If these are the understandings that are important, it is these understandings that should be assessed by teachers.

Assessment is taken to mean the process of collecting data. This data provides a basis for evaluation or judgement of performance, i.e. assessment provides the material for evaluation.

Assessment and evaluation are an integral part of classroom management.

They are of little value if they are used to compare one individual to another.

They can be very valuable when they:

- Form the basis for instructional decisions.
- Provide information about the progress of an individual.
- Lead to an examination of the conditions under which a child is operating.

If assessment and evaluation do these three things, then they are worthwhile.

Any evaluation of reading should relate directly to the philosophical beliefs that underpin the teaching of language. A belief that underpins First Steps is that all aspects of language are interdependent and should be taught and evaluated in contexts that are meaningful for students. It is possible, however, to focus on one aspect (e.g. reading comprehension), providing that the natural connection between all language areas is not forgotten and that the assessment or evaluation is appropriate to children's level of development and cultural or experiential background.

In the past, reading has often been evaluated by asking readers to answer a series of written questions based on previously unsighted texts, completely out of context. This type of evaluation has obvious disadvantages. It assumes that all readers have the **same** cultural knowledge, strategy knowledge, knowledge of the language structures in the particular text, prior knowledge of the topic and motivation or interest in reading. We know this is not true. Most teachers assess children's reading and comprehension continually and have a good understanding of their children's capabilities. Reading must be evaluated the way it is taught, i.e. in context.

Planning for Assessment and Evaluation

Teachers can use classroom activities to observe reading behaviours and strategies used by children.

Observations can be made:

- during silent reading
- while small groups are working collaboratively
- in shared reading sessions
- in discussions
- from children's written responses

The active process of comprehension before, during and after reading should be valued and any evaluation should include processes as well as product outcomes.

Evaluation should also be used to help students take ownership and control over their learning. This empowerment is essential if students are to establish their own purposes for reading (and learning).

The assessment procedures suggested rely heavily on teacher observations of readers at work. It is hoped that the suggestions will help teachers focus on what to look for and how to record information observed.

Remember, before evaluating reading, teachers must ask:

- What do I need to know?
- How can I find out?
- What will I do with the information?
- How will I implement an appropriate program?

PLANNING FOR EVALUATION

<u>WHAT DO I NEED TO KNOW ?</u>

<u>I need to know :</u>

- what knowledge and understandings children have about reading.
- what strategies they are using to read.
- what attitudes they have about reading.

<u>HOW CAN I FIND OUT ?</u>

<u>I can find out by :</u>

- using First Steps Reading Continuum.
- talking to students.
- using students' self assessment.
- analysing:
  - miscues.
  - cloze answers.
  - readers' written
  - responses.
  - word identification
  - strategies.
  - written and
  - oral retells.

<u>WHAT WILL I DO WITH THE INFORMATION ?</u>

<u>I will :</u>

- plan a teaching program. include :
  - strategies for reading.
  - organisation of class.
  - resources.
  - activities.
  - content objectives.
- report to children, parents and teachers.

<u>HOW WILL I IMPLEMENT THE PROGRAM ?</u>

<u>My program will include :</u>

- reading to children.
- shared reading.
- guided reading.
- independent reading.
- language experience reading and writing.
- collaborative learning.
- talking.

Some Suggestions for Evaluating Reading

Using First Steps *Reading: Developmental Continuum*

Talking to Students
- Reading conference
- Interviews

Using Students' Self-Assessment
- Reading logs
- Reading journals
- Personal reading reports

Analysing Responses
- Analysis of retells
- Miscue analysis
- Cloze analysis
- Analysis of readers' written or oral activities
- Analysis of word identification strategies

Using The *Reading: Developmental Continuum*

The Continuum is easy to use because it reflects the knowledge that teachers already have about their children. It offers a framework for teaching and learning, linking the learning behaviours of children with strategies and activities that will ensure that progress is made. It enables teachers to build on solid foundations. Parents will find it helpful and easy to understand, as the Continuum describes behaviours that can be recognised in their own children.

In summary, the Continuum enables teachers to:
- evaluate the development of children's understandings and skills.
- report systematically and accurately on children's current understandings and skills.
- monitor children's progress.
- select from banks of strategies that are directly linked to a child's current level of functioning as mapped on the Continuum, to ensure that satisfactory progress is maintained.
- provide continuity of teaching and learning throughout the school and from year to year.

Procedure:

1 Read 'Beliefs about Reading' (page 15 of the *Reading: Developmental Continuum*).

2 Read through the overview of the *Reading: Developmental Continuum* and become familiar with phase descriptors and key indicators.

3 Read through the complete list of indicators for each phase of development.
It should be noted that behaviours exhibited by children in any one year level may range over a number of phases.

4 Gather information about children's reading behaviours.
The Continuum indicators will inform your observations.

5 Identify the key indicators that describe the reading behaviours exhibited by children in your class and place each child in the appropriate phase.
It should be noted that learners may be spread out on the Continuum. Some learners may plateau at a particular point while others may move ahead at a faster pace. Some may even appear to have regressed, possibly due to the concentration on consolidating a new skill or understanding.

6 Use the key indicator record sheet to record indicators exhibited by your children.
This will provide a total class profile of the children's reading development.

7 Examine the major teaching emphases for each of these phases and select appropriate teaching strategies.
The key teaching strategies described in each phase are considered critical for children's further reading development.

8 Use this information to make instructional plans to meet the needs of the whole class, small groups and individuals.

9 When getting started with the Continuum, it is best to select a small group of children experiencing difficulty with reading for more in-depth analysis and instruction.
Use the reading record form to map individual children's progress and to indicate the focus for future teaching. Note that many of the suggested strategies will also help all children in the class.

10 Work with specific children individually, or as a small group, using appropriate teaching strategies.
Ensure that strategies and activities used are appropriate for the children's phase of development.

Talking with Students

Reading Conference

Student-teacher conferences may be conducted on a one-to-one basis or with a small group. They provide the opportunity for teachers to assess reading understandings and skills in an informal way that gives readers a chance to explain and substantiate their answers, ask questions and discuss any problems encountered.

Conferences are made more effective if some guiding questions or frameworks are established as a basis for discussion.

The following framework was used as a starting point for conferences when children were engaged in selecting and reading books from which they were gathering information for personal Social Studies projects.

Reading Conference Framework

Teacher:
Why did you choose that book?

Child:
I looked at three books but this one had the information I needed and some good diagrams.

Teacher:
Were you able to read the book easily?

Child:
Some of the words were hard but I could work them out by reading around them.

Teacher:
Did the layout of the text help or hinder you? Why?

Child:
The book had a Table of Contents so that was good. Some of the writing was two columns and some wasn't, so it was a bit tricky. Not that bad though…

Teacher:
How did the text help you with your project writing?

Child:
I used the Contents list as headings for my project. I didn't copy out the words though…I already had some other information of my own and it just fitted under the headings.

Teacher:
How did you decide which information you needed?

Child:
It was hard to decide so I talked to some other kids.

The student responses indicate knowledge and understanding about conventions found in non-fiction texts and how knowledge of text organisation can assist comprehension.

The conference framework would change according to the type of text being discussed.

Interviews

Reading interviews can help students and teachers focus on the reading process and the strategies needed to improve understanding.

The following questions are suggested as a guide only and could be modified for different students.

Are you a reader?

What do you do before you start reading?

What do you do if you don't know a word?

When you read, what happens inside your head?

Why do you think other people read?

How do you find the main idea or important things from text?

How do you find answers to questions about things you have read?

How do good readers understand text?

How do you choose material to read?

What is reading?

What is reading for?

What could you do to make you a better reader?

How do you feel about reading?

Do you believe everything you read?

Who is a good reader you know?

When students are involved in self-assessment, they are able to set goals and reflect on their achievements. They can make plans and seek help when it is required. The honest comments given by students, about themselves, can provide teachers with insights into the problems faced by students.

Using Students' Self-Assessment

Reading Logs

A reading log can provide students and teachers with information about the use the child is making of reading.

Procedure:

Provide pages already ruled for students to enter information. Invite children to share their lists. Use a double page of an exercise book.

For example:

Name:					
Date Started	Title	Date Finished	Comments	Activities Completed	Parents/Teacher comment

For younger children some more structure may be needed.

My Reading Log

Title: _____

Author: _____

I Chose This Book...

_____

_____

I Thought That...

_____

_____

I Want to Read...

_____

_____

Reading Journal

A reading journal provides students with an opportunity to reflect upon, and respond to, text. It can provide information about the students' thinking processes and understandings as they interact with text.

Before asking students to start a journal, discuss the idea with them and then brainstorm to produce a range of suggestions for journal entries. Teachers should model the use of a journal and share their entries with students. A journal could include:

- a set of personal goals for reading
- a list of texts read (with commencement dates). This should be separated from the other entries so that teachers can easily see the list
- thoughts or feelings recorded in response to reading
- drawings of settings, characters or events
- phrases or words that have interested, excited or puzzled the reader
- predictions
- suggested changes readers would have made if they'd been the author
- comments on characters, pictures, diagrams or language used

The first pages of students' journals could be set aside to record goals and comments about reading.

For example:

Date	My Goals What do I want to achieve as a reader?	By When	My Successes What have I learned as a reader?	Date

Teachers should take the opportunity to respond in writing to some journal entries. These written responses can pose or answer questions, provide models of language use, offer a sympathetic comment or present a different viewpoint.

Example:

Student:

I read Koala Lou by Mem Fox. I read it to myself but I wanted to read it aloud because I loved the sound of the words. I felt that the story was about me because I never come first at anything.

Teacher:

I love the sound of the words too.
They sound so rhythmical.
Remember, winning isn't everything!
I like you just as you are.

Personal Reading Reports

Students are invited to write a report on themselves as readers. The report can be structured using questions developed by the teacher. A class brainstorming session could provide a useful list of statements or questions to guide student responses.

The following example was constructed after a year four brainstorming session, to which the teacher contributed some ideas. The list is meant to guide students not restrict them.

I think I am a .... reader because ....

My feelings about reading.
My problems with reading.
Help I need.
What I've learned about reading.
What I want to achieve in reading.
Activities I have completed.
Other comments about reading.

Sally's report shows that she has learnt a lot about reading processes. It also gives the teacher an indication of the pressure Sally feels when she is asked to read aloud.

Reading Report
Sally Greenway Year 3 May 1991

I think I am a not too good reader
because I get stuck on some words.
I'm good at USSR.
I have learned that sometimes I can miss out
words when I don't know them and still get
the story. Sometimes I go back and read
things again to see if they make sense. I am
not good at reading aloud because I forget
the story while I concentrate on the words.
I done a story map and a book review.
I want to read more on my own and
choose my own books.

When students are able to take part in evaluating their reading strategies, they can reflect on their practices and decide what works for them. They can begin to take control of their learning.

Analysing Responses

Analysis of Oral or Written Retells

Teachers who wish to use retelling as part of the evaluation process will find it provides valuable information about literacy development. Before using retells for evaluation, it is essential that students have some background knowledge of either texts of the same type (e.g. fairy tales or fables) or the same topic (e.g. a science topic—Frogs, or social studies topic—Early Explorers.)

What could be evaluated?

1 Student's prior knowledge.
2 Behaviours exhibited during reading, writing or sharing times.
3 Knowledge of text structure.

4 Knowledge of language features of particular types of text.

5 Knowledge of language conventions such as spelling, punctuation and syntax.

6 Knowledge of ideas from text.

7 Knowledge of vocabulary.

8 The student's ability to predict, infer, hypothesise and generalise.

Retells can be evaluated by assessing:

Meaning
- Ideas
- Clarity
- Relevance to form/purpose

Organisation
- Sequence
- Unity between parts and whole

Conventions
- Spelling
- Vocabulary
- Punctuation

Cognitive abilities
- To infer
- To predict
- To hypothesise

(See pages 97 to 99 for outline of procedure)

Reference: Brown, H. and Cambourne, B. 1987, *Read and Retell*, Thomas Nelson Australia, 102 Dodds St South Melbourne 3205.

Miscue Analysis

If teachers wish to observe the processes children use as they read, they may need to analyse the errors (or miscues) made by readers when they read aloud. Most readers make errors as they read. They may omit words, make substitutions or add words, sometimes making corrections and sometimes not. By analysing the 'errors' teachers can discover why errors were made. They give clues to what the reader's reading system is trying to do. This information will provide insight into the strategies readers are using or not using.

For example:

Text: The man painted his *house* and then sold it.

Child 1:   The main painted his *horse* and then sold it.

Child 2:   The man painted his *flat* and then sold it.

Both children have made an error or miscue. Child 1's substitution or *horse* for *house* shows that he/she has probably used graphophonic information to arrive at the word *horse* which looks and sounds similar to *house*. It shows also that Child 1 has not used meaning to help decode (it is unlikely that a man would paint a *horse*!). Child 2 on the other hand has substituted *flat* for *house,* indicating that he/she has sought to retain meaning by making use of world or semantic knowledge. Child 2 probably believes, when reading, it is essential to get words that make sense in the context even if this means sacrificing graphophonic information. Both children used words that conformed to the conventional syntactic patterns of the language.

Procedure:

The teacher selects a text that the child might enjoy but at a level slightly more difficult than usual. The child should be able to peruse the text before reading aloud. The teacher requires a copy of the text to make miscues. The teacher needs to prepare literal, inferential and evaluative questions to ask after the passage is read. There are many examples of codes for recording miscue analysis. Teachers need to decide on a code that is easy to use and provides relevant information. The following is a simple coding system adapted for use in a classroom.

Type of error	Coding
Substitution	Write word above
No attempt made	Underline
Insertion	Write word
Omission	Circle omission
Self correction	Write word used and SC

If the miscue does not affect the meaning of the text it can be seen as a positive miscue. If the meaning is lost or altered, it is a negative miscue and shows that the reader may have difficulty understanding the text. The questions asked after the reading will determine the degree to which miscueing has altered meaning.

Many teachers conduct informal miscue analysis as children take part in usual classroom reading activities. The more formal use of this technique can provide specific information about children who seem to be experiencing difficulties with reading comprehension.

Cloze Analysis

Cloze activities can be designed as a teaching strategy to encourage children to use different cueing systems and as a comprehension evaluation method. If cloze is used to evaluate comprehension, it is necessary to analyse the words students use to complete the cloze.

For example:

Original text

Mrs Rodgers drove quickly down the road. Simon and Mandy were sitting in the back of the car. They were both watching for the next set of traffic lights. Mrs Rodgers slowed down as they reached the red light.
'We like traffic lights.
We like traffic lights.
We like traffic lights, but only when they're ... GREEN!'
The children shrieked as the lights changed to green just as they said the word. It was a game they played every time they were in the car. They always tried to guess exactly when the lights would change.
Mrs Rodgers smiled to herself as she drove off. The children were noisy but at least they weren't arguing.

Student's text

Mrs Rodgers drove quickly down the *street*. Simon and Mandy were *sitting* in the back of the car. They were both watching *for* the next set of traffic lights. Mrs Rodgers *slowed* down as they reached the red light.
'*We* like traffic lights.
We like traffic lights.

We like traffic lights, but only *if* they're ... GREEN!'

The *kids* shrieked as the lights changed to *green* just as they said the word. It was a game they *liked* every time they were in the *traffic*. They always tried to guess exactly when the lights would change.

Mrs Rodgers smiled to _____ as she drove off. They children were noisy, _____ at least *then* weren't *fighting*.

Comparison

	Original Text	Reader's Substitutions
1	road	street
2	sitting	sitting
3	for	for
4	slowed	slowed
5	we	we
6	when	if
7	children	kids
8	green	green
9	played	liked
10	car	traffic
11	herself	-
12	but	-
13	they	then
14	arguing	fighting

Name: _____ Date: _____

The substitutions may be made from various categories (some words may fit into more than one category).

Categories

Words which require:

- world or cultural knowledge (1,4 and 14)
- linguistic knowledge (6,7,9,11 and 12)
- the reader to refer back to previous text (7,8 and 10)
- the reader to read on further (2,3 and 13)

Analysis

Exact or meaningful replacement (1,2,4,5,7,8,14)
Partial meaning retained (6,9,10)
Meaning lost (13—forward referencing)
Omissions (11,12—linguistic knowledge)

The use of this type of cloze analysis will give teachers some understanding of what strategies children need to practise and will also provide information about their knowledge and understandings.

Analysis of Reader's Written or Oral Activities

To evaluate children's reading, it may be useful to observe how children are using strategies within the context of classroom reading events, before, during and after reading a text.

The following checklist is suggested as a guide and could be used in conjunction with dated samples of work that illustrate the use of particular strategies.

Strategies	Observed				Comment
Before Reading 1 Ask questions to gain information (or clarify) 2 Uses background knowledge appropriately 3 Can predict outcomes 4 Can describe how to complete activities, i.e. devise and follow a plan					

During Reading
5 Uses picture cues appropriately
6 Locates key words and underlines
7 Can substantiate responses:
   (i) explicit (from text)
   (ii) implicit (from knowledge)
8 Recognises miscomprehension
9 Can self-correct					

After Reading
10 Can summarise key points
11 Can substantiate:
   (1) response
   (2) strategies used
12 Recognises if activity is complete					

The marking key could include information about frequency of use, e.g. A – always, S – sometimes, N – not yet

Analysis of Word Identification Strategies

There are some fundamental strategies that are used by effective readers. Teachers may wish to record children's use of these strategies as various reading tasks are undertaken in the classroom.

Strategies	Observed				Comment

1 Can describe how to identify words (i.e. plan)
2 Can self-correct
   (i) words in isolation
   (ii) words in context
3 Can substantiate attempts at words
4 Uses the following information:
   (1) semantic cues and world knowledge
   (2) syntactic cues
   (3) graphophonic cues
5 Specific strategies relied upon:
   (1) context cues
   (2) focus on initial letters
   (3) focus on word parts
   (4) sounding out
   (5) blending
6 Uses a range of strategies when dealing with unfamiliar words in text
7 Predicts unknown words on basis of semantic or syntactic information
8 Confirms or rejects predictions, often using graphophonic knowledge					

Chapter 5:

Helping Children Who Have Reading Difficulties

Introduction

This section sets out ideas and suggestions for teaching children with reading difficulties. The ideas presented reflect what might be termed as an 'integrated' approach, wherein the child, the teaching approach, the school and the parents all play an important role in helping to design the most suitable instructional program for the child.

The Child		The Teacher		The School		The Instructional Program		The Parent
Has the opportunity to learn to read by reading	↔	Has clearly identified beliefs about teaching children with reading difficulties	↔	Has clearly identified beliefs about helping children who have reading difficulties *across* the school	↔	Links to the regular reading/language program	↔	Is informed about the child's reading difficulties
Is encouraged to take control of his/her learning		Links an intervention program for children who have reading difficulties with the regular reading/ language program		Has a school policy and plan for children with reading difficulties		Takes a diagnostic teaching focus		Understands the instructional program
Is aware of his/her own reading strategies				Has a management information system to monitor children's progress		Encourages 'success'		Is provided with ideas/strategies/ resources to assist the child
Is able to self-monitor his/her own reading		Implements a diagnostic teaching approach when working with children who have reading difficulties (see intervention pathway and example on pages 143–156)				Focuses on strategies		

The view presented in this chapter is that there is no one way of teaching children with reading difficulties, and that teachers and schools need to be flexible in their efforts to diagnose, plan, implement and evaluate children's progress.

Teachers and schools are encouraged to follow the 'Pathway for Intervention' described on page 143, in developing an instructional program. This 'pathway' attempts to link the general beliefs about teaching and learning developed through all the First Steps material, with a specific *diagnostic teaching* approach, which is seen to be of crucial importance in developing effective individualised instructional programs for children with reading difficulties.

Children with Reading Difficulties

For many years there have been different definitions and teaching approaches developed for children who experience difficulties in learning to read. Indeed, the whole area of reading difficulties, and the often related learning and behavioural difficulties, has been controversial, and it has therefore been extremely difficult for teachers, schools and parents to develop effective procedures for helping these children learn to read.

There may be many possible causes for different children's reading difficulties. However, no matter what the causes of reading difficulties might be, good *diagnostic teaching* provides an excellent pathway for helping teachers, the school and the parents identify and understand difficulties their children may be experiencing. More importantly, this approach provides an *educational* program for helping children overcome their difficulties.

Within the proposed diagnostic teaching framework and pathway, those involved in helping children who experience reading difficulties are strongly encouraged to diagnose the nature of the difficulty, and to gather information about the possible causes. This section, however, promotes the belief that the instructional program established by the teachers, the school and the parents must focus on the reading *skills and strategies* that are essential for a child's reading development.

Teachers are encouraged to use a wide range of assessment activities to diagnose and place children on the First Steps *Reading: Developmental Continuum* and to identify each child's specific strengths and weaknesses in reading.

Overview of Beliefs About Helping Children Who Have Reading Difficulties

Focus

Children with reading difficulties ——————————————

Focus

Teaching children with reading difficulties ——————

Focus

Whole school based planning ——————————————

Focus

Parents helping children with reading difficulties ——————

Children with reading difficulties
- need to experience success
- need to develop confidence in themselves as readers
- need more time to develop
- need to see reading as enjoyable
- need to see reading as purposeful
- need to be aware of their own strategies
- need to be able to self monitor their reading
- need to be encouraged to take control of their learning
- need to review their own progress
- need to value independent reading
- need the opportunity to learn to read by reading

Teachers helping children who have reading difficulties need to:
- use a diagnostic teaching approach to identify reader's developing knowledge and understandings, skills and strategies
- use diagnostic information to identify appropriate teaching strategies that will be used to support the child's further development
- plan an instructional program that builds on the child's strengths and ensures they will experience success
- use a variety of approaches/strategies
- ensure there is a balance between explicit and general instruction
- keep natural language teaching principles in mind when planning, e.g. language is for making meaning. Reading and writing are interrelated.
- provide many opportunities for children to apply and practise their skills and strategies
- model/demonstrate all skills and strategies
- provide support in the context of the regular classroom program. (Plan to help children during whole class, small group and individual activities.)
- provide ready access to support materials such as word banks, charts, books, children's writing
- gather information about their reading development across a range of reading activities where children are working in different contexts with varied texts

Schools need to:
- develop a policy that outlines their beliefs in relation to supporting children who have reading difficulties
- identify children at risk and monitor their progress through the different year levels
- develop evaluation/record keeping/reporting strategies that are consistent with program beliefs across the school
- ensure school timetables allow for large blocks of uninterrupted time, to enable class teachers to implement a language program that meets the needs of all children in the class
- ensure there is continuity across the year levels, in the approach used in supporting children who have reading difficulties
- keep in mind the program objectives and the identified needs of the children when selecting resources
- provide opportunities for professional development
- provide support for children experiencing difficulty with reading within the regular classroom program. (If withdrawal is considered it must be linked to the regular classroom program.)

Schools need to:
- ensure parents have a clear understanding about the school's beliefs in relation to supporting children who have reading difficulties
- inform parents about how they can support their child's reading development at home
- identify appropriate ways to involve parents in helping children with reading difficulties at school
- encourage parents to focus on their child's strengths rather than his/her weaknesses
- make use of the developmental continua in parent/teacher interviews, to identify the child's developing knowledge and understanding, skills and strategies
- organise parent information sessions

141

Teaching Children Who Have Reading Difficulties

Pathway for Intervention

Planning for Intervention

The children in a class who are experiencing difficulties with reading are seldom difficult to identify. As well as below-average performances, these children often exhibit low self-esteem through a constant lack of success and may avoid reading altogether.

It is important to recognise that although children experiencing difficulties need increased guidance, they should always be encouraged to take control of their learning, review their own progress and value independent reading. To realise these ends, the children must understand the purpose of anything they are required to do and must be intrinsically motivated to succeed.

To assist each individual to overcome difficulties and increase his or her range of strategies, it is important to diagnose individual strengths and weaknesses. The strengths subsequently are used as springboards for learning new strategies, while weaknesses become the focus for teaching.

To ensure that the child's needs are met in the intervention program, it is important to spend time gathering information about the child's attitude to reading and his or her developing knowledge and understanding, skills and strategies. Through observing, listening and talking to the child during the normal class program, and then plotting the child's development on the *Reading: Developmental Continuum*, the teacher is able to accurately assess and evaluate his or her development as a reader. By analysing the data, the teacher is able to determine which language and literacy behaviours need fostering and to plan an individualised instructional program that will meet the needs of the child.

What the class teacher has to do next is to decide how the identified needs of the child can be met in the context of the regular class program. This aspect of planning is discussed in detail in the section on Class Organisation (page 5). In this section, different organisational structures are explained and it is shown how the needs of the child can be met in a program that allows for whole-class, small-group and individualised teaching/learning.

The pathway for intervention outlined on the following page describes a process that will help teachers to develop an effective individualised instructional program, that can be carried out in the context of the regular class program.

Pathway for Intervention

Step 1

Gather data

Information should be gathered across a range of reading activities; for example:

- Oral retelling following silent reading
- Observing reading behaviours, e.g. selection of books, interest in reading tasks
- Observation during 'Directed Silent Reading', e.g. subvocalisation, finger pointing, use of picture cues
- Teacher questioning about a text
- Teacher-child conference
- Written retelling following silent reading
- Children's self-evaluation comments
- Observing classroom reading activities, e.g. cloze passages, story maps
- Teacher-child interview
- Oral reading and miscue analysis
- General comprehension activities before, during and after reading

Step 2

Plot the child on the *Reading : Developmental Continuum*

- Focus on the key indicators to determine the phase the child is working in
- Having determined the child's phase of development, mark off any other indicators the child is exhibiting

Step 3

Analyse information and identify important teaching strategies

- Analyse information and determine which language and literacy behaviours need developing
- Check which of the 'Children's Reading Strategies' still need to be encouraged
- Examine the Major Teaching Emphases to identify important teaching information
- Look at the *Helping Children Who Have Reading Difficulties* chapter for further ideas. Examine information from the relevant phase for the child
- Identify specific teaching strategies to incorporate in the intervention program

Step 4

Plan intervention program

- Plan a program in which the child's needs will be met during whole-class, small-group and individual activities; for example:

Whole-class
- Shared book experience
- Language experience
- Modelling reading to children
- Content area reading
- Read and retell

Small-group
- Guided instructional reading, e.g. DSR
- Read and Retell
- Request procedure QAR
- Supported reading

Individualised
- Supported reading
- DEAR
- Individualised reading program
- USSR

- Consider how support may be used

Step 5

Organise a parent-teacher conference

- Ask the parents to talk about their child's reading at home
- Use the *Reading: Developmental Continuum* Overview to explain how their child's reading is developing
- Show the parents work samples, e.g. reading log, story map, written retell. Discuss the proposed intervention plan
- Inform the parents about what they can do to support their child's reading development

Step 6

Implement plans

- Begin with a teacher-child conference
- Introduce a reading journal into the language program (if you haven't already done so). Involve the child in some simple goal setting.
- Discuss with the child how s/he can use his/her journal to record titles of books read, feelings about books, questions about books, stories, characters, authors

Step 7

Monitor continuously

- The child's reading development will be monitored continuously
- Information will be gathered about interests, strategies, comprehension, attitude

Step 8

Plot the child on the *Reading: Developmental Continuum*

- After a month, the child's development should be plotted on the *Reading: Developmental Continuum* again
- Analyse information and determine how successfully the needs of the child are being met with the existing program

Step 9

Review plans

- Existing plans should be reviewed and refined or altered to ensure the identified needs of the child are being met

Implementing the Pathway for Intervention

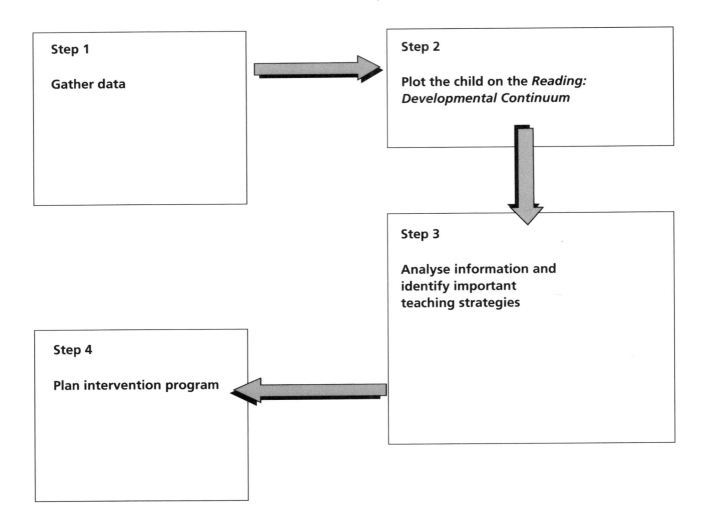

The following pages show how the pathway for intervention can be used to develop an individual program for a particular child, beginning with gathering data and plotting a child on the continuum, then analysing this information and making plans for intervention.

Case Study — Jonathon

The following case study provides an example of an analysis of a child's reading. It shows how the data that was gathered enabled the teacher to identify what the child could do and the areas in which he needed additional support. It links the data gathered, to the indicators of the Continuum to then provide an appropriate program to support and enhance his learning.

Running Record	**E** (Errors)	**SC** (Self-corrections)
Every night	—	
Jim sat on the fire escape	2	
and played his trumpet	—	
for the little people	2	
in the building.	1	
He played eating music	1	
and laughing music.		
He played music for jumping	1	
and music for dancing.	2	
Then he played soft music	1	
for sleeping.	1	
Jim was the little people's friend,	1	
but there were two big people	—	
who didn't like the trumpet music.	—	
'Stop that noise!' they yelled.	1	1
'It isn't noise,' said Jim.	2	
'It's music.'		
'It's noise!' yelled the big people.	3	
'Stop it at once!'		
'I can't stop playing my trumpet,'	—	
said Jim.		
'I'll just have to go,	—	
and live with my sister.'	—	
So he went away	1	
to another part of town.	5	
That night,	—	
the building was quiet.	2	1
No one could get to sleep.	1	
The two big people		
were awake all night.		1
In the morning,	—	
the two big people	—	
went to see Jim	—	
at his sister's place.	1	
'We were wrong	1	
about your trumpet,'		
they said.		
'You don't make noise.	6	
You make music,	1	
and we miss it.	2	
Please, come back!'		
So Jim came back.		
When night came,	1	
there he was on the fire escape,	2	
playing music for eating	2	
and laughing	—	
and jumping		
and dancing.	1	
All the little people		
cheered and clapped	4	
… and so did the two big people.	**48**	**3**

Comments on Jonathon's Miscues

Jim sat on the front — and *played his trumpet* indicates that an initial letter cue is being used.

house for 'building' indicates that Jonathon is reading for meaning

every for 'eating' shows use of initial letter cue.

Substitution of *jellybeans* for 'jumping' makes sense and shows use of initial letter cue combined with his knowledge of the world.

The similar configuration of *for* and *soft* probably caused this miscue.
Jonathon is not responding to syntactic cues

It makes sense to replace *noise* by 'music'.
Nose looks like *noise* but doesn't make sense.

Yelling for 'yelled' indicates a lack of response to syntactic cues

So he went away down his sisters place is an excellent substitution in terms of meaning.

These substitutions seem to show an attempt to make meaning, which is not supported by word identification strategies.

The similarity between *make* and *awake* seems to have prompted this misuse.

This substitution makes sense.

An impulsive guess prompted by the initial letter. Meaning is maintained.

The substitution shows an attempt to make meaning.

Once again *and we want it* makes sense

An initial letter guess — *we* for 'when'

The substitution for *fair special* for 'fire escape' seems to be based on initial letters and configuration rather than meaning

Once again *played music for him* is an attempt to make meaning.

Jonathon provides a classic ending to the story *all went to sleep*

Text: *Jim's Trumpet*, Joy Cowley, 1989, Level 4 Sunshine Books, Rigby

145

Summary of conventions

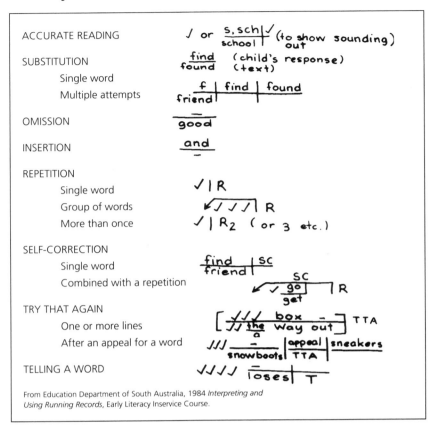

From Education Department of South Australia, 1984 *Interpreting and Using Running Records*, Early Literacy Inservice Course.

Analysis of Running Record

Jonathon makes many substitutions, but shows little evidence of substantiating his predictions through self-monitoring and self-correction. He does not appear to return to the text to have a 're-run' or to have another go if he has not got it quite right. This may indicate that he thinks he *has* got it right and is not picking up syntactic and semantic cues, e.g. his reading of *there he was on the fire escape* as *there he was on the fair special* and *yelling the big people* for *yelled the big people*.

Some of his substitutions are semantically acceptable, e.g. *house* for *building* and *music* for *noise*. His use of overall meaning can be quite effective, e.g. ... *played his trumpet for a little bit* for ...*played his trumpet for the little people*; *So he went down his sister's place* for *So he went away to another part of town*; and *All the little people all went to sleep* for *All the little people cheered and clapped* and *That night the people were...* instead of *That night the building was...* These substitutions seem to show that he is impulsively having-a-go at creating meaning without regard for graphophonic cues when the going gets too hard.

Jonathon sometimes uses initial letter cues such as *every/eating*, *jelly beans/jumping*, *worried/wrong*, *we/when*. Other substitutions also indicate that he sometimes leaps to a conclusion after approximating the visual image of a word, for instance, *front/fire*, *for/soft*, *sleep/sleeping*, *yell/yelled*, *making/awake*. Very often, however, he fails to use graphophonic cues, and, when he does, he jumps to a conclusion without following his prediction through by sounding out or pausing to verify it by looking at the letter patterns.

Oral Retell

A boy with a trumpet. All the people didn't want him and then when he went away they did want him. (Why didn't they want him?) *He wasn't very good and bursted their ear drums.* (And then what happened?) *Then he went away and they all wanted him because he could play better.* (Anything else?) *And because they couldn't get to sleep without music.*

Comment

Orientation – not evident
Identified the problem
Identified some important information
Dependence on questions/prompts
The retell was poorly structured
Syntax – weak

Question and Answer

Q What sort of music did Jim play for the people?
A *Trumpet music.*
Q What sort of things did the people do when Jim played music?
A *Throwed up jelly beans.*
Q Did he play any special music when they were sleeping?
A *Yes, quiet music.*
Q Why didn't the big people like his music?
A *Because it was too slow.*
Q Why did Jim decide to go away?
A *Because no one liked his music.*
Q Where did he go?
A *To his sister's place.*
Q Do you think that was a good idea?
A *No. He should have stayed there.*
Q What would you have done if you had been him?
A *How old was he? Hide from them.*
Q What do you think the people discovered while Jim was away?
A *They missed the sounds.*

Analysis of Oral Retell and Question and Answer

Jonathon did not provide any introduction or orientation in his retelling of the story, although he captured the central problem concisely. His retell lacked structure, maybe because he did not appear to see the need to elaborate further.

Jonathon clearly understood what had happened in the story, as his retelling was couched in his own words, showing that his overall comprehension was good, even if his mastery of syntax was weak. He was able to supply some detail but was dependent on questions and prompts to elicit further information.

In the questioning session it is interesting to note that his answer to the question 'What would you have done...?' was 'How old was he?', showing that he was thinking about the character in relation to what could be expected of a person of that age, before answering that he himself would hide.

Reading Teacher-Child Interview

Q **What is reading?**

A *Just talking.*

Q **What is reading for?**

A *For fun.*

Q **What makes a person a good reader?**

A *Practise a lot.*

Q **What would you like to do or could you do that would make you a better reader?**

A *Read every night.*

Q **When you are reading and you come to a word that you don't know (recognise), what do you do?**

A *Sound it out.*

Bruinsma Reading Questionnaire

Q **When you are reading and you come to a word that you recognise (can decode or sound out) but don't know the meaning of, what do you do?**

A *Ask someone.*

Q **Do you ever read something over again? Why or why not?**

A *Yes, because it's easy—you've already read it.*

Q **What do you do to help you remember what you read?**

A *Read it over and over again.*

Q **How do you get the main idea (the most important point) of the story?**

A *By reading it.*

Analysis of Teacher-Child Interview

The teacher-child interview shows that Jonathon does not have a great deal of insight into his reading processes and is inclined to think that constant practice and repetition will solve everything. He identifies two valid strategies for word identification—sounding out and asking someone. It is good that he feels that reading is 'for fun'.

Me as a reader:

Name **Jonathon**

Make this face look how
you feel as a reader.

The kinds of reading I like to do are *plans*

I like reading when *at thit*

I am getting better at *haveing a goat wris*

Now I want to get better at *riing*

Analysis of Self-Evaluation

Jonathon's self-evaluation is interesting. Jonathon clearly has no sense of control over specific strategies but feels that if he does things over and over again everything will come right in the end.

The picture that the data presents of Jonathon as a reader is extremely consistent throughout. It enables his teacher to make an accurate diagnosis of his strengths and his needs and so to construct a supportive and productive program for him.

Placement on Developmental Continuum — Jonathon

Indicators from Reading Developmental Continuum

Experimental Reading Phase

Making Meaning at Text Level	
◆ realises that print contains a constant message, i.e. that the words of a written story remain the same, but the words of an oral story may change	✓
◆ is focused on expressing the meaning of a story rather than on reading words accurately	✓
• knows that print goes from left to right and from top to bottom of a page	✓
• responds to and uses terminology such as: letter, word, sentence, chapter	✓
• is beginning to demonstrate awareness of literary language, e.g. 'a long, long time ago...', 'by the fire sat a cat', 'No, no, no', said the....'	✓
• identifies the subject matter of a story through the use of titles and illustrations, e.g. 'I want the story about the big black cat'	✓
• shows an ability to connect ideas and events from stories heard or viewed by retelling events in sequence, using pictures, memory of the story and knowledge of story structure	✓
• expresses personal views about the actions of a character and speculates on own behaviour in a similar situation, e.g. 'If I had been...I would have...'	✓
• sub-vocalises or whispers when reading 'silently'	✓
Making Meaning Using Context	✓
◆ uses prior knowledge of context and personal experience to make meaning, e.g. uses memory of a text to match spoken with written words	✓
• demonstrates understanding of one-to-one correspondence between spoken and written words, for instance, the child slows down when dictating to an adult	✓
• asks for assistance with some words. May be aware that own reading is not accurate and may seek help, re-read or stop reading	✓
• uses patterns of language to predict words or phrases	✓

Experimental Reading Phase

Making Meaning at Word Level	
◆ recognises some personally significant words in context, e.g. in job roster, weather chart or books	✓
◆ matches some spoken words with written words when reading a book or environmental print	✓
• is developing the ability to separate a word from the object it represents. For instance, the child realises that 'Dad' is a little word, not that 'Dad' is a big word because Dad is big	✓
• recognises some letters of the alphabet and is able to name them	✓
• demonstrates some knowledge of letter-sound relationships, for instance, the sound represented by the initial and most salient letters in words	✓
• points to specific known words as they are read	✓
• uses initial letter sounds to predict words in texts	✓
Attitudes	
• is beginning to see self as a reader and talks about own reading	✓
• may ask for favourite stories to be read	✓
• joins in and acts out familiar stories	✓
• selects books to read for pleasure	✓
• self-selects texts on basis of interest or familiarity	✓

Behaviours observed ✓
Literacy behaviours that need developing *

150

Placement on Developmental Continuum — Jonathon

Indicators from Reading Developmental Continuum

Early Reading Phase

Making Meaning at Text Level	
◆ is beginning to read familiar texts confidently and can retell major contents from visual and printed texts, e.g. language experience recounts, shared books, simple informational texts and children's television programs	✓
◆ can identify and talk about a range of different text forms such as letters, lists, recipes, stories, newspaper and magazine articles, television dramas and documentaries	not known
◆ demonstrates understanding that all texts, both narrative and informational, are written by authors who are expressing their own ideas	not known
• identifies the main topic of a story or informational text and supplies some supporting information	*
• talks about characters in books using picture clues, personal experience and the text to make inferences	emerging
• provides detail about characters, setting and events when retelling a story	*
• talks about ideas and information from informational texts, making links to own knowledge	not known
• has strong personal reaction to advertisements, ideas and information from visual and written texts	not known
• makes comparisons with other texts read or viewed. The child's comments could relate to theme, setting, character, plot, structure, information or the way the text is written	not known
• can talk about how to predict text content, e.g. 'I knew that book hadn't got facts in it. The dinosaurs had clothes on.'	*

Making Meaning Using Context	
◆ may read word-by-word or line-by-line when reading an unfamiliar text, i.e. reading performance may be word centred. Fluency and expression become stilted as the child focuses on decoding	
◆ uses picture cues and knowledge of context to check understanding of meaning	✓ impulsive
• generally makes meaningful substitutions, however over-reliance on graphophonics may cause some meaning to be lost	✓
• may sub-vocalise when reading difficult text 'silently'	
• is beginning to use self-correction as a strategy	*
• uses knowledge of sentence structure and punctuation to help make meaning (syntactic strategies)	*
• sometimes reads-on to confirm meaning	*
• re-reads passage in order to clarify meaning that may have been lost due to word-by-word reading. May re-read a phrase, a sentence or a paragraph.	*
• can talk about strategies used at the sentence level, e.g. 'If I think it doesn't sound right, I try again'	*
• is beginning to integrate prediction and substantiation	*

Early Reading Phase

Making Meaning at Word Level	
◆ has a bank of words which are recognised when encountered in different contexts, e.g. in a book, on the blackboard, in the environment or on a chart	✓
◆ relies heavily on beginning letters and sounding-out for word identification (graphophonic strategies)	✓ *
• carefully reads text, demonstrating the understanding that meaning is vested in the words	
• may point as an aid to reading, using finger, eyes or voice, especially when reading difficult text	not known
• locates words from sources such as word banks and environmental print	not known
• when questioned can reflect on own word identification strategies, e.g. 'I sounded it out'	*

Attitude	
• is willing to have-a-go at reading unknown words	✓
• enjoys listening to stories	
• reads for a range of purposes, e.g. for pleasure or information	
• responds sensitively to stories read	
• discusses favourite books	
• talks about favourite author	
• selects own reading material according to interest, purpose and level of difficulty and, with teacher support, can reconstruct information gained	

Analysis of Information

Early Reading Phase

From the data gathered so far it is clear that Jonathon is exhibiting the following indicators:

Making Meaning at the Text Level

- talks about characters in books, using picture clues, personal experience and the text to make inferences (*Jonathon relates playing music to being rewarded with jelly beans and asks the age of the boy when deciding what he would have done*)

Making Meaning Using Context

- generally makes meaningful substitutions, however over-reliance on graphophonics may cause some meaning to be lost (*in this case, Jonathon sometimes makes wild guesses based on initial letter cues*)

Making Meaning at the Word Level

- has a bank of words which are recognised when encountered in different contexts (*it is clear that Jonathon can read many words without thinking*)

Attitude

- is willing to have-a-go at reading unknown words (*Jonathon makes wild guesses that are in tune with his perception of the meaning of the text. He needs to check his guesses by paying more attention to actual word identification strategies*)

It is impossible to tell if Jonathon has achieved some of the indicators, as direct observation would be needed to obtain this data, e.g. 'points as an aid to reading'.

The data indicates that the following indicators have not yet been fully achieved:

Key Indicators

The key indicators that Jonathon is not yet fully exhibiting are:

Making Meaning Using Context

- **uses picture cues and knowledge of context to check understanding of meaning (*Jonathon does not read reflectively*)**

Making Meaning at Word Level

- **relies heavily on beginning letters and sounding-out for word identification (graphophonic) strategies. (*Jonathon does not sound out.*)**

Other Indicators

Jonathon's profile as an Early Reader, using available data, shows that he is not yet exhibiting the following indicators:

Making Meaning at Text Level

- identifies the main topic of a story or informational text and supplies some supporting information (*no supporting detail given*)
- talks about characters in books using picture clues, personal experience and the text to make inferences (*only one small indication of this*)
- provides detail about characters, setting and events when retelling a story

Making Meaning Using Context

- is beginning to use self-correction as a strategy
- uses knowledge of sentence structure and punctuation to help gain meaning (syntactic strategies)
- sometimes reads on to confirm meaning

- can talk about strategies used at the sentence level, e.g. 'If I think it doesn't sound right I try again.'
- re-reads passage in order to clarify meaning that may have been lost due to word-by-word reading
- is beginning to integrate prediction and substantiation

Making Meaning at Word Level
- when questioned can reflect on own word identification strategies (*his reflection shows little insight*)

Important Teaching Strategies/Intervention Plan

Name: Jonathon Smith   **Phase:** Early Reading
Behaviours to be encouraged:

Making Meaning at Text Level
- Using prediction combined with confirmation of text outcomes
- Critical thinking, questioning, commenting on content and intention
- Recognising important information in texts and identifying supporting detail
- Self-monitoring of reading strategies

Making Meaning Using Context
- Using knowledge of oral language patterns
- Re-reading and reading on to establish meaning
- Using self-correction

Making Meaning at Word Level
- Sounding out
- Blending sounds and word parts

Attitude
- Discussing authors, stories and other texts
- Selecting own reading material
- Responding sensitively to stories

Teaching Strategies:

Making Meaning at Text Level (taken from major teaching emphases of Early Phase)
- Ask Jonathon about ideas and information he has found in books. Encourage him to talk about his opinions and reactions, particularly in regard to stereotypes and generalisations.
- Ensure that Jonathon participates regularly in individual conferences to discuss aspects of his reading particularly his reading strategies.
- Model strategies such as re-reading and self-correction during shared reading sessions in which Jonathon is participating.
- Ensure that there is time for Jonathon to demonstrate his understanding of a text by discussing the story he has read, delving into the ways in which characters are depicted, possible motivations, alternative outcomes etc. Encourage Jonathon to relate the context, people and events to his own experiences. Talk about the author's intentions and how the choice of words influences the way we interpret what has been written. Promote discussion before, during and after reading.
- Ensure that Jonathon reads independently every day.
- Foster Jonathon's ability to predict through questioning and discussion before, during and after reading.
- Talk together about roles, assumptions, stereotypes. Encourage critical and divergent comment.

- After reading, ask Jonathon to draw a picture of their favourite scene and then re-tell the story beginning from that part. Provide many opportunities for retelling stories, emphasising the need to provide appropriate detail. Jonathon could work in a small group to produce a written retell that could be presented to children in Year One.
- Plan language experience activities that require Jonathon to participate actively in talking, reading and writing for a real purpose.
- Provide opportunities for Jonathon to take part in circle stories.
- At all times encourage reflective reading. While Jonathon needs to be praised for having-a-go, he must realise the need to check some of his impulsive 'goes' against meaning, syntax and more scrupulous word identification. Help Jonathon to reflect on the strategies he is using and to further develop strategies he doesn't use very often.

Additional strategies from next segment of this chapter linking strategies to key indicators:
- *Enable Jonathon to take part in paired reading.*
- *If miscues are meaningful, do not draw attention to them.*
- *Create opportunities for Jonathon to dramatise stories or television episodes.*
- *Encourage Jonathon to explore the wide range of materials in the reading corner.*

Making Meaning Using Context (taken from major teaching emphases of Early Phase)
- Encourage use of personal experiences, knowledge of oral language patterns and text structure to help children make meaning.
- Provide opportunities for children to demonstrate understanding of a text through activities such as:
  - substantiating answers by reading from the text
  - sequencing text
  - developing a story map
  - making comparisons with other texts
  - identifying the main idea of a story and providing some supporting information
  - identifying character traits.

Additional strategies including some from the next segment of this chapter linking strategies to key indicators:

If Jonathon is an impulsive reader who makes wild guesses on the basis of an initial letter or a similar looking word, encourage him to pause after reading a short but 'complete' chunk of text so that he can think about the meaning: did it make sense? did it seem to say what was suggested in the picture? did it sound right? Do not worry if there is a long pause while Jonathon does a 're-run' in the head to check understanding. Let Jonathon talk about it if he wishes, but do not initiate conversation yourself, in case this disrupts the process of reflection. Be careful that you reassure Jonathon that it is good to have-a-go and guess, but it is also important to check that guesses were reasonable ones. Model 'reflective reading' in shared reading sessions, so that Jonathon knows what expert readers do to check understanding of a word, a sentence or a chunk of text.

Take every opportunity to discuss the probable meanings of unknown words in shared book sessions, talking about the word in relation to other words in the text, the general context and the word in relation to other words with the same root or a similar letter pattern.

- *Begin each day by reading a 'Big Book' together, after initial reading for enjoyment focus on modelling the reading behaviours listed above, especially reading on and re-reading to establish and confirm meaning.*
- *Involve the child in a number of supported reading activities, for example:*
  - *Shared Book reading*
  - *Choral reading from class charts of poems or extracts from texts*
  - *Paired reading*
- *Involve the child in small group Directed Silent Reading activities each day.*
- *Involve the child in before and during reading activities, for example, before reading:*
  - *making predictions from title and illustrations*
  - *discussing vocabulary that will be encountered in the text*
  - *developing 'What I know' and 'What I want to find out' charts during reading:*
  - *reading from the text to substantiate a prediction*
  - *re-reading a sentence if meaning is lost*
  - *reading-on to clarify the meaning of an unknown word*
- *Encourage Jonathon to re-read when he has lost meaning or become confused over an unknown word.*
- *Allow time for Jonathon to self-correct and expect that he will do so.*
- *Provide opportunities for Jonathon to manipulate and sequence words, phrases and sentences after reading a text.*
- *Use cloze activities to focus on different aspects of language, especially on using syntactic cues.*

Making Meaning at Word Level (taken from major teaching emphases of Early Phase)

- Model strategies for attacking unknown words, e.g. identifying similar word beginnings, common word patterns, chunking parts of a word.
- Develop class word banks containing topic words, high frequency words, linking words etc.

Additional strategies including some from next segment of this chapter linking strategies to key indicators:

- *Help Jonathon to listen to and reproduce the order of sounds in a word, using sound frames as an aid.*
- *Reinforce the understanding that letter-sound correlations may be different in different words, e.g.*
  - *one letter can represent a number of sounds*
  - *the same sound can be represented by different letters.*
- *Use shared book experience to focus on words after Jonathon is familiar with the text, e.g. word endings, letter clusters and sound-symbol relationships. Value any discoveries made by Jonathon and ensure that they are written onto the appropriate class chart.*
- *After shared reading sessions give children opportunities to play with an interesting word of his choice. For instance, let him see how many words he can make using the same letters, first in order and then in any order. Challenge him to find rhyming words. Encourage him to classify words from the text and from classroom print according to visual pattern and sound. Delete word endings from a sentence or short paragraph and ask Jonathon to fill them in.*
- *Encourage Jonathon to:*
  - *sound out the whole word instead of just the initial letter*

- *identify letter patterns such as blends, digraphs and common endings such as '...ing', '...ed', ...ious', '...tion'*
- *find short words in longer words*
- *identify prefixes*
- *look for rhyming words.*

- *Help Jonathon to segment and blend with confidence by using Secret Message activities (see page 224).*
- *Involve Jonathon in daily Sound Sleuth activities (see page 222).*
- *At all times encourage children to think about whether a word makes sense in context. Model this reflective decoding in shared reading sessions.*

Attitude

- Continue to encourage Jonathon to immerse himself in books.
- Listen carefully to and place high value on Jonathon's thoughts and opinions, particularly if they differ from your own.
- Show enthusiasm for and help Jonathon to pursue individual interests.

Additional strategies taken from the next segment of this chapter linking strategies to key indicators:

- *Encourage Jonathon to reflect on the successes that have been experienced. Make sure that these are acknowledged and valued in the classroom context.*
- *Give Jonathon time and opportunity to pursue an interest and share texts on the topic of his choice with the class or a small group.*
- *Ensure that Jonathon has the opportunity to participate in motivating and varied reading games that demand a concrete response to small amounts of text.*
- *Involve Jonathon in goal setting, giving him opportunities to identify small, achievable goals which can then be monitored to demonstrate success.*
- *Undertake regular reading conferences with Jonathon to assist with the self-monitoring process and provide encouragement and reinforcement. Include his parents if possible.*
- *Encourage Jonathon to identify a favourite author and talk about favourite books.*
- *Help Jonathon to develop self-selection strategies to ensure that he can access books effectively:*
  - *read the summary on the inside cover.*
  - *flick through the book to gain a general impression*
  - *read a paragraph or two to see if the text is accessible. If the book is being chosen for the pictures this does not matter.*

Case Study – Mark

Mark is a fun-loving ten-year-old, though quite shy, initially, with adults. During the third term of Year 5, Mark was exhibiting behaviours which are fairly typical of children who are unsure of what they are doing; he was:

- well-behaved and quiet in class
- tense
- lacking in confidence

He enjoyed looking at books and drawing, but as soon as reading or writing were on the agenda, he avoided the tasks by visits to the toilet, finding pencils, or drawing.

When his reading was observed, it was clear that he had developed some skills; for example:

- he used picture cues
- he had a reasonable sight vocabulary
- he memorised stories well (short-term)
- he enjoyed listening to stories if he found them interesting

Mark has caring parents, who were concerned about his progress and worked with Mark at home.

First Stage of Intervention

Mark's teacher decided that the best approach would be to work initially on his confidence and general enjoyment of reading.

To this end, *small-group* work was used as often as possible and activities chosen which were *motivating* and gave him a high level of *success*.

Activities included:

- Choral reading — Commercially-produced stories and poems class/group stories and poems
- Reading activities — Following instructions to colour a picture
- Colouring activities — These activities all involved Mark responding to
- Construction activities — written instructions in a purposeful way
- Making books — Narrative text / Informational text
- Taped stories

After a few weeks, Mark showed a notable increase in confidence and his tenseness was less evident. He was eager to participate in activities.

Second Stage of Intervention

At this stage it was decided to concentrate on more specific strategies to improve his reading skills. In order to do this effectively, Mark was asked to read a familiar text—*Book Beetle's Dreadful Fright*. (A. Dewsbury et al., The Jacaranda Press) and his oral reading behaviours were recorded. This process helped us identify his strengths and weaknesses.

Analysis

Mark began reading quite fluently. He remembered the story context well and used picture cues effectively. He also made use of semantic cues and syntactic cues. He seemed comfortable with the task for a while, then lost concentration or confidence. At this point he began to read word by word and made an increasing number of errors.

Intervention

Mark's behaviour pattern during reading indicated a teaching strategy which would be necessary to make all his learning effective, i.e. keep tasks clear, concise and captivating! It would also be necessary to encourage risk-taking.

His artistic skills are strong and should be used as a resource for reading and writing and for maintaining his confidence.

The number of refusals he made, particularly as the task became more stressful, was a concern and indicated a need to heighten his awareness of word identification skills and other strategies which emphasise the importance of meaning.

Reading strategies needed to be frequently modelled and encouraged; that is:

- Omit the word and read on to the end of the sentence
- Substitute a word and check

Placement on Developmental Continuum — Mark

Indicators from Reading Developmental Continuum

Early Reading Phase

Making Meaning at Text Level	
◆ is beginning to read familiar texts confidently and can retell major contents from visual and printed texts, e.g. language experience recounts, shared books, simple informational texts and children's television programs	✓
◆ can identify and talk about a range of different text forms such as letters, lists, recipes, stories, newspaper and magazine articles, television dramas and documentaries	✓
◆ demonstrates understanding that all texts, both narrative and informational, are written by authors who are expressing their own ideas	✓
• identifies the main topic of a story or informational text and supplies some supporting information	✓
• talks about characters in books using picture clues, personal experience and the text to make inferences	✓
• provides detail about characters, setting and events when retelling a story	✓
• talks about ideas and information from informational texts, making links to own knowledge	✓
• has strong personal reaction to advertisements, ideas and information from visual and written texts	✓
• makes comparisons with other texts read or viewed. The child's comments could relate to theme, setting, character, plot, structure, information or the way the text is written	✓
• can talk about how to predict text content, e.g. 'I knew that book hadn't got facts in it. The dinosaurs had clothes on.'	✓
Making Meaning Using Context	
◆ may read word-by-word or line-by-line when reading an unfamiliar text, i.e. reading performance may be word centred. Fluency and expression become stilted as the child focuses on decoding	✓
◆ uses picture cues and knowledge of context to check understanding of meaning	✓
• generally makes meaningful substitutions, however over-reliance on graphophonics may cause some meaning to be lost	✓
• may sub-vocalise when reading difficult text 'silently'	✓
• is beginning to use self-correction as a strategy	✓
• uses knowledge of sentence structure and punctuation to help make meaning (syntactic strategies)	✓
• sometimes reads-on to confirm meaning	*
• re-reads passage in order to clarify meaning that may have been lost due to word-by-word reading. May re-read a phrase, a sentence or a paragraph.	*
• can talk about strategies used at the sentence level, e.g. 'If I think it doesn't sound right, I try again'	✓
• is beginning to integrate prediction and substantiation	✓

Early Reading Phase

Making Meaning at Word Level	
◆ has a bank of words which are recognised when encountered in different contexts, e.g. in a book, on the blackboard, in the environment or on a chart	✓
◆ relies heavily on beginning letters and sounding-out for word identification (graphophonic strategies)	✓
• carefully reads text, demonstrating the understanding that meaning is vested in the words	✓
• may point as an aid to reading, using finger, eyes or voice, especially when reading difficult text	✓
• locates words from sources such as word banks and environmental print	✓
• when questioned can reflect on own word identification strategies, e.g. 'I sounded it out'	✓
Attitude	
• is willing to have-a-go at reading unknown words	✓
• enjoys listening to stories	✓
• reads for a range of purposes, e.g. for pleasure or information	*
• responds sensitively to stories read	*
• discusses favourite books	✓
• talks about favourite author	*
• selects own reading material according to interest, purpose and level of difficulty and, with teacher support, can reconstruct information gained	*

Behaviours observed ✓
Literacy behaviours that need developing ∗

Placement on Developmental Continuum — Mark

Indicators from Reading Developmental Continuum

Transitional Reading Phase

Making Meaning at Text Level	
◆ shows an ability to construct meaning by integrating knowledge of:	
– text structure, e.g. letter, narrative, report, recount, procedure	
– text organisation, e.g. paragraphs, chapters, introduction, conclusion, contents, page index	*
– language features, e.g. descriptive language connectives such as because, therefore, if… then	
– subject specific language, e.g. the language of reporting in science and the language of a journalistic report	
◆ can retell and discuss own interpretation of texts read or viewed with others, providing information relating to plot and characterisation in narrative or to main ideas and supporting detail in informational text	*
◆ recognises that characters can be stereotyped in a text, e.g. a mother looking after children at home while the father goes out to work or a prince rescuing a helpless maiden from an evil stepmother, and discusses how this could be changed	*
◆ selects appropriate material and adjusts reading strategies for different texts and different purposes, e.g. skimming to search for a specific fact; scanning for a key word	*
• makes inferences and predictions based on information which is both explicit and implicit in a text	*
• makes generalisations based on interpretation of texts viewed or read, i.e. confirms, extends, or amends own knowledge through reading or viewing	*
• uses a range of strategies effectively to find relevant information in texts, e.g. makes use of table of contents and index	not known
• reads orally with increasing fluency and expression. Oral reading reflects personal interpretation	*
• makes comparisons with other texts read	
• selects texts effectively, integrating reading purpose and level of difficulty	
• recognises devices which influence construction of meaning such as the attribution of 'good' or 'bad' facial characteristics, clothing or language and the provision of emotive music and colour, and stereotypical roles and situations in written or visual texts	not known

Behaviours observed ✓
Literacy behaviours that need developing *

Transitional Reading Phase

Strategies for Making Meaning Using Context	
◆ is becoming efficient in using most of the following strategies for constructing meaning:	
– makes predictions and is able to substantiate them	
– self-corrects when reading	*
– re-reads to clarify meaning	
– reads-on when encountering a difficult text	
– slows down when reading difficult texts	✓
– substitutes familiar words	
– uses knowledge of print conventions, e.g. capitalisation, full stops, commas, exclamation marks, speech marks	*
◆ makes meaningful substitutions, i.e. replacement miscues are meaningful, e.g. 'cool' drink for 'cold' drink. The integration of the three cuing systems (semantic, syntactic and graphophonic) is developing	developing
◆ is able to reflect on and describe some of the strategies of the strategies for making meaning	*
Making Meaning at Word Level	
◆ has an increasing bank of sight words, including some difficult and subject-specific words, e.g. science, experiment, February, Christmas	✓
◆ is becoming efficient in the use of the following word identification strategies for constructing meaning:	
– sounds out to decode words	
– uses initial letters as a cue to decoding	
– uses knowledge of common letter patterns to decode words, e.g. th, tion, scious	*
– uses known parts of words to make sense of the whole word	
– uses blending to decode words, e.g. string	
– uses word segmentation and syllabification to make sense of the whole word	
Attitude	
• is self-motivated to read for pleasure	*
• reads for a range of purposes	*
• responds sensitively to stories	✓
• discusses favourite books	
• may discover a particular genre, e.g. adventure stories (may seek out other titles of this type)	
• shows a marked preference for a specific type of book or author	
• makes comparisons with other texts read	
• demonstrate confidence when reading different texts	*

Case Study – Mark
Intervention Plan

Name: Mark   **Phase**: Transitional

Behaviours to be encouraged

Making Meaning at Text Level
- Using language cues and knowledge of conventions of print.
- On-going monitoring to ensure that reading is making sense.
- Reflective and critical reading resulting in discussion and argument.

Making Meaning Using Context
- Prediction and confirmation strategies, re-reading, reading-on and having-a-go.
- Using cues such as sentence patterns, picture cues, language appropriate to the text.
- Using textual cues to identify words: sentence patterns, picture cues.

Making Meaning at Word Level
- Graphic and Phonic Knowledge: sounding out, blending, knowledge of letter and word patterns.
- Using knowledge of syllabification and knowledge of root words and word components such as prefixes and suffixes.

Attitude
- having-a-go and reading for pleasure

Teaching strategies (plain text from major teaching emphases; italic from key indicator links)

Making Meaning at Text Level
- Create a climate which fosters critical thinking.
- Ensure that Mark reads a range of texts for a variety of purposes.
- Provide opportunities for:
  - identifying the main issues in a text and providing supporting detail; identifying cause and effect and predicting outcomes; discussing concepts and vocabulary and extracting and organising information.
- Ensure that charts, notices, lists, wall stories/poems/recounts/reports etc. are topical and in constant use as referents.
- Provide opportunities for individual conferences when Mark can talk through his use of reading strategies, his perceived strengths and specific needs and other issues that are on his mind.
- Involve Mark in discussion and a range of activities before, during and after reading.
- Focus on the use of print conventions during shared book sessions, proof reading and editing activities.
- Provide opportunities for retelling complex stories.
- *Discuss with Mark his interpretation of a text in relation to background knowledge and world experience. Role-play strategies may help children to look at an event or concept from a range of view-points.*
- *Set up situations in which children react to a narrative text solely from the standpoint of one of the characters. Discuss and compare reactions.*
- *After reading a text, ask Mark to compare his reading with that of a peer.*

Making Meaning Using Context

- Model and discuss prediction and confirmation strategies, use of syntactic and semantic cues, use of picture cues, use of context cues, re-reading, reading-on, substituting words.
- *Encourage Mark to make predictions before reading and then read-on to confirm or reject ideas. Sometimes encourage him to discuss the initial predictions and then substantiate claims by reading aloud from the text.*
- *Avoid correcting Mark's miscues as he reads; give him the opportunity to read-on and self-correct. If Mark does not self-correct, stop the reading after a meaningful section of text has been completed and ask him to have another go.*
- *Help Mark to develop self-monitoring strategies, i.e. the awareness that meaning has been lost.*
- *Model self-questioning.*
- *Encourage Mark to have-a-go at a word and keep on reading and model re-reading of a text during shared book reading.*
- *Involve Mark in oral cloze activities. A word is covered, he makes a substitution and keeps on reading.*
- *Provide opportunities for text innovation. Mark works with a familiar framework and changes specified words.*
- *When Marks is stuck on a word, re-read the previous text for him to re-establish the flow.*

Making Meaning at Word Level

- Model and discuss word identification strategies: use of graphophonic knowledge and 'sounding out', blending, letter and word patterns, sight words, using syllabification and segmentation, using knowledge of root words and word components.
- *Involve Mark in pattern searches, e.g. find other words that have the 'was' or 'er' pattern.*
- *Model a process for working out words, e.g. predict what would make sense, look at the beginning of the word, syllabify, sound it out and/or identify a sequential letter pattern, divide a word into morphemes.*
- *Involve Mark in cloze activities where words have been deleted, leaving only the initial letters or initial blends.*
- *Develop charts with Mark. Find words with similar visual patterns, sound patterns and meaning-based relationships.*
- *Ask Mark, when correcting spelling errors, to compare his words with the correct version and tick the parts spelt correctly and circle the part causing a problem.*
- *Mark needs to understand that words must not only sound right, but they must also look right. Teach Mark to look for and focus on the highly predictable sequential letter patterns of English.*
- *Praise Mark for identifying patterns in new words. Add these to any pattern lists you have around the room. Help Mark to look for the common patterns in words. Encourage the child to mark the patterns, e.g. n**ee**d, f**ee**d, s**ee**d and group words which contain common patterns, e.g. **other**, br**other**, m**other**, b**other.***
- *Involve Mark in Secret Message and Sound Sleuth activities (see pages 222–6).*

Case Study – Jason

Jason caused his teacher concern at the beginning of Year 4 because of his obvious lack of skill development.

Jason was good at sport and frequently at odds with authority in the playground. However, he appeared to be quite a diligent worker in class and had managed to cover up the severity of his reading problem by becoming extremely adept at picking up cues from his environment. These cues ranged from the teacher talking to other children to copying directly from other children as he borrowed a pencil, felt pen or ruler or walked across the room for some reason or other. He was also a quiet master of avoidance.

The teacher observed Jason's reading habits and skills. She asked him if he had a favourite book which he would like to read to her. He answered in the negative.

The teacher asked Jason if he ever read at home—he didn't. He chose comics and sports magazines to read during silent reading time.

It was clear that Jason had little understanding about the process of reading. He seemed to lack purpose in mastering the skills and there was no interest or motivating force.

His lack of success had compounded these feelings.

First Stage of Intervention

Assisting Jason to find some purpose for learning how to read was the first priority. It was decided to utilise his interest in sport.

The teacher was lucky to find a volunteer (male physical education student) who agreed to meet with Jason for half an hour each week. Jason responded very positively to this interaction. He looked forward to each visit and his self-esteem grew.

Initially, the volunteer just chatted with Jason as they walked around the oval or sat in the deputy principal's room. The volunteer kept in contact with Jason's teacher and kept a written record of each meeting, noting Jason's interests and concerns and discussing any work Jason brought along.

As a result, Jason and the volunteer developed a good relationship, which became the base for skill development.

The teacher organised a basketball identity (Ricky Grace) to visit the school. Articles from newspapers and magazines concerning Ricky Grace and basketball were collected. These were enlarged for student reading and some put on overhead projector transparencies to be used for class discussion. They were all used extensively to prepare the class for the visit. Parallel programming was used successfully to engage the children. One group of children collected information to put on a graph; another group answered questions on a particular article, while Jason was required to underline specific words in the same article and do a 'Word Sort' with them. (At another stage he had to do 'Sound Sleuth' activities and, at another, he joined a group having a specific task to do which helped the completion of the group's task). He became immersed in these activities as a direct result of his interest.

Placement on Developmental Continuum—Jason
Indicators from Reading Developmental Continuum

Early Reading Phase

Making Meaning at Text Level	
◆ is beginning to read familiar texts confidently and can retell major contents from visual and printed texts, e.g. language experience recounts, shared books, simple informational texts and children's television programs	✓
◆ can identify and talk about a range of different text forms such as letters, lists, recipes, stories, newspaper and magazine articles, television dramas and documentaries	✓
◆ demonstrates understanding that all texts, both narrative and informational, are written by authors who are expressing their own ideas	✓
• identifies the main topic of a story or informational text and supplies some supporting information	✱
• talks about characters in books using picture clues, personal experience and the text to make inferences	✱
• provides detail about characters, setting and events when retelling a story	✱
• talks about ideas and information from informational texts, making links to own knowledge	✱
• has strong personal reaction to advertisements, ideas and information from visual and written texts	not known
• makes comparisons with other texts read or viewed. The child's comments could relate to theme, setting, character, plot, structure, information or the way the text is written	✱
• can talk about how to predict text content, e.g. 'I knew that book hadn't got facts in it. The dinosaurs had clothes on.'	✱

Making Meaning Using Context	
◆ may read word-by-word or line-by-line when reading an unfamiliar text, i.e. reading performance may be word centred. Fluency and expression become stilted as the child focuses on decoding	✓
◆ uses picture cues and knowledge of context to check understanding of meaning	✱
• generally makes meaningful substitutions, however over-reliance on graphophonics may cause some meaning to be lost	✱
• may sub-vocalise when reading difficult text 'silently'	✓
• is beginning to use self-correction as a strategy	✱
• uses knowledge of sentence structure and punctuation to help make meaning (syntactic strategies)	✱
• sometimes reads-on to confirm meaning	✱
• re-reads passage in order to clarify meaning that may have been lost due to word-by-word reading. May re-read a phrase, a sentence or a paragraph.	✱
• can talk about strategies used at the sentence level, e.g. 'If I think it doesn't sound right, I try again'	✱
• is beginning to integrate prediction and substantiation	✱

Early Reading Phase

Making Meaning at Word Level	
◆ has a bank of words which are recognised when encountered in different contexts, e.g. in a book, on the blackboard, in the environment or on a chart	✓
◆ relies heavily on beginning letters and sounding-out for word identification (graphophonic strategies)	✓
• carefully reads text, demonstrating the understanding that meaning is vested in the words	
• may point as an aid to reading, using finger, eyes or voice, especially when reading difficult text	✱
• locates words from sources such as word banks and environmental print	✓
• when questioned can reflect on own word identification strategies, e.g. 'I sounded it out'	✱

Attitude	
• is willing to have-a-go at reading unknown words	✱
• enjoys listening to stories	✓
• reads for a range of purposes, e.g. for pleasure or information	✱
• responds sensitively to stories read	✓
• discusses favourite books	
• talks about favourite author	
• selects own reading material according to interest, purpose and level of difficulty and, with teacher support, can reconstruct information gained	

Behaviours observed ✓
Literacy behaviours that need developing ✱

Placement on Developmental Continuum—Jason

Indicators from Reading Developmental Continuum

Jason isn't displaying any Transitional Phase Indicators.

Transitional Reading Phase

Making Meaning at Text Level	
◆ shows an ability to construct meaning by integrating knowledge of:	
– text structure, e.g. letter, narrative, report, recount, procedure	
– text organisation, e.g. paragraphs, chapters, introduction, conclusion, contents, page index	
– language features, e.g. descriptive language connectives such as because, therefore, if... then	
– subject specific language, e.g. the language of reporting in science and the language of a journalistic report	
◆ can retell and discuss own interpretation of texts read or viewed with others, providing information relating to plot and characterisation in narrative or to main ideas and supporting detail in informational text	
◆ recognises that characters can be stereotyped in a text, e.g. a mother looking after children at home while the father goes out to work or a prince rescuing a helpless maiden from an evil stepmother, and discusses how this could be changed	
◆ selects appropriate material and adjusts reading strategies for different texts and different purposes, e.g. skimming to search for a specific fact; scanning for a key word	
• makes inferences and predictions based on information which is both explicit and implicit in a text	
• makes generalisations based on interpretation of texts viewed or read, i.e. confirms, extends, or amends own knowledge through reading or viewing	
• uses a range of strategies effectively to find relevant information in texts, e.g. makes use of table of contents and index	
• reads orally with increasing fluency and expression. Oral reading reflects personal interpretation	
• selects texts effectively, integrating reading purpose and level of difficulty	
• makes comparisons with other texts read	
• recognises devices which influence construction of meaning such as the attribution of 'good' or 'bad' facial characteristics, clothing or language and the provision of emotive music and colour, and stereotypical roles and situations in written or visual texts	

Transitional Reading Phase

Strategies for Making Meaning Using Context	
◆ is becoming efficient in using most of the following strategies for constructing meaning:	
– makes predictions and is able to substantiate them	
– self-corrects when reading	
– re-reads to clarify meaning	
– reads-on when encountering a difficult text	
– slows down when reading difficult texts	
– substitutes familiar words	
– uses knowledge of print conventions, e.g. capitalisation, full stops, commas, exclamation marks, speech marks	
◆ makes meaningful substitutions, i.e. replacement miscues are meaningful, e.g. 'cool' drink for 'cold' drink. The integration of the three cuing systems (semantic, syntactic and graphophonic) is developing	
◆ is able to reflect on and describe some of the strategies of the strategies for making meaning	
Making Meaning at Word Level	
◆ has an increasing bank of sight words, including some difficult and subject-specific words, e.g. science, experiment, February, Christmas	
◆ is becoming efficient in the use of the following word identification strategies for constructing meaning:	
– sounds out to decode words	
– uses initial letters as a cue to decoding	
– uses knowledge of common letter patterns to decode words, e.g. th, tion, scious	
– uses known parts of words to make sense of the whole word	
– uses blending to decode words, e.g. string	
– uses word segmentation and syllabification to make sense of the whole word	
• uses print conventions on an aid to understanding e.g. capitalisation, full stops, commas, exclamation marks, speech marks	
Attitude	
• is self-motivated to read for pleasure	
• reads for a range of purposes	
• selects texts effectively, integrating reading purpose and level of difficulty	
• responds sensitively to stories	
• discusses favourite books	
• may discover a particular genre, e.g. adventure stories (may seek out other titles of this type)	

165

Intervention Plan

Name: Jason   **Phase:** Early

Behaviours to be encouraged

Making Meaning at Text Level
* Using personal knowledge and experience
* Responding to and reflecting on text meaning
* Using previous knowledge of stories or informational text
* Using prediction combined with confirmation of text outcomes
* Critical thinking, questioning, commenting on content and intention

Making Meaning Using Context
* Using pictures and context to predict words
* Re-reading and reading-on to re-establish meaning
* Using own knowledge and experience to create meaning

Making Meaning at Word Level
* Using knowledge of letters and visual letter patterns
* Sounding out
* Blending sounds and word parts
* Locating words from word banks and environmental print

Attitude
* Having-a-go
* Discussing authors, stories and other texts
* Selecting own reading material and reading for a range of purposes
* Responding sensitively to stories

Teaching Strategies

(plain text from major teaching emphases; italic from key indicator links)

Making Meaning at Text Level
* Ask Jason about ideas and information he has found in books. Encourage a range of opinions and reactions.
* Provide opportunities for individual conferences where Jason can discuss aspects of his reading.
* Model strategies such as substituting, re-reading and self-correction.
* Ensure that Jason has the opportunity to select his own books to read independently every day.
* Foster Jason's ability to predict through questioning and discussion before, during and after reading.
* Encourage Jason to share experiences related to his reading.
* Provide opportunities for Jason to retell stories or impart information he has gained from books.
* *Enable Jason to take part in paired reading with an adult, each reading a sentence or paragraph. Give him taped stories to read.*
* *If miscues are meaningful, do not draw attention to them.*
* *Set up situations where children dramatise a story or television episode, using a narrator and characters. Give Jason a chance to take different parts. Help him adopt appropriate 'voices' and intonation patterns.*
* *Encourage Jason to make contributions to reading corner from home. Compare and contrast two items such as a community newspaper article about a pet and a favourite story about the same animal. After extensive discussion list similarities and differences.*

166

- *Provide purposes for Jason to experiment and interact with different text forms, e.g. to contribute a recipe from home, to write a thank-you letter to the librarian and to cut out and display interesting articles from magazines.*

Making Meaning Using Context

- Encourage use of personal experiences, knowledge of oral language patterns and text structure.
- Provide opportunities for Jason to demonstrate understanding of a text through activities such as: substantiating answers by reading from the text, sequencing text, story mapping, identifying character traits.
- *Involve Jason in a number of supported reading activities, e.g. Choral reading from class charts of poems.*
- *Involve Jason in small group Directed Silent Reading activities each day.*
- *Involve Jason in before and during reading activities.*
- *Involve Jason in oral cloze activities, so he is involved in chunks of meaning rather than individual word decoding.*
- *Encourage Jason to substitute words and read-on, rather than worry over individual words.*
- *Involve Jason in sequencing activities after reading a text. Ensure that the sequencing is intrinsically meaningful.*
- *Work with Jason to develop a 'Reader's Theatre' script from a book he is reading.*

Making Meaning at Word Level

- Model strategies for attacking unknown words, e.g. identifying similar word beginnings, common word patterns, chunking parts of a word.
- Model 'reflective reading' in shared reading sessions, so that children know what expert readers do to check understanding of a word, a sentence or a chunk of text.
- Construct 'Secret Messages' for children (see pages 224–6).
- Give children opportunities to take part in 'Sound Sleuth' activities (see page 222).
- At all times encourage children to think about whether a word makes sense in context. Model this reflective decoding in shared reading sessions.

Attitude

- Continue to encourage Jason to immerse himself in books.
- Praise and encourage risk-taking.
- Listen carefully to and place high value on Jason's thoughts and opinions.
- Show enthusiasm for and help Jason to pursue individual interests.
- *Encourage Jason to reflect on the successes. Make sure that these are acknowledged and valued in the classroom.*
- *Give Jason time and opportunity to pursue an interest and share texts on the topic of his choice with the class.*
- *Ensure that Jason has the opportunity to participate in motivating and varied reading games that demand a concrete response to small amounts of text.*
- *Involve the child in goal setting, giving him/her opportunities to identify small, achievable goals which can then be monitored to demonstrate success.*

Teaching Strategies Linked to Key Indicators

When observing children's behaviours in relation to the key indicators and the attitude indicators of the *Reading: Developmental Continuum*, it may become clear that a child is having problems in a specific area. In the following pages, key indicators and attitude indicators are linked to a range of teaching strategies that will help children make progress.

The strategies are designed to encourage readers in whole-class, small-group or individual reading activities.

Instructional programs for children with reading difficulties are most effective if they develop from the classroom teacher's regular reading/language program. However, if children are experiencing difficulties, there will be times when they require additional, short, intensive, explicit, individual teaching.

Role Play Reading Phase

Making Meaning at the Text Level
- **The child displays reading-like behaviour:**
  - **holding the book the right way up**
  - **turning the pages appropriately**
  - **looking at words and pictures**
  - **using pictures to construct ideas**
- Read to the child every day and encourage him or her to 're-read' the stories.
- Point to interesting words as you read a book.
- Differentiate clearly between talking about a picture and reading print.
- Discuss the pictures and encourage the child to use them to make predictions.
- Sometimes ask the child to turn a page or point to a special word as you read.
- Sometimes ask the child to point to the words as she or he reads.
- After reading a book to the child ask him or her to find a particular part of the story, e.g. 'Can you find the part where Red Riding Hood met the wolf?'.

- **The child realises that print carries a message, but may read the writing differently each time, e.g. when 'reading' scribble to parents.**
- Read and re-read the same favourite story many times.
- Refer frequently to familiar classroom lists and labels in context to create an awareness of the constancy of print.
- Model writing for different purposes in front of the child. Discuss what you are writing while you are writing and talk about what you have written afterwards.
- During a cooking session refer to the recipe, matching the direction to the action each time.
- Involve children in reading print around the room every day for specific purposes.
- Make the child responsible for a task involving print every day, e.g. looking after the weather chart or changing the helper's roster.
- With the child make word/picture cards to label objects on the science table.
- Write the child's favourite rhyme on a card to his/her dictation, then give the child the card to keep. Put simple pictures above key words. Encourage the child to read the rhyme back to you and take it home to read to siblings or adults.

- **The child focuses on the meaning of a television program, story or other text viewed, listened to or 'read'. Responses reflect understanding.**
  - Read familiar books to the child and encourage her/him to read them back to self, you or others.
  - Stop reading when half way through a familiar story and ask the child what is going to happen next.
  - Before you start to read an unfamiliar story, discuss the title and pictures with the child and encourage her/him to predict what the story might be about.
  - Have the child arrange the pictures from a story in the correct sequence and then use them to assist her/him to retell the story.
  - Encourage children to role play parts of stories that they relate to and enjoy.
  - Encourage the child to tell others a well-known story or episode on television. If the television episode is part of a sequence, encourage the child to predict what will happen in the next episode.
  - Provide the child with the opportunity to respond to a story or television sequence through drawing, modelling, role play, discussion and finger puppets.
  - Read 'real-life' stories to the child and encourage discussion about similarities to people and events in the child's own life.

- **The child makes links to own experience when listening to or 'reading' books, e.g. points to illustration, saying 'My dog jumps up too.'**
  - Before reading to or with the child discuss the title and pictures, relating these to the child's own experiences and word knowledge. Encourage the child to predict what will happen in the story after having such a discussion. After reading the story discuss the setting, characters and happenings in relation to the child's predictions and his/her own life experiences.
  - Encourage the child to draw characters or scenes from stories, relating these to people or contexts known to her or him.
  - Ensure that the child's comments are always listened to and given value (even if they are not always clearly understood). Follow up all comments, relating them to texts and happenings in the classroom.
  - Ensure that the teacher's perceptions are not unconsciously imposed on a child, so that the child feels that conformity rather than individuality is what is required.
  - Include parents or caregivers in conferences and in informal conversation. Demonstrate through interest that the child's home life is extremely important.
  - In shared reading experiences, or when reading to the children, relate what is being read to your own personal life and experience, to provide a role model for the children.

Making Meaning Using Context

- **The child uses pictorial and visual cues when watching television, listening to or 'reading' stories, i.e. talks about television program, advertisement or picture in magazine or book, relating it to own knowledge and experience**
  - Ask the child to choose some pictures from the community newspaper or a magazine. Use these as a trigger for group discussion. Children hypothesise about the context and what is happening or what the picture represents.
  - Make a collection of toy advertisements or take segments from a catalogue. Discuss the content and message of the advertisement with the children and encourage them to make contributions from their own experiences.
  - Encourage the child to recount a segment from a television program viewed at home or school. Give the child an opportunity to talk about reactions, relating to

feelings, likes and dislikes, comparisons with own experience, etc. Try and elicit why the child feels the way he/she does about it. If the child has seen a film recently, focus on this also.

– Discuss the pictures in books, drawing attention to the way in which they illustrate the meaning of the text.
– Make use of textless picture books for oral story telling.
– Encourage the child to relate illustrations to own experience, e.g. point to a picture and say 'Is that like your bike at home?'.
– Encourage the child to use the illustrations to predict what might happen next and to make inferences.
– Encourage the child to retell a story from the illustrations.
– Slowly reveal a picture, asking a child to guess what is in the rest of it.

Making Meaning at Word Level

- **The child recognises own name, or part of it, in print.**
– Label the child's table, chair and peg. Ask the parent to write the child's name inside all his or her books and let the child 'help' with the writing.
– Draw up class lists, e.g. the Helper's Rosters and draw attention to the child's name in context.
– Write the child's name and stick it to her/his table so that it can be copied when required.
– Encourage the child to write her/his name on paintings and 'writings'.
– Comment on the child's name and related features ,e.g. 'I love your name, my little nephew is called Sam too!', 'Look — that stop sign has an S at the beginning, just like your name!', 'Let's count and see how many letters there are in your name.', 'Can you go on a name hunt and find how many times you can find your name written in the classroom?'.
– Make a 'name frame' for the child to use which follows the contours of the letters and provides a box for each letter.

Attitude

- The most important factor is to notice and praise the child for all small successes, valuing them highly and creating opportunities to share them with others.
- Praise the child for risk-taking behaviours and for having-a-go, even if the result is not absolutely right.
- Read and re-read old favourites.
- After reading a book, leave it around so that the child can read it for him/herself.
- Encourage the child to join in with you when you are reading well known or repetitive parts of the text.
- Praise the child for using print around the room in context.
- Provide many opportunities for the child to write, purposes for writing and attractive paper and pencils to write with.
- Always refer to reading-like behaviour as reading.
- Encourage the child to talk about, illustrate and role play favourite parts of stories. Ensure that there are many opportunities to respond to stories in any way that the child wants.
- If the child has a particular interest, ensure that he/she is able to pursue it.
- Provide an attractive reading corner and reward the child as often as you can by offering opportunities to use it creatively.
- For older children in this phase, select high interest, colourful and motivating reading material.

Experimental Reading Phase

Making Meaning at Text Level

- **The child realises that print contains a constant message, e.g. that the words of a written story remain the same, but the words of an oral story may change**
- Read and re-read favourite stories, sometimes pointing to words as you read.
- Use sentence makers (transparent plastic holders into which words can be inserted) to construct sentences. For instance, start with a sentence suggested by the child such as *I have a new school bag.* Each word is written on a separate card, which is given to the child to insert in the sentence maker.
  The child can experiment by changing one word at a time and gradually transforming the sentence, e.g.
    I have a new school bag
    I have a new school hat.
    I have an old school book.
    I have an exciting school book.
    I have an exciting library book, etc.
  Re-read the sentence with the child each time. Leave the sentences on display for a while and then give the words to the child to put in a personal word bank.
- Select stories with repetitive refrains and encourage children to chant them as they point to the words.
- Select books that use familiar oral language patterns so that children are able to match words, phrases and sentences as they are read.
- Write a short, meaningful sentence on a strip of card. Let the child cut the strip into single words, then reconstruct the sentence, first using a model and then, if completely confident, trying without one.

– Put the child in charge of one of the classroom charts that needs to be manipulated daily by inserting word-cards, e.g. a helper's roster or the weather chart. If the child is unable to read the words to be inserted independently, provide support by pairing the word-cards with pictures.

– Write familiar rhymes in front of the child, then give him/her the text to take home.

- **The child is focused on expressing the meaning of a story rather than reading the words accurately.**

– Read books that contain an abundance of cues on which to base prediction and confirmation.

– Encourage the child to make predictions based on the title and illustrations of a book.

– Before reading a book, talk about what you expect will be in it, encouraging comment.

– During reading, draw attention to the way in which illustrations support the text, e.g. 'Doesn't Cinderella look sad sitting alone by the fireplace?'.

– After a book has been read encourage children to comment about the text, offering their own interpretations; relating it to their own experiences; comparing fictional situations with real life as they know it; and expressing their reactions honestly.

– Encourage the child to retell the story, using illustrations as cues if necessary.

Making Meaning Using Context

- **The child uses prior knowledge of context and personal experience to make meaning, e.g. uses memory of a text to match spoken with written words.**

– Encourage the child to have-a-go at a word and then read-on to confirm that meaning has been maintained.

– If a child is unsure of a word, help him/her to re-read the sentence to predict what the word might be from the context.

– Before reading a text discuss the probable content and brainstorm words that may be used. Relate these to the child's current understandings and previous experience. Create a word bank under the topic heading for on-going reference.

– Use language games that involve a concrete response to sentences containing repetitive language patterns in clear contexts.

– Talk about reading print around the classroom and why the children read it so well. Discuss the use of high frequency words in classroom texts and find some of these in books children are reading. Talk about other words used in specific contexts such as colour charts, weather reports and helpers' rosters, exploring other contexts where such words might be found.

– Use repetitive texts to show how a reader can refer back to the text to decode a word.

– Use well-known and favourite stories and informational texts to model strategies of prediction and confirmation.

Making Meaning at Word Level

- **The child recognises some personally significant words in context, e.g. in job roster, weather chart or books.**

- Scribe the child's news and then ask the child to find all the words beginning with the initial letter of the child's name. Extend this activity to finding words displayed in the classroom. Choose other letters on other occasions. Give the child a 'special' notepad on which to record some of the words if he/she would like to do so. These could be used to form the basis of a personal dictionary.

- During the re-reading of a shared book, ask the child to find words starting with the initial letter of her/his name.

- Explore alphabet books with the child.

- Teach the names of the alphabet using alphabet rhymes and songs, books, blocks and charts.

- Involve the child in creating class books exemplifying common language patterns such as:

  We can jump.
  We can hop.
  We can skip. or
  We like oranges.
  We like bananas.
  We like apples.
  We hate warm drinks.
  We hate stale bread, etc.

- Encourage the child to carry out word sorting activities involving initial letters and familiar words.

- During modelled writing sessions use print around the room to check the spelling of a word.
- Involve the child in oral cloze activities, using familiar and frequently used words.
- Play Sound Sleuth activities with children (see page 222).
- Put the child in charge of the weather chart. Make sure that the word-cards that need changing each day display a word combined with a word-picture, e.g. 'sunny' with a picture of the sun; 'rainy' with a picture of rain; 'cloudy' with a picture of clouds. The names of the months and days of the week from which the children can choose should be displayed in the order in which they are chanted by the children, so that the correct one can be picked. The job roster can be treated in a similar way.
- In shared reading sessions encourage the child to choose a 'special' word that attracts him or her. Write this on a card for the child to add to his or her personal word bank. If the child is inclined to forget the word the next day, make sure you combine it with a word-picture. Let the child decide when she or he no longer needs the picture clue.
- Ask the child to find interesting or funny words at home and bring these to school. Show them at news time and display them on the wall. Praise the child for sharing these word discoveries with others.

- **The child matches some spoken words with written words when reading a book or environmental print.**
- Read to the child every day and encourage the child to read the text with you.
- Select books with repetitive texts and read turn and turn about, letting the child read the refrain.
- After the child has 'read' the text, ask her/him to go through the book and tell you any words she/he knows.
- Read a sentence or phrase from a book which is being read and ask the child if he/she can find the words. Then ask the child to read the words to you.
- Write short and meaningful sentences such as *Dinosaurs are ferocious*, cut the words up and encourage the child to reconstruct the sentence. Some children might need the original sentence to refer to.
- Use sentence makers (transparent plastic holders into which words can be inserted) to construct, deconstruct, expand and transform sentences. For instance, start with a sentence suggested by the child such as 'I saw an elephant' and gradually expand it by adding words and phrases. Each word is written on a separate card, which is given to the child to insert in the sentence maker. After the child has put the card in place, read the sentence together and decide whether or not the word is in the right place. If not, let the child have another go. Do not, however, let the child become discouraged and if she/he finds it difficult to place the card, offer some broad hints. An example could be:

  I saw an elephant.
  I saw a big elephant.
  I saw a big gray elephant.
  I saw a big gray elephant at the zoo.
  I saw a big gray elephant at the zoo squirting water.

  Alternatively, start with a longer sentence such as:
  The slimy green monster slowly slithered across the grassy river bank, looking for something fat and tasty to eat for its supper.
  The child can experiment by removing one word at a time and then, with help, read the sentence to see if it still makes sense. If it doesn't the word is restored to its place and another is removed.

The child will also enjoy taking a simple sentence and, by changing one word at a time, making a nonsense sentence which is still grammatically accurate:

> *I saw a cat sitting on the roof.*
> *I chased a cat sitting on the roof.*
> *I chased a teacher sitting on the roof.*
> *I chased a teacher dancing on the roof, etc.*

– Write children's sentences and/or well known sentences from favourite books, such as *Run, run, run as fast as you can. You can't catch me, I'm the gingerbread man.* on card. Write with the child, read with the child and then give them to the child to take home and read.
– Involve children in Secret Messages activities daily (see page 224).

Attitude

– Ensure that all efforts are valued and praised. Use successes as an example to others.
– Listen carefully to and consider the child's comments, making sure that her/his opinions and insights are not overridden by your own or those of other children.
– Encourage the child to bring favourite reading materials from home—story books, magazines, comics, factual texts or anything else that is valued.
– Give children time to browse in the reading corner.
– Make sure there is time for personal reading during the day.
– Encourage the child to select his or her own books and make opportunities for the child to talk about them and recommend them to others.

Early Reading Phase

Making Meaning at Text Level

• **The child is beginning to read familiar texts confidently and can retell major content from visual and printed texts, e.g. language experience recounts, shared books, simple informational texts and children's television programs.**

– Read and re-read favourite stories. Allow the child to take favourite books home and read them with a care-giver.
– Enable the child to take part in paired reading with an adult, each reading a sentence or paragraph.
– If miscues are meaningful, do not draw attention to them.
– Set up situations where children dramatise a story or television episode, using a narrator and characters. Give children a chance to take different parts. Help them adopt appropriate 'voices' and intonation patterns.

• **The child can identify and talk about a range of different text forms such as letters, lists, recipes, stories, newspaper and magazine articles, television dramas and documentaries.**

– Provide a wide range of materials in the reading corner, including all those print materials listed above. Encourage children to make their own contributions from home. Compare and contrast two items such as a community newspaper article about a pet and a favourite story about the same animal. After extensive discussion list similarities and differences.
– Provide purposes for children to experiment and interact with different text forms, e.g. to contribute a recipe from home, to write a thank-you letter to the librarian and to cut out and display interesting articles from magazines.

- Ensure that a wide range of text forms are read together in shared reading sessions. Encourage children to use these forms in their personal writing.

- **The child demonstrates understanding that all texts, both narrative and informational, are written by authors who are expressing their own ideas.**

- In shared book sessions make a point of discussing the author and illustrator, pointing out their photographs if possible. If the child feels strongly about a book, suggest that the author or illustrator might like to receive a letter about their work.

- Whenever possible enable children to interact with different versions of the same story. Discuss similarities and differences, relating these to the authors responsible for the texts.

- Collect different articles about the same topic whenever possible. These could be taken from simple informational texts, children's sections of the newspaper, school magazines, children's encyclopaedias etc. It could be helpful if parents and friends are persuaded to look for a range of such texts. Children are usually interested in topics such as animals and magic or any current 'craze' that is receiving attention in the media. Help children to understand that authors wrote these texts for specific purposes such as to persuade, to inform, to amuse etc. With the children classify these according to perceived purpose and then let the children decide whether they think the purpose has been achieved. Use one or two of the articles in a shared writing session, writing about the same topic from a different standpoint or with a different purpose. For instance, turn a factual account of dinosaurs into a fantasy, or an amusing account of animal behaviour into an instructional piece. Help the children to realise that each piece of text represents the ideas and reflects the purpose of the particular author.

- Talk about television productions, using photographs and information about actors or participants from television magazines.

- Dramatise a favourite story, discussing the process of script writing, production and direction with the children. Draw parallels with well-known films or television productions.

- Take a well known television drama or a favourite story and radically change one of the characters, talk about the difference this might make to the plot.

- Introduce the children to a 'back-to-front' version of a well-known fairy tale in a shared book session.

- Highlight instances of gender, age or cultural stereotyping. Compare fiction with reality, e.g. in the story of Cinderella. It is very difficult for children to realise that a commonly accepted view of a person, role or situation may not actually be true. Encourage them to look for examples that do not fit or that challenge the stereotype. Move from gross examples to more subtle representations. Encourage critical thinking and comment at all times, but do not expect too much too quickly.

- Encourage children to bring commentaries or previews of children's television programs to school so that these can be discussed in the light of the childrens' experience.

Making Meaning Using Context

- **The child may read word-by-word or line-by-line when reading unfamiliar text; i.e. reading performance may be word-centred. Fluency and expression become stilted as the reader focuses on decoding.**
- Involve the child in a number of supported reading activities; for example:
  Shared Book reading
  Choral reading from class charts of poems or extracts from texts
  Paired reading
  Reading with good commercial tapes, or ones that you have made of favourite stories.
- Involve the child in small group Directed Silent Reading activities each day.
- Involve the child in before and during reading activities; for example:
  Before reading:
  - making predictions from title and illustrations
  - discussing vocabulary that will be encountered in the text
  - developing 'What I know' and 'What I want to find out' charts
  During reading:
  - reading from the text to substantiate a prediction
  - re-reading a sentence if meaning is lost
  - reading-on to clarify the meaning of an unknown word
- Provide opportunities for the child to adapt familiar stories, rhymes or poems by changing some of the words.
- Involve the child in oral cloze activities, so that he/she is involved in chunks of meaning rather than individual word decoding.
- Encourage the child to substitute words and read-on, rather than worry over individual words.

– Involve the child in sequencing activities after reading a text. Ensure that the sequencing is intrinsically meaningful, i.e. that it involves a logical ordering of events or concepts, and is not merely a listing of characters or actions.
– Read the child different versions of traditional stories and encourage her/him to make comparisons between them.
– Work with the child to develop a 'Reader's Theatre' script from a book she/he is reading.

- **The child uses picture cues and knowledge of context to check understanding.**
– If a child is an impulsive reader who makes wild guesses on the basis of an initial letter or a similar looking word, encourage him or her to pause after reading a short but 'complete' chunk of text so that she or he can think about the meaning: Did it make sense? Did it seem to say what was suggested in the picture? Did it sound right? Do not worry if there is a long pause while the child does a 're-run' in the head to check understanding. Let the child talk about it if she or he wishes, but do not initiate conversation yourself, in case this disrupts the process of reflection. Be careful that you reassure the child that it is good to have-a-go and guess, but it is also important to check that guesses were reasonable ones.
– Model 'reflective reading' in shared reading sessions, so that children know what expert readers do to check understanding of a word, a sentence or a chunk of text.
– Take every opportunity to discuss the probable meanings of unknown words in shared book sessions, talking about the word in relation to other words in the text, the general context and the word in relation to other words with the same root or a similar letter pattern

Making Meaning at Word Level

- **The child has a bank of words which are recognised when encountered in different contexts, e.g. in a book, on the blackboard, in the environment or on a chart.**
– Ensure that the child is aware that he/she is encountering high frequency words across a range of contexts.
– After the child has finished reading a text, give her/him the opportunity to re-read the text and note some high frequency words that she/he considers to be important. Encourage the child to note these words in a personal dictionary.
– Use a familiar text to focus attention on high-frequency words by preparing a cloze passage and deleting some of these words. The missing words are written on cards, the children discuss where they fit in the text.
– Use sentence frames to help the child become familiar with high frequency words, e.g. *What is round?*
    A ball is round.
    A wheel is round.
    A hoop is round, etc.
– When reading the child's writing or scribing for him/her, comment on the 'useful' words that we are always using.
– Provide activities which involve the child in using words from his/her personal word bank to construct sentences, complete word matching games and undertake word sorts.
– Involve the child in text innovation activities.
– Provide opportunities for the child to play reading games such as those provided in this book.

178

- **The child relies heavily on beginning letters and sounding-out for word identification. (graphophonic strategies).**
  - Involve the child in activities which involve alliteration, e.g. using her/his name to create a nonsense sentence such as *Conrad catches catfish carefully.* or *Tanya tiptoes through the terrible turnips.*
  - Teach children to listen to the order of sounds in a word and represent these with a letter or letters in correct sequence.
  - Sound frames can be used to assist children to identify the place of individual letters within a word. If a child asks for the spelling of jumped, the teacher might prepare a frame to help the child fill in as many letters as possible, J U M P E D .
  - Reinforce the understanding that letter-sound correlation is different in different words. Re-teach the concept that:
    - one letter can represent a number of sounds, e.g. 'a': cat, able, car. probable, apparent, father, any
    - the same sound can be represented by different letters, e.g. sound 'ay': ate, ray, rain, obey, steak, veil, gage, reign.
  - Reinforce the understanding that sounds need to be represented by one or more letters. If letter frames are set up for words (as shown in 'order of sounds' above), the following questions can be asked:
    - What is the very first sound you hear?
    - Do you know what letter can be used for that sound?
    - In which box do you think it should be written?
  - Give the child opportunities to sort words into groups according to beginning letters.
  - Set up games for the child which involve writing words in an unbroken chain or pattern, joining the last letter of one word to the matching initial letter of the next. Children can be challenged to discover whether the two letters sound the same or different in the two words, e.g. *hopot* (hop/pot) where the letters represent the same sound and *wasit* (was/sit) where the same letter represents different sounds. Children could use red and blue circles to note the differences. Children may need support as they attempt this task. Once they become confident they can be further challenged to go on a 'Word Hunt' and find other words which contain letters representing one sound or the other, e.g. was/is/his/nose/dogs - sit/sad/past/us/sing.
  - Different types of alphabet books can be constructed. Children can make up their own alphabet books, which they can illustrate and use themselves or donate to younger children.
  - An alphabet book could become a personal dictionary in which children can write words which they know or want to learn.
  - Children could be challenged to make an alphabet book which contains two examples of each way a sound can be represented by the same letter, for instance: cat/come, circle/Cynthia, church/chair, Christmas/chemist. They might take a long time to discover and collect examples, but this can be an on-going activity.
  - Construct Secret Messages for children (see page 224)
  - Give children opportunities to take part in Sound Sleuth activities (see page 222)
  - At all times encourage children to think about whether a word makes sense in context.
    Model this reflective decoding in shared reading sessions.

179

Attitude

- Provide a selection of books with tapes so that the child can experience success by 'reading-along'.
- Encourage the child to reflect on the successes that have been experienced. Make sure that these are acknowledged and valued in the classroom context.
- Give the child time and opportunity to pursue an interest and share texts on the topic of his/her choice with the class or a small group.
- Ensure that the child has the opportunity to participate in motivating and varied reading games that demand a concrete response to small amounts of text. Some examples are offered at the end of this book.
- Involve the child in goal setting, giving him/her opportunities to identify small, achievable goals which can then be monitored to demonstrate success.
- Undertake regular reading conferences with the child to assist with the self-monitoring process and provide encouragement and reinforcement. Include care-givers if possible.
- Encourage the child to identify a favourite author and talk about favourite books.
- Help children to develop self-selection strategies to ensure that she/he can access books effectively:
  - read the summary on the inside cover
  - flick through the book to gain a general impression
  - read a paragraph or two to see if the text is accessible. If the book is being chosen for the pictures this does not matter.

Transitional Reading Phase

Making Meaning at Text Level

- **The child shows an ability to construct meaning by integrating knowledge of:**
  - **text structure, e.g. letter, narrative, report, recount, procedure**
  - **text organisation, e.g. paragraphs, chapters, introduction, conclusion, contents page, index**
  - **language features, for instance descriptive language, connectives such as because, therefore, if...then**
  - **subject-specific language, e.g. the language of reporting in science and the language of a journalistic report**
- Involve the child in before, during and after comprehension activities, such as

Before
  - discussing the structure of the text
  - predicting content from the cover and illustrations
  - identifying what is known about the topic
  - relating topic to own experience and prior knowledge
  - brain-storming likely vocabulary and language features
  - draw attention to the organisation of the text, highlighting aspects such as the table of contents, index, glossary, headings and sub-headings, captions and footnotes

During
- focus attention on the way the author has used particular conventions such as abbreviations, inverted commas, compound words, similes
- comment on structural aspects of the text as they occur
- draw attention to introductory statements, signal words and concluding statements

After
- talk through difficult concepts and new words
- discuss how the structure of the text assisted the reader to comprehend the topic
- relate the content to the child's own experience and knowledge of the topic.
- Provide opportunities for the child to re-read for different purposes, e.g. to develop an interesting words chart or construct a skeleton outline.
- Encourage the child to look for words in a text that signal:
  - cause and effect (because, as a result of, consequently)
  - explanation (for instance, for example, this means..)
  - comparison and contrast (but, however, similarly, on the other hand)
  - time order (now, then, after, before, next, soon and dates or times).
- Have the child retell the information or story orally, using props such as flow charts, strategic overviews or story maps and plot profiles.
- Have the child construct a written retell, either as an individual effort, in a group or with a partner.
- Encourage the child to make inferences about characters in stories. Thought bubbles could be created showing implications of events or interactions on people.
- Introduce a self-evaluation checklist. Children are encouraged to tick off any strategy they use. This can be used in conjunction with a reading log. This will help a child become aware of and develop control over the use of specific strategies.

- **The child retells and discusses own interpretation of texts read or viewed with others, providing information relating to plot and characterisation in narrative or to main ideas and supporting detail in informational text.**
- Discuss with the child his/her interpretation of a written or visual text in relation to background knowledge and world experience. Encourage the child to try and adopt the viewpoint of a person with a different cultural background or life experience. Role-play strategies may help children to look at an event or concept from a range of view-points.
- Encourage the child to look underneath the text of a book, film or video to try and identify the stance of the author. Discuss this with others to see if there is consensus on this matter.
- Set up situations in which children react to a narrative text solely from the stand-point of one of the characters. Discuss and compare reactions.
- After reading a text, ask the child to compare her/his reading with that of a peer. Help the children structure their discussion to include the reasons why each drew specific conclusions and the reasons why their conclusions may have been different.

- **recognises that characters can be stereotyped in a text, e.g. a mother looking after children at home while the father goes out to work, or a prince rescuing a helpless maiden from an evil stepmother; and discusses how this could be changed.**
- Use alternative versions of familiar fairy stories as a springboard for an investigation into gender bias. Pursue this further with other texts, praising children when they recognise bias and stereotyping. Collect examples for class consideration and discussion.
- Read or view selected texts with the children that typify stereotyping in literature, e.g. Little Black Sambo, The Seven Little Australians, Cinderella. Discuss passages carefully looking first at the images engendered, comparing them with reality; after which the impact of such texts on people's perceptions can be considered. Finally, examine linguistic features that embody bias and convey emotive impressions.

- **The child selects appropriate material and adjusts reading strategies for different texts and purposes, e.g. skimming to search for a specific fact, scanning for a key word.**
- Have the child work with a group of children to answer questions about a piece of text that they have chosen. Discuss with them the ways in which they chose the topic, such as personal preference or previous knowledge and the processes they used to make decisions about the specific text, e.g. skimming and scanning to determine suitability. Each group will decide how best they will present what they have learnt through and about the text, e.g. written report, oral report, dramatic presentation.
- Model and discuss appropriate use of diagrams to help readers extract and organise important information. Once students are experienced in using a number of diagrams, they can then decide which diagram to use in a particular situation; for example:
  - labelled diagrams
  - sequenced pictures
  - hierarchies

- flow charts
- cycles
- structured overviews
- modified structured overviews
- retrieval charts
- Venn diagrams
- tree diagrams
- Model the use of an 'Interesting Words' chart as a strategy to help a child make use of context clues to work out word meanings and identify key words.

Making Meaning Using Context

- **The child is becoming efficient in using most of the following strategies for constructing meaning:**
  - **makes predictions and is able to substantiate them**
  - **self-corrects when reading**
  - **re-reads to clarify meaning**
  - **reads on when encountering a difficult text**
  - **slows down when reading difficult texts**
  - **substitutes familiar words**
  - **uses knowledge of print conventions, e.g. capitalisation, full stops, commas, exclamation marks, speech marks.**
- Encourage the child to make predictions before reading and then read on to confirm or reject ideas. Sometimes encourage the child to discuss the initial predictions and then substantiate claims by reading aloud from the text.
- Avoid correcting the child's miscues as he/she reads; give her/him the opportunity to read on and self-correct. If the child does not self-correct, you might want to stop the reading after a meaningful section of text has been completed and ask the child to have another go at the word.
- Help the child to develop self-monitoring strategies, i.e. the awareness that meaning has been lost.
- Model self-questioning.
- Encourage the child to have a go at a word and keep on reading.
- Model re-reading of a text during shared book reading.
- Involve the child in oral cloze activities. A word is covered and the child is encouraged to make a substitution and keep on reading.
- Provide opportunities for text innovation. The child works with a familiar framework and changes specified words.
- When a child has become stuck on a word, re-read some of the previous text for him/her to re-establish the flow of the language.

- **The child makes meaningful substitutions, i.e. replacement miscues are meaningful, e.g. 'cool' drink for 'cold' drink. The integration of the three cuing systems (semantic, syntactic and graphophonic) is developing.**
- Ask the child to find a synonym for each word underlined in a piece of text. The child can then compare notes with a partner and discuss the words they have chosen. Stress that there may be a whole range of acceptable words.
- Promote the use of semantic knowledge and content by helping children develop lists of related words drawn from their own experience. The teacher names a category and the class suggests words which belong. These lists can be developed throughout the term:
    agriculture
    seeds

harvester
grain
vehicle
truck
car
motorcycle

– Help children develop the ability to make associations and thus promote the use of semantics when decoding words. The teacher establishes a topic such as 'flowers'. The children take turns in suggesting flowers which commence with letters of the alphabet, e.g. daisy, delphiniums, etc. When they cannot think of flowers beginning with each particular letter, they move to the next letter of the alphabet

– Involve the child in reading texts that relate to a particular theme or topic. Provide a range of different types of books for selection, such as informational texts, narratives, poetry, reports.

– Have the child complete a cloze passage and then explain why particular words were chosen. Delete only content words such as nouns, verbs, adjectives and adverbs. Start by concentrating on only one class of words so that it is easier for the child to make generalisations.

– After a child has read a text ask her/him to retell it to you.

- **The child is able to talk about some of the strategies used for making meaning.**

– Use 'talk-aloud' protocol to model and reinforce the use of meaning-making strategies in modelled reading and shared book sessions.

– Talk with the child about the strategies readers use to establish meaning. Read a difficult piece of text together and demonstrate some techniques like slowing down, sub-vocalising, re-reading, reading on, self-correcting, prediction and substantiation. Discuss when a reading strategy can be used appropriately in context. Encourage the child to practise one or two of the techniques in order to gain conscious control over it. Suggest that the child talks about this during reflection time.

– Make use of class or small group reflection times to highlight a strategy used successfully by another child. Talk about the strategy, put it on a chart and encourage other children to add to it or make alternative contributions

– At the end of a one-to-one reading session, help the child to think back and reflect on strategies used when difficulties were encountered. Discuss alternative strategies that could have been used if the 'first run' was not successful.

– Provide opportunities for the child to talk about his/her perceptions of the reading process. Try and foster a conscious awareness of the strategies employed on different occasions. Praise the child for expressing insights into his/her learning.

Making Meaning at the Word Level

- **The child has an increasing bank of sight words, including some difficult and subject-specific words, e.g. science, experiment, February, Christmas.**

If children are having problems with some common high frequency words, it is of fundamental importance that they learn to focus on the critical (most significant) features of a word, e.g. ca**l**m, ca**l**f, wh**a**t.

Encourage the child to:

– Look at a word
  Focus on the part which is causing a problem.

Shut your eyes

Think about the word

Write it down

- Mnemonics can be used to help them memorise these critical features.
- Make the words into a crossword puzzle
- Write the word

Think about it

Fold the paper over

Write the word

Check back

Correct if necessary

- Write a nonsense sentence including as many of your spelling words as you can
- Make a design using the spelling words printed end to end, e.g. a circle, a triangle, a spiral
- Take one of your spelling words. Make as many other words from it as you can by adding to it and making other words from it, e.g. reference: referenced, referencing, references, referee, referent; refer
- Use spelling words to make a spelling step ladder.

Each word should start with the letter which ends the word before.

Other words may need to be added to create links between the spelling words

- Write out the spelling words leaving out some letters.

Fill in the missing letters the next day.

- Jumble up the letters of the spelling words.

Sort them out the next day.

- Find words that rhyme with the spelling words.

Decide if they are spelled the same or differently.

- Make a grid.

Insert a friend's spelling words into the grid, either horizontally or vertically.

Fill the gaps with random letters.

Challenge the friend to find and circle the words.

Some other suggested activities are:

- Cloze activities can be used to focus on high frequency words. Prepare a passage by deleting any high frequency words you want to focus on.
- Use high frequency words in the traditional game of Bingo.

  1 Write the words on the board for the children to look at closely.

  2 Cover the words and call them out. Children write their words onto their Bingo cards.

  3 Uncover words. Children check their spelling and correct any words incorrectly spelt.

  4 Play Bingo.

- **The child is becoming efficient in the use of the following word identification strategies for constructing meaning:**
  - **sounds out to decode words**
  - **uses initial letters as a cue to decoding**
  - **uses knowledge of common letter patterns to decode words, e.g. th, tion, scious, ough**
  - **uses known parts of words to make sense of the whole word**
  - **uses blending to decode words, e.g. str-ing**
  - **uses word segmentation syllabification to make sense of the whole word**
- Ensure that the child is writing every day in all curriculum areas.

185

- Involve the child in pattern searches, e.g. find other words that have the 'was' or 'er' pattern
- Model a process for working out words, e.g. predict what would make sense, look at the beginning of the word, syllabify, sound it out and/or identify a sequential letter pattern, divide a word into morphemes.
- Involve the child in cloze activities where words have been deleted, leaving only the initial letters or initial blends, e.g. *On Friday it rained so hard that the r——overflowed and fl—— the town.*
- Involve the child in cloze activities where syllables or common English letter patterns have been deleted.
- Develop class charts with the child. Words with similar visual patterns, sound patterns and meaning-based relationships may be recorded.
- Ask the child, when correcting spelling errors, to compare his/her words with the correct version and to tick the parts spelt correctly and circle the part causing a problem, i.e. the critical feature of that word.
- The child needs to understand that words must not only *sound* right, but they must also *look* right. Some children have a sound understanding of graphophonic relationships but have not developed any alternative strategies that they can apply when a graphophonic strategy is not appropriate. One of the major strategies they need to develop is the use of common letter patterns which characterise the spelling of English words. Children need to be taught to look for and focus on the highly predictable sequential letter patterns of English.
- Word sorting and categorising are important activities in developing recognition of common English letter patterns. Praise the child for identifying patterns in new words. Add these to any pattern lists you have around the room. Help the child to look for the common patterns in words. Encourage the child to mark the patterns, e.g. n**ee**d, f**ee**d, s**ee**d and group words which contain common patterns, e.g. **other**, br**other**, m**other**, b**other**
- Pick the Pattern activities will involve the child in finding words which exhibit the same patterns, although they may be pronounced differently, and different patterns which represent the same sound.

Attitude

- If a child is a reluctant reader ensure that instant success is possible by providing texts that are rich in rhyme, rhythm and repetition.
- Try and make sure that texts are read together in a natural way before a child attempts to read them independently. Sometimes give a synopsis of the plot or content so that prediction is made easy. For instance, you can say, 'This is a great book about spiders. I found it really interesting. Look, each part has a heading to show what the section is about (*show and read through*) and it has a lot of diagrams that illustrate what is being said…'
- Praise and encouragement are crucial, but make sure that all that is said is genuine. Make sure that the child's contributions are listened to and valued. Remove all pressure and tension. Talk with parents or caregivers to make sure that reading is not associated with worry and stress. Do not set reading for homework if this is the case. Avoid reading conferences for the time being if these represent an affirmation of failure—wait until the child is set up for success before discussing how well something has been accomplished.

- Find out from the child or caregiver what interests the child is currently pursuing. Tap into the school or local library to get hold of appropriate material. Do not present this as 'reading material' but make it available to serve another purpose, e.g. a child who is a football addict could be asked to construct a weekly quiz for the class relating to players, goals, incidents etc. Much of this material could come from the local paper. Involve the parents or caregivers in the activity, asking them to support the child as she or he looks for information or needs help with difficult words. Make the weekly quiz sheets into a 'Footy Book' that could be used in subsequent sessions to provide a basis for comparison. If the child is interested in something that you know little about, capitalise on this by showing real interest and making sure the child realises he/she is teaching you something. Always make sure that there is a lasting record of what has been achieved and that this is given high status in the classroom.
- Find a book of exciting short stories and read one each day to the class. Stop just before the denouement. Let the child take the book home to find out what happens. It doesn't matter if the child reads the ending him or herself or asks for it to be read.
- If the child is daunted by books, do not try to 'push' them. Instead, encourage the child to read short texts that are of topical interest, e.g. instructions for building a model aeroplane or setting up a science experiment; cartoons that use speech bubbles; games that involve small amounts of reading; treasure hunts where one clue leads to another; computer programs that involve minimal reading; mathematical conundrums if these are enjoyed; jokes and riddles.

Alternative Approaches for Teaching Children with Reading Difficulties

The following specific teaching strategies have been identified from the literature published on teaching children with reading difficulties. They have been included in this chapter to introduce teachers to the wide range of excellent teaching suggestions that are developing a strong research base for the whole area. Teachers are actively encouraged to incorporate these specific teaching strategies within their regular classroom reading program, as many of them can be easily adapted for whole-class, small-group or individual activities. (For a more detailed explanation of these teaching strategies, teachers are encouraged to read the original references.) Also see Language Games beginning on page 227.

Reading Recovery – Marie Clay

Marie Clay, 1987. *Implementing Reading Recovery: Systemic Adaptations to an Education Innovation.* New Zealand Journal of Educational Studies.

Reading Recovery is a specific program designed by Marie Clay in New Zealand to focus on children with reading difficulties. The program is designed to be implemented with children in Years 1/2 who have been identified as at risk in their reading development. The children are withdrawn from the regular classroom for a period of between twelve to fifteen weeks, wherein they receive individualised instruction for approximately forty minutes with a tutor trained in the Reading Recovery procedures.

The program takes a diagnostic teaching approach focusing on developing children's understanding of the skills and strategies required for successful reading. The program requires the teacher to actively 'scaffold' the instructional activities using a structured lesson sequence each day. The lesson sequence always includes the following (in sequence):

- Reading familiar stories.
- Taking running records of oral reading.
- Working on word identification (letters and sounds).
- Daily writing (similar to a language experience session).
- Reading a new book.

Parents are encouraged to observe the lessons, and to continue to work with the child at home. There is a 'phasing in' period when the child returns to the regular classroom reading program.

The Reading Recovery program is gaining in popularity in Australia and America and early research results indicate the program is successful in working with children experiencing reading difficulties.

Re-Quest Reading Program

A.V.C. Manzo, 1969. *The Re-Quest Procedure.* Journal of Reading, November 1969.
© The International Reading Association.

The Re-Quest program focuses on teaching children reading comprehension strategies by having them develop their individual self-questioning strategies as they read. The program was originally designed as a one-to-one teacher-child activity where the teacher initially modelled the questioning (*and* how to answer the question) and then the children gradually took responsibility for the questioning. The lesson format involves the following procedures:

- Selection and preparation of the material to read.
- Read the first sentence/passage and identify possible questions.
- Student asks the teacher questions, evaluates the response, and they discuss the questions.
- The teacher asks questions about the next sentence/passage, respond and review.
- Teacher and child are required to substantiate their answers.
- The child is encouraged to integrate all the information about the text, the questions, the responses.

Many teachers have taken the general procedures outlined above and adapted them to include small-group, and peer teaching, and a more across-the-curriculum reading focus for content area reading development.

Bridge Reading

Alison Dewsbury: Ontario Institute for Studies in Education, 252 Bloor Street West, Toronto, Ontario M5S IV6, Canada

Learning to read is like constructing a jigsaw puzzle. Children have to see the picture before they come to terms with the individual pieces, and even when they are dealing with an individual piece they need to keep the big picture very much in mind.

Children who are experiencing difficulties with reading are often trying to tackle conventions of print before they really understand the relationship between spoken and written language and how the written language is used to enable people to communicate with each other.

Children learn by doing. They watch their parents turning on the television and then they have-a-go themselves. They learn to build a tower by trial and error when playing with blocks. It is difficult for them to play with words to find out how the written language works because printed words seem to be beyond their control. Print is set on a page or a road sign and it is often not clear to children how it got there. The relationship between the spoken and written word is not immediately obvious to them. It is crucial that children build understandings by interacting with environmental print, story telling, scribbling and all the other vital literacy experiences of early childhood. It can also make a big difference if children participate in very concrete experiences which enable them to construct and refine understandings about the written language and how it works.

Bridge Reading makes language concrete for children by pairing words with word-pictures, thus enabling children to construct meaning for themselves through play. Abstract words are given meaning by pairing them with gestures in context and drawing the gestures. This gives children instant access to and control over writing and reading. They learn through play, manipulating words and sentences to build messages for each other and reading treasure hunt clues, instructions for games and little books. This enables them to learn concepts of print through purposeful activity in a real-world situation. They are able to learn to read by reading and to write by writing because the relationship between written and spoken language is clear and concrete.

Children do not need the support offered by Bridge Reading for very long and research carried out at the Ontario Institute for Studies in Education shows clearly that the initial success and impetus which they gain from the program is maintained long after they have ceased to use it.

Reciprocal Reading

A. Palincsar, 1984. *The Quest for Meaning from Expository Text: A Teacher Guided Journey.*

This instructional strategy was the forerunner of a large number of studies focusing on 'interactive teaching' for teaching children *strategies* for comprehension. 'Reciprocal' means the teacher and student exchange roles and teach each other to answer different types of questions; that is:

- Self-questioning
- Clarifying
- Predicting
- Summarising
- Evaluating

The teacher initially models the types of questions *and* how to solve them, while both the teacher and the children engage in activities to substantiate and evaluate both the answers and *how* the answers were obtained. The children take turns at being the teacher in questioning and substantiating answers across a wide range of different texts.

This strategy has proven to be *very* popular and successful with children experiencing difficulties (and most other children as well!).

Question and Answer Relationships (QAR)

T. Raphael, 1982. *Question Answering Strategies for children.* The Reading Teacher, November 1982. © The International Reading Association.

This is a very simple yet very effective instructional strategy for teaching children how to recognise the relationships that exist among different question types, and where answers can be found in the text. This strategy has been adapted and implemented successfully by teachers across all Year levels and with children of all ability levels.

The instructional strategy requires the teacher to teach the following explicitly:

1 Identify the *type* of question (i.e. literal, inferential, evaluative, appreciative) by using Raphael's revised classification.
   - 'Right There' Questions – The answer is stated explicitly in the text and is easy to find because the words in the question match the words in the text.

190

- 'Think and Search' Questions – The answer is in the text but is not stated explicitly and the reader may need to read several paragraphs to relate information.
- 'On My Own' Questions – The answer is not explicitly in the text but inside the reader's head (background knowledge).

2 The teacher models the different question types, how to recognise them, *and* how to find the answers.

3 The teacher and students take turns in modelling and finding the relationships between questions and responses (with lots of repetition and 'thinking aloud' about *how* and *why* the answers were obtained).

4 Gradually, the students take ownership of the strategy and the teacher provides transfer and maintenance activities across the curriculum.

Concept – Text – Application Approach (CTA)

J. Wong, and K. Au, 1985. *The Concept – Text – Application Approach: Helping elementary students comprehend expository text.* The Reading Teacher, March 1985. © The International Reading Association.

This teaching strategy was devised for children in the Hawaiian school system whose first language was not English. It has since been found to be successful with almost all children. It provides teaching ideas/activities to guide children through pre-reading, guided reading, and after-reading activities. In each 'phase' of the lesson, the teacher encourages the children to use their background knowledge of the 'concept' (topic), through careful teacher scaffolding of the discussion about the text.

- Concept Phase   Find out what children know about the concept/topic extend/ enrich vocabulary by semantic mapping etc. Assess their level of understanding.
- Text Phase   Review purposes for reading, use guided reading strategies (e.g. DSR), ongoing discussion/elaboration. Examine the structure of the text and set out the information in an overview. Help the children 'make connections' between their knowledge and the text.
- Application Phase   Children discuss the whole text, complete a retelling of the text, summarise the content and review the text overview. Complete follow-up extension activities (short-term and long-term projects).

Think-aloud

B. Davey, 1983. *'Think Aloud'—Modelling the cognitive processes of reading comprehension.* Journal of Reading.

Because reading is a cognitive activity, a major problem for children who experience reading difficulty is that they usually do not have a model or example of *how* good readers solve the reading puzzle. A simple yet very effective strategy is to have the teacher always clearly model (think-aloud) how s/he is using strategies when s/he reads—strategies for gaining meaning, strategies for answering questions *and* strategies for word identification.

Davey developed a simple lesson sequence to make reading more overt; that is:

- Make predictions (explain why and how).

- Describe the idea (picture) inside your head as you read each sentence/paragraph (explain why/how).
- Share an analogy (i.e. make connections to background of knowledge, explain how/why).
- Monitor reading (self-question, i.e. this is not making sense).
- Problem Solving (How will I find the solution, to my problem?).

Read and Retell

The 'read and retell' strategy as described by Hazel Brown and Brian Cambourne in their book *Read and Retell* is a most effective learning activity. It focuses children on *meaning* as they are involved in predicting, sharing, listening, justifying, reading and writing. It has been found that one of the most important effects of the retelling procedure is the 'almost unconscious learning of text structures, vocabulary and conventions of writing language taking place'. (Brown and Cambourne, 1987, *Read and Retell,* Thomas Nelson Australia, page 10).

Retelling procedures can be varied to accommodate different levels of language ability. There are different forms of the retelling procedure; for example:

- oral to oral retelling
- oral to written
- oral to drawing
- written to oral
- written to written
- written to drawing
- diagram to oral or written
- drama to written
- written to drama

Directed Silent Reading (DSR)

The 'directed silent reading' strategy develops reading as a thinking process. Children are encouraged to make predictions and then read to confirm their ideas. It is a useful strategy to use when introducing an unfamiliar topic in the content area.

Procedure:
- Each student is given a copy of the text which should be short and meaningful.
- Discuss pictures which encourage prediction and familiarise the students with background information, ideas and vocabulary which might appear in the text.
  If fiction is to be read, the pictures can be linked to create a story.
  The students offer suggestions freely. It is important to value all contributions.
- Discuss basic word attack strategies:
  - picture cues
  - context cues (read around the word)
  - graphophonic cue (symbol-sound relationships; small words in big ones; familiar parts)
  - confirmation (does it make sense?)
- Set a directing question (purpose)
- Students read silently (mark difficult words and/or make notes if appropriate). Teacher models silent reading behaviour.

- When all students have finished, teacher asks for answer to the directing question.
- Teacher asks further questions, encouraging students to read 'on the lines', 'between the lines' and 'beyond the lines'.
  Answers must be sustained by the student referring to the particular part of the text which provides the answer.
- Discuss the words which the students found difficult in terms of the word attack strategies.
- Use the text to develop any language skills which the students are finding difficult.

Assessment of Children With Reading Difficulties

Assessment Activities

- Observation and analysis of children's reading skills and strategies during regular classroom reading activities.
- Teacher-made 'tasks' designed to identify specific strengths and weaknesses; e.g. word identification strategies; Comprehension-answering inference questions or constructing story maps.
- Teacher-child interviews or conferences designed to focus on *what* children understand and *how* they use reading skills and strategies.
- Questionnaires, rating scales, interest surveys, attitudes to reading surveys.
- Using children's self-evaluation comments or checklists.
- Published diagnostic tests that help identify children's strengths and weaknesses.

The following assessment activities are recommended to provide a *basis* for assisting teachers and schools to place children on the Reading Continuum and diagnose specific strengths and weaknesses. Schools are encouraged to develop a school-wide Management Information System to record and monitor children's progress across the school.)

Knowledge and Understanding of Reading

- Observation of children during reading sessions (teacher checklists of Reading Continuum Indicators).
- Teacher-child interviews about reading strategies, interests, habits.
- Analysis of children's work in reading/language activities.
- Questionnaires/surveys.

Comprehension: Meaning-making Strategies

- Re-telling (oral and written re-tells)
- Answering comprehension questions (various levels of questions).
- Cloze passages.
- Teacher-child interviews.
- Questionnaires/surveys focusing on reading strategies.
- Oral reading and miscue analysis.
- Analysis of comprehension activities, e.g. story maps.

Word Identification Strategies

- Observation of children's oral and silent reading strategies.
- Oral reading and miscue analysis.
- Cloze and modified cloze activities.
- Analysis of children's reading activities.
- Teacher-child interviews on word identification strategies.
- Graphophonic knowledge.

Concepts of Print

- Observation of children's reading.
- Concepts of print checklists.

- Re-telling activities.
- 'Approximation to text' activities.
- Teacher-child interviews.

Attitude

- Teacher observation of reading habits, attitude and interests.
- Records of books read.
- Questionnaires/Surveys/Attitude scales.
- Teacher interviews on reading attitudes.
- Parent-teacher interviews.

At all times, First Steps encourages teachers and parents to identify both the strengths and weaknesses of the child and to plan a program that develops both areas together.

Supporting Children's Oral Reading

If children ...

make a mistake and correct the error	come to a word they don't know and pause	make a mistake which does not make sense	make a mistake which does make sense
• offer praise or support for their self-correction	• wait to give them time for problem solving • if they're successful, encourage them to read on to maintain meaning • if meaning is lost and the word is likely to be known, ask them to go back to the beginning of the sentence and take another 'run' at it or ask them to predict a word which begins with the correct letter and would make sense or ask a question which will give a clue to the meaning, e.g. 'How do you think Johnny feels—angry?' • if the word is not likely to be known, say it quickly and encourage reading on to maintain fluency	• wait to see if self-correction occurs and offer praise if it does • if there is no self-correction, ask 'Does that make sense?' or ask a question which will give a clue to the meaning of the sentence, e.g. 'What do you think is going to happen?' or 'Where will he go to catch the train?' • if the word is not likely to be known, say it quickly and encourage the child to read on. Later, when the whole text is read, go back to unknown words and help children use secondary word identification strategies, i.e. – sound out and sequence syllables in the word – identify the base or root of the word, add prefixes and suffixes – look for smaller words inside larger words – consult an authority (e.g. someone else or the dictionary)	• do nothing until the children have finished • when they have finished, go back to the word and say 'You said this word was__; it made sense but it begins (or ends) with the letter__ so what do you think it could be?' • you may wish to discuss the structure of the word with the children and see if they can think of any other words with a similar pattern

Chapter 6:

Supporting Diversity Through Reading, Writing and Spelling

The approach to literacy development taken by First Steps is based on a holistic view of learning. It is argued that the four modes of language are interrelated and that children become literate through meaningful interaction in specific contexts. Thus literacy is seen as a language process which begins long before children come to school. Children are becoming literate through their everyday interactions and experiences at home and in the wider community. The literacy 'events' that children are involved in and the way in which these are 'done', e.g. story reading, reading religious texts, choosing videos, making shopping lists etc., construct for children a view of 'what counts' as literacy.

If this view is accepted, then literacy is seen as a social phenomenon which is embedded in cultural norms and values. Clearly the understandings children bring to school about how text is constructed and what it is used for will differ according to their cultural, religious and linguistic background. Thus the context in which children are becoming literate will influence the way in which they approach reading and writing in school.

Children who do not speak English as their first language, may have a wide range of competencies in other languages. As well as speaking other languages, some children may be becoming literate in their community languages. They may be constructing meaning through numerical, pictorial or scriptural representation at a number of different levels. Their writing may range from marks on a page to sophisticated text construction. Their reading may range from a 'beginning' understanding of concepts of print to reading complex text.

If the learner's understanding and use of literacy is seen as central to development, then clearly it is important to build on the range of skills that children bring to school. For teachers who do not share the learner's community languages, the task may seem daunting. However, to deny the learner's expertise may actually make the process of becoming literate very difficult and for some children the development of literacy in English may be at the expense of literacy in their community languages.

1 **What do I know about the literacy skills that are being fostered in the home and community?**
2 **What information do I have about the languages spoken and written by the children in my class?**
3 **Where can I get information and resources to help establish a multi-lingual context?**

A classroom displaying language relevant to the children. This can be in English and/or their community languages.

I go ih Water ahd sitting underwater

I paly runing ih the water

I can swimihthewater

I go in the watering kicking

I diveing in the water

I cah floating in the water

I cah go ih thewater

I can go in the deep water

I cah go ta get dinosaur inwater

I cah go to ih the waterdeep

I cah go to get dihosaurin the deep water

I go vwth bus go to Beatty park

This child has used the print in the environment as a resource to produce this text.

Creating a Context to Support Diversity

A Print Rich Environment

In order to build on and extend children's knowledge and literacy experiences, it is important that the classroom context reflects the cultural and linguistic diversity of both individual children and the wider community. This is equally important in classrooms where all the children are monolingual. Recognising diversity through print raises the status and value of community languages and extends the children's experience of language.

A print rich environment includes different forms of print in a range of languages from a variety of sources. The joint construction of the classroom environment by the children and the teacher ensures that print is contextualised and therefore meaningful. As children interact with print in a number of different ways, the environment becomes a resource which supports independent learning and enables children to work at their own level. In addition to this, as children display, change, develop and discuss aspects of their reading and writing they are able to:

- demonstrate and develop their skills in reading and writing in languages other than English
- build on their own and others' knowledge of what writing is and what can be done through writing
- develop an understanding of a range of different scripts and meanings
- recognise the similarities and differences by comparing various scripts both visually (by looking) and orally (by reading)
- share and experiment with a range of different scripts.

1 **Does the classroom context reflect the diversity of languages used by the children?**
2 **Does the classroom context reflect the diversity of languages used by the wider community?**
3 **How can I share what I hope to achieve with parents/carers and gain their support?**
4 **How can I involve the children, colleagues, parents and the community in creating a multi-lingual environment?**

Opportunities to Create Text in Community Languages and English

All children need a variety of opportunities to construct text for different purposes and audiences. Encouraging children to write and read in their community languages enables them to:

- experience success and continue to value the languages they bring to school
- demonstrate their skill and 'expertise' in a language other than English
- use their home languages for learning as well as social communication
- share their skills with their peers thereby raising the status of their home languages
- 'teach' their peers to read and write in a new language.

1 **How can I create a context in which children feel confident to write and read in their community languages?**

2 How can I incorporate the children's languages into the curriculum?

3 How can I encourage the children to learn from each other about different languages?

4 How can I challenge negative attitudes from children, colleagues and parents about linguistic diversity?

Samples of scripts within a classroom

This writer is developing concepts in both English and Vietnamese simultaneously. She was unable to write a complete sentence in her first language upon arrival at school.

Once upon a time there was a very poor couple. One day the wife bought a duck. One morning the duck laid a golden egg. The couple was very happy. As the duck laid an egg everyday. The couple became very rich. One day the wife said "Kill her, then we will have lots of gold". Then she killed the duck. But she did not have gold. She was very angry.

Key Features in Supporting Reading and Writing

As well as supporting community languages, for children who do not speak English as their first language, the following seven features are particularly important in the development of reading and writing skills:

Integration of the Four Modes of Language

By integrating speaking, listening, reading and writing through meaningful activities children are able to make connections and build on their developing competency, as each area complements and reinforces the other. Clearly this has implications for creating a 'whole language' context rather than dividing learning into discrete curriculum areas.

By developing a theme or topic, children are able to hear and use language arising from related activities, for different purposes and audiences in a range of contexts. This helps them to gain confidence in using English and their community languages, thereby consolidating and extending learning.

An integrated program can also maximise the use of resources from the school and community.

In addition to this, if a support teacher is available, an integrated program enables the support teacher to:

- plan programs of work with the classroom teacher which they help to implement within the classroom, minimising disruption and feelings of exclusion for both children and some support teachers who may be working in isolation from the rest of the class
- ensure continuity by working on a theme or topic, while supporting particular aspects of language development
- swap roles with the classroom teacher. If time allows it may be useful for the teacher to work with particular children while the support teacher manages the class as a whole.

Supporting Reading and Writing Through Talk

Creating learning situations where talking, reading and writing are an integral part of the context (for example structured play) enables children to:

- choose which language seems most appropriate to talk, read and write in, while developing code switching skills
- jointly construct meaning through interaction with other children, ensuring that reading and writing evolves from talk
- write for specific purposes and audiences ensuring that writing is meaningful
- write at their own level without the pressure of more formal situations, giving room for experimentation and collaboration, while learning from other children
- see and hear English being used for specific purposes in highly contextualised situations. This gives the learner a framework on which to build and the opportunity to try-out and practise new structures.

In contexts in which reading and writing are more teacher-directed or structured then, where possible, talk needs to be built into the activity. This enables the children to:

- make connections between spoken and written English
- clarify ideas and organise their writing, to ensure that writing is meaningful rather than 'reproductive' with little understanding
- develop 'meta-linguistic' awareness. Reflecting upon language enables children to become aware of the structure, function and meaning of language
- develop strategies for supporting reading and writing. Through discussion and conferencing, children can be encouraged to use word banks, dictionaries, the library, computers, story maps, environmental print, picture clues, tapes and other children etc. All these strategies will help children to become independent learners.

However, it must be added that initially some learners (especially older children) may not want or need to talk about their writing. They may find the demands of talk (to produce an immediate response) greater than those of producing a piece of writing. When children are writing they have more time to compose their thoughts and express their ideas.

Opportunities to Produce Text in Different Ways

In the early stages of developing English as a second language, some children may become so absorbed in the mechanics of writing that meaning may become limited or lost. By reducing the cognitive demands required by handwriting and spelling, children can concentrate on creating meaning. Depending on the age and experience of the learner, there are a number of ways in which this can be done:

- Collaborative group work. This enables children to work together and contribute at their own level. Each learner may have a different role e.g. scribe, illustrator, proof reader etc. This allows all children to be involved, making writing a positive and non-threatening experience as they build on each other's understanding.
- Using formulas. Very often in speech and writing children will 'tune into' particular structures of language. Initially these are usually phrases that are in common use around the classroom. Children will use these in a variety of contexts and begin to replace specific elements. This gives them a feeling of success and confidence and gives them a basis on which to extend their repertoire.
- Retellings and recounts. These provide the children with a 'given' structure which supports writing because the structure and content is less demanding than other forms of writing. The writing is based on language which is familiar to the children and they have had practice is using.
- technical support, e.g.
  tape recording of text to be written later
  word processing
  writing centres
  different scribes (teacher, peers, parent)
  concept keyboard
- Extending Reading and Writing. As children become more competent in reading and writing in English it is important to continue to support their development in structured and explicit ways. Enabling them to move from personal to more formal uses of reading and writing gives them access to increasingly complex academic uses of language.

Teacher talking with child about the language used in an activity

Collaborative Group Work — making a group story map following reading of and oral work on *The Three Little Pigs*.

Recognition of Cultural Values and Practices

It is important to consider if there are any 'key classroom practices' that may conflict with the learner's understanding and expectations of reading and writing.

If possible it is helpful to discuss cultural values and practices with children and parents, to avoid conflict and jointly create the classroom context. This also avoids stereotyping and misunderstanding about what children and parents feel is appropriate, as this will vary in and across cultures.

Clearly this is not an easy task, especially if children are from a range of different cultural backgrounds and if some of the cultural 'norms' conflict with your own. However it may be useful to consider the following questions:

Are some 'topics' unacceptable for children to talk, read and write about?
e.g. Some parents may feel it is not acceptable for their children to be involved in particular celebrations (Jehovah Witnesses).

Do some religious texts have to be presented and read in particular ways?
e.g. The Koran must be handled with utmost respect

Are some reading and writing practices related to gender?
e.g. Some parents feel that boys are expected to be more educated and the girls more domesticated.

Does the structure of genres differ in different languages?
Does the logical structure and presentation of information differ in different languages?
e.g . Some children may present work which may seem jumbled and confused but they are actually transferring knowledge from their first language structure.

Are some of the practices used in a 'whole language' approach to learning inappropriate?
e.g. Some children may not feel comfortable with the notion of 'risk taking' and find practices such as 'invented spelling' difficult. Initially they may prefer to ensure what they write is 'correct'.

How do you confirm the value of those cultures which are not 'print' oriented?
e.g. Model the oral telling of stories, illustrating the story while going along.

Awareness of the Learner's Community Language

Reading and writing are clearly complex skills that are embedded in cultural values, but given the opportunity, children who are literate in their first language will transfer their knowledge of reading and writing to their second language. However, there may be children who need extra support in developing particular aspects of English.

Research has shown that understanding particular concepts about print is important to the development of reading and writing in English. In texts written in English these concepts include recognition that:

- print conveys meaning and is different to pictures
- there is a connection between the spoken and the written word
- books are read from front to back
- print runs from left to right and down the page
- the left page precedes the right page
- writing obeys particular grammatical rules (syntactic awareness)

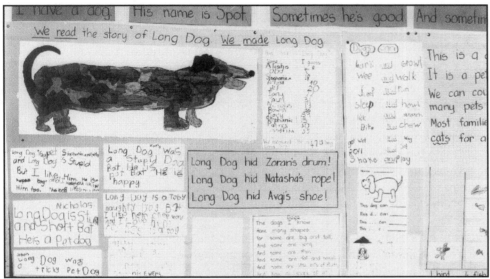

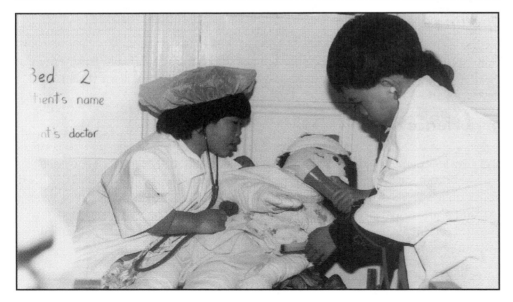

- sentences are made up of words (word awareness)
- words are make up of sounds (phonological awareness).

Where *conventions of print* differ from the learner's community language, this may not pose major difficulties, as children soon learn to distinguish between the two languages. However when the written system is constructed in a completely different way to English, some children may have particular difficulties.

This may be particularly noticeable in languages that are not based on an alphabetic system e.g. Japanese, Mandarin. These languages are based on an ideographic system, in which a character symbolises the idea of a thing without expressing the sequence of sounds in its name. The English language is based on an alphabetic system, in which the 26 letters of the alphabet are combined to produce 44 or so phonemes.

Phonological Awareness

In English, phonological awareness is thought to be an important part of developing reading and writing. The ability to break words up into sounds helps children to read and spell new words. For children who are unfamiliar with a phonetic system, recognising the relationship between sounds and letters may be a very difficult task.

There are a number of ways of developing grammatical, phonological and word awareness through meaningful and contextually appropriate activities. They are as follows:

- using a musical instrument or clapping hands once for each word in a sentence or rhyme as part of a musical activity
- singing simple rhymes, this helps children focus on individual words by replacing rhyming words with other rhyming words, in a story telling or music session
- rhymes can help children focus on sound/symbol relationships
- games such as 'I Spy' help focus on initial sounds
- making class books that repeat the rhyming and alliteration patterns of shared books
- creating a collage or classroom display of food labels that begin with the same letter e.g. bread, beans, butter, burfi, bomboniere, etc., collected by the children
- computer programs and concept keyboards.

Spelling

For those children who are not accustomed to the English phonological system, even hearing the sounds to make phonetic approximations may be difficult. For these children helping them to recognise the visual patterns in words will assist spelling development.

Importance of Time

It is very important to give children time to make sense of the new classroom context and new language. Children who are learning English as a second language need time to become familiar with the forms, patterns and functions of English. They need opportunities to consolidate and reinforce learning in a number of different ways, working at their own pace. Working in a second language places high cognitive demands on the learner, thus time is needed to process and use new information without pressure to produce 'finished' products or respond instantly.

Thus it helps if learning is not divided up into short time chunks and children are able to:

- design and manage their writing and reading e.g. writing corner, structured play
- discuss their work
- work at their own pace
- return to their work
- collaborate with their peers.

Importance of Children's Attitudes

Children's attitudes towards each other are central to developing a positive view of other languages and cultures. This is reflected in the way in which children interact with each other in both formal and informal situations.

Children can learn a tremendous amount about different cultures and languages from each other. The success of collaborative work depends upon the children's willingness to share, listen and respond to each other. The teacher's commitment to the recognition of diversity is crucial to genuine collaboration and exchange of ideas. This includes recognition of the need to counter negative attitudes and work with parents as well as children, in creating a positive context.

Topics on 'language' can be developed to enable children to explore the nature and make-up of different languages in depth. In addition to this, topics which deal with issues which are notoriously difficult can also help to challenge racism and affirm diversity e.g. one school confronted children's verbal abuse in the playground by doing an extended project on 'Name Calling'. This involved all children and took the emphasis off 'individual silliness' and demonstrated the seriousness with which this kind of behaviour was viewed. This led to work on language in literature and the media which developed from an exploration of stereotyping through language and illustrations.

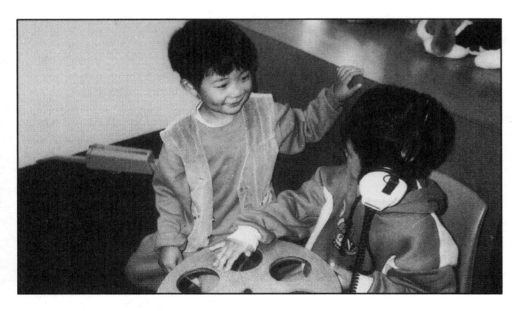

Monitoring and Assessing Development

Taking Account of Community Languages

Children who are learning English as a second language may be becoming literate in other languages. In order to get a true picture of the learner's communicative competence, it is necessary to take all languages into account. Recognising the skills children have in their community languages brings a new dimension to evaluation and planning. There are a number of ways to build up a profile of development:

- collect samples of work over a period of time to identify changes
- talk to children in English about their writing and reading
- observe their behaviour before, during and after reading and writing activities when possible
- translate writing into English
- talk with their peers (in the early stages of development)
- try to get outside help, e.g. bilingual assistant, parents.

Using Languages Interchangeably

Even in the early stages of development, many children are able to move from one language to another. In both speaking and writing children seem to 'code switch' for a variety of reasons:

- to make the meaning clearer, not all concepts are transferable and children will choose the most appropriate word or words, e.g.
  I got **guthli** for hapy birtdy
  (guthi - a special money bag made out of material)
- to use language in a more effective and efficient way
- to overcome frustration due to lack of vocabulary
- to express particular content more easily. Even children who are fluent in English may find some topics easier to talk and write about in their community language
- to take account of the audience, e.g. if the audience shares the same language and culture, then it may be more appropriate to write in the community language.

These substitutions can be looked upon as deliberate choices rather than mistakes or confusion, indicating a sophisticated use of language. They also give the teacher and the children the opportunity to discuss particular aspects of languages, developing further meta-linguistic awareness.

Language Transfer

It is very useful to have some knowledge of the learner's community language. This enables identification of aspects of English development that have been transferred from the learner's other languages. Transfer may include pronunciation, grammatical structure, vocabulary and semantics and occur in talking, reading and writing.

For example Tony has transferred the pronunciation of Croatian, his first language, to English and this is reflected in his writing. Amran frequently replaces 'a' and 'the' with 'one', this could be a reflection of his first language (Punjabi), which does not distinguish between the definite and indefinite article.

These examples suggest that the learners are attempting to make meaning by using a range of strategies derived from more than one language. Through interaction and observation the teacher sees the children as creatively constructing meaning rather than making mistakes. With support the learners will gradually begin to distinguish between the languages.

Initially, when the teacher glanced at the child's effort it caused some concern but when the child read the story with his own accent it was quite an excellent piece of writing.

Mr Kanganas
Mr Gilbert will you play with me.
I like Mr Gilbert. You come here play helicopter. No hat no play. Mr Gilbert I like Mr Gilbert

Sharing Assessment

The context in which children are using language affects the choices they make about language. Thus, assessment needs to take account of context and content in order to accurately judge what the learner is able to do with language. In doing this the teacher is able to make decisions about what is needed and how this can best be done.

Involving child and parent can give great insight, especially in relation to the learner's community language. It is very important to discuss progress with the learner as this provides a joint picture and gives the learner feedback.

Teacher Intervention

Continual, on-going assessment enables the teacher to judge what type of intervention is appropriate and when this is going to be most effective. In addition to the on-going help and support that is part of a 'whole language' approach to learning, there may be times when it is appropriate to identify specific or re-occurring difficulties and focus upon these. Modelling is a useful strategy as it enables the teacher to focus on certain aspects of writing and reading while taking the pressure off the individual.

Patterns of Development

In relation to the First Steps Reading, Writing and Spelling Continua, older children who are in early stages of developing English will not necessarily display early indicators because of their maturity and developmental level.

209

Strategies for Second Language Learners

Read and write for self and for children everyday — this extends the children's literacy experiences, word bank and knowledge of a number of genres.

Immersion — learners are exposed to demonstrations of how language is used.

Whole-Language Integration — skills and strategies are taught and continually reinforced throughout the various curriculum areas.

Community Language — allow learners to write in their first languages. Display their writing in the classroom. This encourages them and they feel that their languages and culture are valued.

Collaborative Group Work — this enables children to work together and contribute at their own level. The children share and clarify ideas with other children and develop their confidence in a non-threatening situation.

Provide a wide range of reading texts around the classroom. Encourage children to use the library.

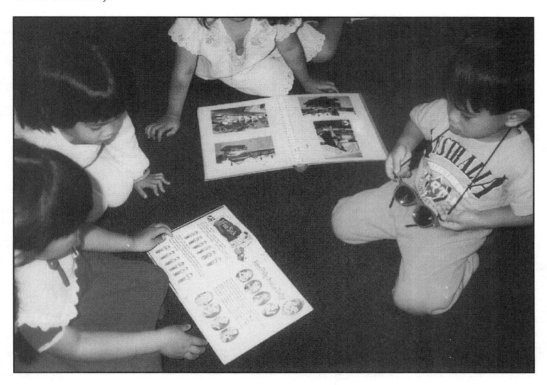

Modelled Writing — the teacher is able to demonstrate language knowledge in a context familiar to the children. The teacher can focus on the way print works in a meaningful context.

Shared Book — children can hear the sounds of English and simultaneously see them in print. Books chosen with care and related to the children's experiences can help develop a positive attitude to reading and writing. Teachers can introduce and provide examples of print conventions within a context children understand.

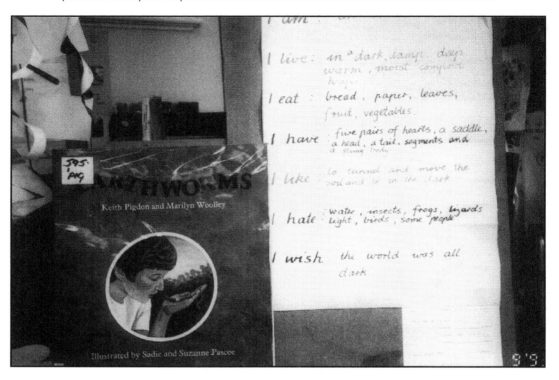

Display print in different contexts.

Provide and read a range of books, including different versions of the same story, to the children so that they can see how text can be manipulated.

Sharing — allowing a sharing time at the end of sessions helps children to clarify their ideas.

Make class books related to children's current needs and experiences and incorporating text that is familiar to them. The children enjoy reading them and refer to them regularly.

Caroline Barratt-Pugh
Anna Sinclair

Appendix 1: Reading Comprehension Resource Sheets

Police Report Form (see p. 107)

POLICE REPORT FORM

WANTED

SUSPECT'S NAME :

CRIME :

DESCRIPTION OF SUSPECT :

DISTINGUISHING FEATURES :

DESCRIPTION OF CRIME :

PAST CRIMES :

Character Self-Portrait (see p. 105)

CHARACTER SELF-PORTRAIT

I am :

I live :

I eat :

I have:

I like :

I hate:

I wish :

Plot Profile (see p. 102)

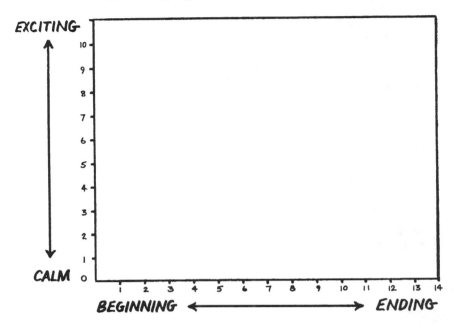

LIST MAIN EVENTS IN ORDER :

1. _____
2. _____
3. _____
4. _____
5. _____
6. _____
7. _____
8. _____
9. _____
10. _____
11. _____
12. _____
13. _____
14. _____

Story Grammar (see p. 100)

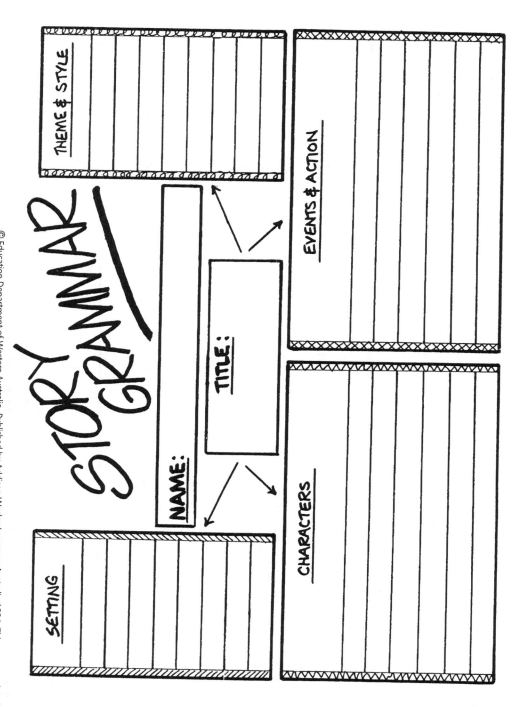

Character Rating (see p. 106)

	VERY	QUITE	NEITHER/BOTH NO INFORMATION	QUITE	VERY
BRAVE					COWARDLY
COMMENTS :					
QUIET					NOISY
COMMENTS :					
KIND					MEAN
COMMENTS :					
IMAGINATIVE					DULL
COMMENTS :					
CHEERFUL					SAD
COMMENTS :					

A Time Line <small>(see p. 101)</small>

A TIME LINE

ABOUT :

TIME	NOTES	ILLUSTRATIONS

Report Card (see p. 107)

REPORT CARD

SCHOOL: _____

STUDENT'S NAME: _____

YEAR: _____ TEACHER'S NAME: _____

GRADES:
A – VERY GOOD
B – GOOD
C – NEEDS TO IMPROVE

SUBJECTS	GRADE	COMMENTS

Wanted (see p. 107)

NAME :

LAST KNOWN ADDRESS :

PHYSICAL DESCRIPTION :

SPECIAL FEATURES :

OTHER INFORMATION:

Appendix 2: Sound Sleuth

(taken from First Steps *Spelling: Resource Book*)

This activity underpins the teaching of graphophonic relationships. Children can become 'Sound Sleuths' in any context where they are involved with meaningful print. A few of these contexts are suggested in the following section.

Suggestions are offered regarding possible focuses for teaching and learning at different phases of development. Teachers will find, however, that they are led by the children. Sometimes children will pursue an understanding far beyond the limits which an externally structured program would impose on them. On other occasions children may miss something which seems very simple, in which case the teacher will say nothing, but will ensure that they encounter the same concept again in a different context so that they are again challenged by the concept.

If children's discoveries are charted on the class chart, as suggested in the *Spelling: Developmental Continuum* book, the teacher will have a precise record of the learning which has occurred and will be able to re-visit any gaps which are apparent.

Preliminary Phase

A major focus for teaching in the preliminary phase is placed on the sounds represented by initial letters. Before they make any connections between symbol and sound, children will make connections between the initial letter of their names and the same letter when they see it in another word, especially when the letter is written in upper case. The children's names make a good starting point for graphophonic teaching, enabling children to make connections between the initial letter and sound of their names and the same initial letter and sound when they encounter it in other well-known words.

- Talk to the children about their first day of school and write one or two simple sentences on the blackboard. Break the sentences into chunks of meaning.
- Read the sentences several times and get the children to 'read' them with you.
- Ask the children if anyone knows what an 'm' looks like. Use the letter name, not the sound.
- Write M, m on the blackboard.
- Ask if anyone has a name which starts with M. Write it/them down.
- Get children to draw rings around the words with M, m in them.
- Say the words with the children and get them to listen to the sound the M, m makes.
- List all the words with M, m in them.
- Ask the children to hunt for more M, m words to add to the list.
- Go through the list at the end of the day and ask the children to see if M, m always makes the same sound.
- Chart the most interesting M, m words and draw pictures next to them so the children can 'read' them.
- Stick a piece of paper to the bottom of the chart for adding new words.

Semi-Phonetic Phase

In the Semi-Phonetic phase children are encouraged to investigate the range of sounds represented by a single letter. Again, a good starting point is a name, e.g. Carol, Charles, Celeste. Praise children for their discoveries and place them on the class chart. Give children time and be prepared to wait for them to extend their understandings as they continue to collect evidence. They will not find out everything at once, but will gradually work out extensions of rules as they are confronted by a new challenge, e.g. that 'c' sometimes sounds like 's'. In this phase children will focus on the most obvious sound in a word. Children will also become increasingly aware of vowel sounds and will often connect these with names of the vowels.

Phonetic Phase and Beyond

In the Phonetic phase children explore different ways of representing the same sounds, e.g. door, saw, more. A major focus is placed on medial vowel sounds and children find that breaking words into syllables helps them to work out the sounds of words effectively.

A recount, report or other text-type can be written on the blackboard or on butcher's paper in a shared writing session. Children can be challenged to list words according to letter patterns which represent a specific sound, e.g. E. The words containing this sound can be written on the class chart, having been classified according to the letter pattern. A piece of paper can be appended to the chart so that children can add more words as they come across them during their daily work.

Appendix 3: Secret Messages

(taken from First Steps *Spelling: Resource Book*)

The ability to segment and blend letters and letter clusters is an important skill in decoding. The 'Secret Message' activity provides children with the opportunity to decode messages by manipulating letters and letter clusters to make new words.

- **To get started, put a secret message on the blackboard every day and work it out as a class. As children become proficient, they can begin to work independently. Remember to put the alphabet at the bottom of each message for easy access.**
- Although it is not appropriate to focus heavily on segmenting and blending until children reach the Phonetic phase, it is very helpful if the concept of secret messages is introduced in the Preliminary phase.
- Give the children 'Spy Pads' so they can work out the solutions by writing the words, crossing out bits and adding to them.
- If children are not competent readers, put a picture by the key word; for example, Take 'b' off *book* and put in 'l.'
- After modelling, older children may attempt to write their own secret messages.
- Keep copies of all activities and build a permanent collection of them.

Some examples of Secret Messages constructed to suit children at different phases of development are shown in subsequent pages.

Preliminary Phase

Write a simple message which combines words with word-pictures and help children decode it, e.g.

Sit on the mat

Children love this activity and soon learn to decode messages by themselves. Although at this phase there is no focus on letters and sounds, this activity will help children to develop their understandings about the relationship between the spoken and written language and their concept of a word.

Semi-Phonetic Phase

At this phase children can deal with secret messages which involve rhyming words and initial letter sounds, provided that support is given by the teacher. Always have the alphabet displayed where children can use it for a reference.

A variety of clues, such as those shown over, can be used; for instance initial letters (1), alphabet knowledge (2) and word knowledge (3).

A B C D E F G H I J K L M N O P Q R S T U V W X Y Z

1   Take 'B' off 'Bit' and add 'S' __ __ __

2   The letter after 'N' and the letter after 'M' __ __

3   The first word in this sentence __ __ __

4   Take 'd' off 'door' and put in 'fl' __ __ __ __ __

__ __ __ __ __ __ __ __ __ __ __ __ __.

Note

It is important when giving a clue that the new word has the same sound as the old word; for example: Take 'st' off 'stood' and put in 'h'; **not** take 'bl' off 'blood' and put in 'h'.

Phonetic Phase

In this phase the children can decode clues independently and may focus specifically on segmenting and blending as in the examples shown below.

A B C D E F G H I J K L M N O P Q R S T U V W X Y Z

Take 'mo - - - r' off 'mother'.   __ __ __

Add 'ball' to 'foot'.   __ __ __ __ __ __ __

Take 'h' off 'his'.   __ __

Rhymes with 'pin'.   __ __

Take 'fa - - - r' off 'father'.   __ __ __

Rhymes with 'you' but starts with 'sh'.   __ __ __ __

Rhymes with 'fox' and starts with 'b'.   __ __ __

__ __ __ __ __ __ __ __ __ __ __ __ __ __ __

__ __ __ __ __ __ __ __ __ __.

A B C D E F G H I J K L M N O P Q R S T U V W X Y Z

Take 'b' off 'book' and put in 'l'.   __ __ __ __

Take 'p' off 'pin'.   __ __

Take 'cr' off 'cry' and put in 'm'.   __ __

Take 'fl' off 'flag' and put in 'b'.   __ __ __

Take 'h' off 'hand'.   __ __ __

Take 'p' off 'pet' and put in 'g'.   __ __ __

Take 'fl' off 'fly' and put in 'm'.   __ __

Take 'h' off 'hen' and put in 'p'.   __ __ __

__ __ __ __ __ __ __ __ __ __ __

__ __ __ __ __ __ __ __ __ __ __ __ __

Transitional Phase

From this phase onwards secret messages can be used to focus on any aspect of spelling which seems to merit special attention. An example of this could be syllabification, as shown below:

1. Put the first syllable of compose before 'p' and the last syllable of delete after 'p'.
2. A one-syllable word which begins with 'y' and sounds like 'door'.
3. The first syllable is the prefix 'pro' and the second syllable of 'injection'.
4. A one-syllable word which rhymes with high and begins with 'b'.
5. The first syllable is the first three letters of fright and the second syllable is the same as the third syllable of Saturday.

— — — — — — —   — — — —

— — — — — —   — —   — — — — —

Appendix 4: Language Games

Introduction

Language games can provide an extremely effective means of helping children who are experiencing difficulties with reading.

- They provide a stimulating context which makes sense to children.
- They enable children to interact independently and successfully with small segments of text.
- They demand an immediate, active response from children, reinforcing the understanding that reading is an interactive process.
- They can be structured to address specific language needs of children (for instance, to give children practice in the correct use of prepositions such as 'beside' or 'near 'and conjunctions such as 'but,' 'although,' 'until').

Language games have been based on the four pictures at the back of this book. All of the materials may be photocopied for use with students. Three of the games offer models of language use at three different levels of difficulty. The fourth set of three games is made up of sections which focus on specific aspects of language (questioning words and conjunctions). This last section is not suitable for beginning readers. The materials are intended to provide models of language use for other, similar games. Each of the four pictures could be used as a context for any of the games.

- Any of the pictures can be used for following directions and colouring-in.
- A grid can be drawn on transparent plastic and placed over the other three pictures (or any other picture), or drawn directly onto a picture, to enable the 'mapping' game to be played.
- The small pictures in squares can be used in conjunction with any other picture to give additional practice in following directions. Small toys, such as those from crackers, could also be used for this purpose.
- Any picture can be used to highlight a language feature by playing 'Sentence Jigsaw', as in game four, where conjunctions and questioning words provide a focus.
- Older children enjoy making game cards for others to use. The teacher must ensure, however, that children's writing is legible, or that their work is typed before being used by other children.
- Children need a great deal of practice in using features of language such as conjunctions. Language games provide a means of giving practice which is interesting and fun. The context should be changed frequently.

Language Game 1

Learning Objective: The children will follow directions to colour in a picture.

Teaching Instructions

| Picture A | City Roads | Individual activity |

1 Put an appropriate spot of colour above the colour word in the Level One sentences.
2 Photocopy the directions and cut out the language cards.
3 Talk about the picture with the children.
4 Model the playing of the game while the children watch.
5 Photocopy a picture (page 250) for each child. Give them language cards at the appropriate level of difficulty (page 229, 230, or 231).
6 Children pick up a language card, read it and do what it says.

Children who are in the role play phase of reading will be able to follow the directions competently if the teacher tells them the sentence pattern and models the activity for them.

This game can be made challenging for much more advanced children by using complex sentences; for instance, *Draw a black and white spotted dog chasing a boy with a football along the pavement.*

Language Game 1: (Level 1)

Learning Objective: The children will follow directions to colour in a picture.

Picture A: City Roads   **Language Cards**

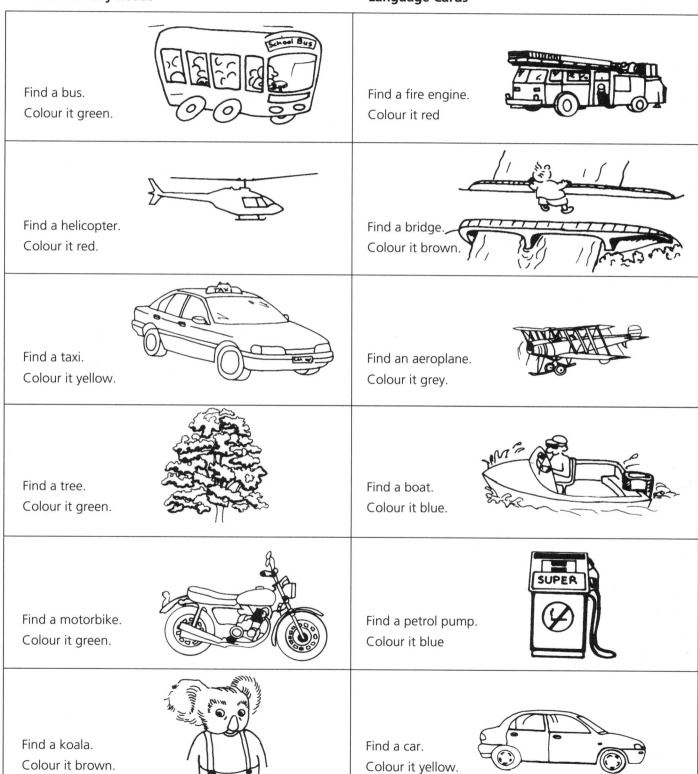

Find a bus.
Colour it green.

Find a fire engine.
Colour it red

Find a helicopter.
Colour it red.

Find a bridge.
Colour it brown.

Find a taxi.
Colour it yellow.

Find an aeroplane.
Colour it grey.

Find a tree.
Colour it green.

Find a boat.
Colour it blue.

Find a motorbike.
Colour it green.

Find a petrol pump.
Colour it blue

Find a koala.
Colour it brown.

Find a car.
Colour it yellow.

Language Game 1: (Level 2)

Learning Objective: The children will follow directions to colour in a picture.

Picture A: City Roads   **Language Cards**

Look for a father koala. Colour his coat brown	Look for a girl koala. Colour her dress blue.
Look for a hot air balloon. Colour it yellow and red	Look for a person on a motorbike. Give the person a red helmet.
`Can you see an ambulance? Give it a red light on top.	Can you find two petrol pumps? Colour one yellow and one blue.
Find a koala wearing glasses. Colour her coat pink.	Draw a koala by the petrol pump. Give the koala a big basket.
Can you see a tree? Draw a little bird in it.	Draw a letterbox by the crossing. Draw a koala posting a letter.
Look for a police car. Make its light blue.	Find the tallest building. Draw windows in it.
Can you see the plumber's van? Draw a dog in the window.	Draw a boat under the bridge. Colour it red.
Can you see the helicopter? Draw a bird under it.	Draw some trees on the hill. Colour the trees green.
Can you see the hills? Colour them red.	Can you see a boat on the river? Colour it red.
Find the fire engine. Colour it red.	Draw a bicycle on the bridge. Colour it black.

Language Game 1: (Level 3)

Learning Objective: The children will follow directions to colour in a picture.

Picture A: City Roads   **Language Cards**

Two koalas are walking on the crossing. Colour the large one brown. Make his suit blue and his tie red. Give the little koala a red dress with yellow stripes.
Draw a little black dog running after the two koalas on the crossing. Draw a man with a flag standing by the crossing.
Draw four birds flying in the sky under the big aeroplane. Draw another bird sitting on a lamp post on the bridge. Colour the aeroplanes
Can you see a tree by the self-service garage? Draw a nest in it. Colour the tree green and the nest brown.
Draw a woman by one of the petrol pumps. Draw the taxi driver beside her. Put a flag on one of the posts.
Can you see the big buildings on the other side of the river? Draw some windows in them.
Draw a person sitting in the empty seat in the bus. Colour the bus green and yellow.
Draw a koala sitting behind the person on the motorbike. Make sure the koala has a helmet on. Colour both helmets red.
Can you see a van crossing the bridge? Write FROZEN FOODS on the side of it. Now colour the van yellow.
Look for the plumber's van. Write the plumber's name on it. Colour the van green.
Can you see a koala with glasses driving a car? Draw a dog on the seat beside her. Colour the koala, the dog and the car any colour you like.
Draw a telephone box in the bottom corner of the picture. Now draw a tree by the telephone box. Draw a koala waiting outside it.

Language Game 2

Learning Objective: The children will follow directions to place small pictures on the large picture.

Teaching Instructions

    Picture B   **Playing in the Park**   **Individual or group activity**

Before playing this game, children would enjoy *following directions to colour in the pictures*.

1. Photocopy the large picture (page 251) for each child or group of children.
2. Talk about the picture with the children.
3. Photocopy the page of small pictures (page 254) and the language cards (page 233, 234 or 235) for each child or group of children.
4. Laminate the pictures if you wish to use them again.
5. Cut up the small pictures and the sets of language cards.
6. Give each child or group of children a large picture, a set of small pictures, a set of language cards and some adhesive putty.
7. Children pick up a language card and follow the directions, sticking a small picture in place on the big picture. Children can either do this as an individual activity, or take turns in a group situation.

Language Game 2: (Level 1)

Learning Objective: The children will follow directions to place small pictures on the large picture.

Picture B: Playing in the Park	Language Cards
Put an elephant by the basket.	Put a bin by the path.
Put a kangaroo by the birds.	Put a dog by the bears.
Put a koala by the tree.	Put some flowers by the water.
Put a rabbit by the seesaw.	Put two mushrooms by a tree.
Put an umbrella by an elephant.	Put a bird by the bat.
Put a stool by the hat.	Put a house by the swing.
Put a slide by the butterflies.	Put a pig by the seesaw.
Put a chick by the swan.	Put a mouse by a stone.
Put a tortoise by the steps.	Put a football by the basket.
Put an aeroplane by the kite.	Put the bike by an elephant.

233

Language Game 2: (Level 2)

Learning Objective: The children will follow directions to place small pictures on the large picture.

Picture B: Playing in the Park	Language Cards
Find a little house. Put it on the grass.	Find a mouse with three balloons. Put her on the hill.
Find a mouse with a basket. Put her on the path.	Find a koala painting. Put him on the grass.
Find a bird with a worm. Put it under a tree.	Find a big dog. Put it near the pigs.
Find a mouse in a wheelchair. Put the wheelchair on the path.	Find a kangaroo with a ball. Put her on the grass.
Find a mouse in a boat. Put the boat on the water.	Find a big bike. Put it near the bat and ball.
Find a bird on a bird bath. Put the bird bath on the grass.	Find a toy aeroplane. Put it in the sky.
Find an eski. Put it near the picnic basket.	Find five flowers. Put them on the grass.
Find a mouse on a scooter. Put it near the water.	Find a rabbit with a bat. Put him near the seesaw.

Language Game 2: (Level 3)

Learning Objective: The children will follow directions to place small pictures on the large picture.

Picture B: Playing in the Park	**Language Cards**
Find a tyre hanging from a rope. Put it on the tree by the swing.	Find a mouse who is going fishing. Put him on the path by the water.
Find a rabbit peeping out of a log. Put the log on the grass by the water.	Find a koala painting a picture. Put him under one of the trees.
Find a bear playing in a toy truck. Put the toy truck below the elephants.	Find a rabbit with a cricket bat and ball. Put him by the cricket stumps.
Find a little mouse holding three balloons. Put her near the rabbit with the kite.	Find a mouse with skipping rope. Put her near the kangaroos playing ball.
Find a cake, a pear, a sandwich and a drink. Put them on the grass by the rug.	Find a koala with a baseball bat and ball. Put her on the path near the elephants.
Find a pig with a ring and flippers. Put him by the edge of the water.	Find a mouse with glasses and a basket. Make her walk on the path.
Find a notice which says: 'DO NOT PICK FLOWERS' Stick it in the grass.	Can you find two tiny mice playing in a toy engine? Put them on the grass.
Find a climbing frame. Put it near the seesaw.	Find an elephant with a beach ball. Put it near the other elephants.

Language Game 3

Learning Objective: The children will follow directions and locate the grid reference.

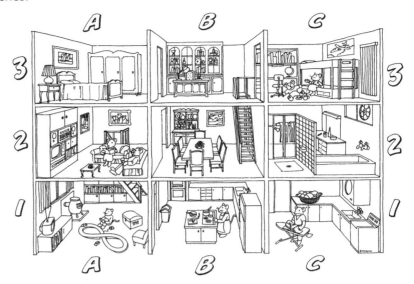

Teaching Instructions

| Picture C | The Mouse House (Mapping Game) | Group activity |

Children would enjoy following directions to colour in this picture before they use it to play the mapping game.

1 Talk about the picture with the children
2 Photocopy a large picture (page 252) and a set of language cards (page 237, 238 or 239) for each group of children.
3 Obtain two envelopes or small containers for each group of children. Write YES on one and NO on the other.
4 Teach the children to use a grid reference. An easy way to do this is by giving children two rulers. Show them that if the reference is B2 they place one ruler between the top B and the bottom B. They then place the other ruler so that it lies between the two numerals 2. The square, or room in the case of this picture, where the two rulers cross is called B2.
5 Use a small group of children to model the playing of this game for the remainder of the class.
6 Put the children in small groups (2-4 children in each group).
7 Children take it in turns to pick up a language card. They read the question, locate the grid reference, and see if they can find the object in that room (square). If they can, they put the card in the 'YES' container. If not, the card is placed in the 'NO' container.

At the end of the game, make sure the cards have been placed in the right containers. If a card is not where you expect it to be, always talk with the child about it. There may be a logical reason behind the child's decision. When the children put the game away, make sure they mix the language cards up thoroughly.

The questions can be changed at intervals to keep the children on their toes!

Children in pre-primary can play this game at Level 1 with a minimum of support from an adult, provided the sentence patterns and the procedures are carefully modelled for them.

Language Game 3: (Level 1)

Learning Objective: The children will follow directions and locate the grid reference.

Picture C: The Mouse House (Mapping Game)	**Language Cards**
Look in A 3 Can you see a bed?	Look in C 1 Can you see an iron?
Look in B 2 Can you see a mouse?	Look in C 2 Can you see a mouse?
Look in C 3 Can you see a flower?	Look in B 1 Can you see a chair?
Look in B 1 Can you see a saucepan?	Look in B 2 Can you see some stairs?
Look in C 2 Can you see a fan?	Look in A 1 Can you see a toy box?
Look in A 1 Can you see a bed?	Look in B 3 Can you see a saucepan?
Look in A 1 Can you see a television?	Look in A 1 Can you see some fruit?
Look in A 3 Can you see a lamp?	Look in C 1 Can you see a lamp?
Look in B 3 Can you see a mouse?	Look in B 1 Can you see a mouse?
Look in B 2 Can you see a picture?	Look in B 3 Can you see a television?
Look in C 2 Can you see two taps?	Look in A 2 Can you see two dogs?

Language Game 3: (Level 2)

Learning Objective: The children will follow directions and locate the grid reference.

Picture C: The Mouse House (Mapping Game)	**Language Cards**
Find A 1 Can you see two little cars?	Find C1 Can you see washing in a basket?
Look in A 3 Can you see a mouse in the bed?	Look in A 1 Can you see a big ball?
Look in B 2 Can you see some fruit on the table?	Look in C 3 Can you see lots of books?
Look in B 1 Can you see a baby mouse on the floor?	Look in A 3 Can you see a big chair?
Find 3 Can you see a picture on the wall?	Look in C 1 Can you see a mouse ironing?
Find C 2 Can you see two mice playing?	Look in C 3 Can you see a mouse with a cup?
Find A 2 Is mother mouse reading a book?	Look in B 3 Can you see a lamp on a desk?
Look in B 2 Is there a cup on the table?	Find A 3 Can you see a mouse in the bed?

Language Game 3: (Level 3)

Learning Objective: The children will follow directions and locate the grid reference.

(Note: The children will need pencil and paper to answer the questions in the right-hand column.)

Picture C: The Mouse House (Mapping Game)	**Language Cards**
Locate A 2 Can you see a mother and father mouse sitting down?	**1** How many mice can you find? Where are they?
Find A 1 Can you see a mouse playing with cars on a track?	**2** Can you find a washing machine? Which room is it in?
Find A 2 Is the mother mouse watching the television?	**3** Which bedroom do you think mother and father mouse sleep in?
Locate C 3 Can you see a ladder at the end of the bunk beds?	**4** Can you see a picture of an aeroplane? Which room is it in?
Locate A 3 Can you find a clock by the bed?	**5** Two of the rooms have lamps in them. Which rooms are they?
Find B 1 Can you see some rubbish on the floor?	**6** Four of the rooms have no mice in them. Which rooms are they?
Look in A 2 Is father mouse reading the newspaper?	**7** Two of the rooms have bowls of fruit in them. Which rooms are they?
Find C 1 Can you see a lot of washing in a basket?	**8** Can you find four rooms with pictures on the walls? Which rooms are they?

Language Game 4

Learning Objective: The children will match sentence beginnings with the correct endings.

Teaching Instructions

Picture D   Gum Leaf Shopping Village   Activity for pairs

1 Talk about the picture with the children. Make sure the children can read/locate the signs on the shops.
2 Photocopy the picture (page 253), a set of sentence strips (page 241) for each pair of children (which will be cut up to make cards) and an extra copy of the sentence strips, which children will use to check their answers.
3 Put a distinguishing mark on the back of the first segments of the sentences. This will help children to sort them at the end of the game.
4 The first segments of the sentences are divided between two children.
5 Mix the sentence endings well and place them face downwards.
6 Children take turns to turn over a card to see if it can be matched with a card in their hand to make a correct sentence. Completed sentences should be checked before being displayed. If a sentence ending can not be matched, it is put back face downwards.
7 When a child displays a correct sentence, she or he has another turn.
8 If a child displays a sentence beginning which is matched with the wrong ending, she or he puts the sentence ending back and the other child has a turn.
9 The first child to match all her or his sentence beginnings with the appropriate ending wins the game.

When making up other games, make sure that a sentence beginning can only be matched with one ending.

Language Game 4: (Level 1)

Learning Objective: The children will match sentence beginnings with the correct endings.

Picture D: Gum Leaf Shopping Village	Language Cards
The ice-cream will melt <u>unless</u>	The rabbit eats it quickly.
The rabbits will all go home <u>when</u>	the shops close.
The baby rabbit will eat a cake <u>if</u>	mother rabbit buys her one.
Mr Rabbit has bought a new suit <u>because</u>	it was half-price in the suit sale.
The car park barrier will be lifted up <u>when</u>	a car wants to go out.
The rabbit will run up the stairs <u>because</u>	he wants to get to the bank quickly.
The rabbit sliding down the tree root will fall <u>if</u>	he doesn't slow down.
Mrs Rabbit would like to buy some new shoes <u>but</u>	she has no money left.
The rabbit will pay the bill <u>after</u>	he has finished his dinner.
The rabbit is peeping out of the window <u>because</u>	she wants to talk to the post bird.
First the rabbits will go to the chemist, <u>then</u>	they will go to the bank.

Language Game 4: (Level 2)

Learning Objective: The children will match sentence beginnings with the correct endings.

Teaching Instructions

Picture D   **Gum Leaf Shopping Village**   **Activity for 3-4 children**

1 Talk about the picture with the children. Make sure they can read/locate the signs on the shops.
2 Photocopy one picture (page 253) for each group of children.
3 Photocopy two sets of sentences (pages 243–6) for each group. One will be cut up to make playing cards, the other will be used to check answers.
4 Mark the back of the sentence beginnings. This will facilitate the sorting of the cards at the end of the game.
5 Give each child one sentence beginning (when children are confident they may be given two sentence beginnings).
6 Place the sentence endings which match the beginnings in a pack. Shuffle them thoroughly. Place pack face down. Turn over top card. Place beside pack.
7 Children place their sentence beginnings face upwards in front of them.
8 Children take it in turns to pick up a card. They may either choose the card they can read, or pick one from the top of the pack which they cannot see.
9 If they can match their sentence beginning with an ending, they place the ending with the sentence beginning card in front of them. They then have another turn. If the ending does not match their beginning, they put the card back at the bottom of the 'face upward' pile.
10 When the last card has been picked up, the pack is turned over and the game continues.
11 The game continues until a child is 'out', having matched his or her sentence beginning with the set of four alternative endings.

Language Game 4: (Level 2)

Learning Objective: The children will match sentence beginnings with the correct endings.

Picture D: Gum Leaf Shopping Village   **Language Cards**

The rabbit will push her shopping trolley to the car
<u>because</u> the parcels are too heavy to carry.
<u>then</u> she will put the parcels in the boot.
<u>but</u> she will not leave it in the middle of the car park.
<u>now that</u> she has finished her shopping.
The little rabbits will fall off the tree root
<u>if</u> they slide down it too quickly.
<u>because</u> they have nothing to hold on to.
<u>then</u> they will cry for their mothers.
<u>but</u> they will climb up and slide down again.

Language Cards

The rabbit will finish her drink
<u>because</u> she is thirsty.
<u>then</u> she will ask for another.
<u>unless</u> she knocks the glass over.
<u>but</u> she will not have anything to eat.
The ice-cream will melt
<u>unless</u> the rabbit eats it quickly.
<u>because</u> it is very hot.
<u>then</u> the rabbit will want another one.
<u>while</u> the rabbit talks to her friend.

Language Cards

Baby Rabbit will eat a cake

<u>if</u> her mother buys one from the shop.

<u>when</u> the baker gives her one.

<u>but</u> her mother will not let her eat two cakes.

<u>then</u> her Mother will give her a drink.

The rabbits will go to the bank

<u>after</u> they have been to the chemist.

<u>because</u> they need some more money.

<u>before</u> they buy some new shoes.

<u>but</u> they may find that it has shut.

Language Cards

The rabbit will run up the stairs
<u>because</u> he wants to get to the bank before it shuts.
<u>although</u> he feels very tired.
<u>but</u> he will need to stop for a rest at the top.
<u>then</u> he will run down them.
The postbird will talk to the rabbit
<u>when</u> he takes the letter out of his beak.
<u>after</u> he has delivered the letter.
<u>but</u> he must not stay and chat for too long.
<u>then</u> he will go and deliver the letter.

Language Game 4: (Level 3)

Learning Objective: The children will match sentence beginnings with the correct endings.

Teaching Instructions

Picture B   Playing in the Park   **Activity for two children**

1 Talk about the picture (page 251) with the children.
2 Make two copies of the question and answer pages (pages 248–9). One copy will be cut up to make cards, the other used by children to check their answers.
3 Mark the back of the questions to facilitate sorting at the end of the game.
4 Divide the questions between the two participants.
5 Place the answers face downwards.
6 Children take turns to turn a card over to see if it is the answer to a question which they hold. If they have a matching pair, this is displayed in front of them. If not, the card is replaced face downwards.
7 If a children matches a question with a correct answer, she or he has another turn.
8 If a child pairs a question with the wrong answer, she or he puts the answer back and the other child has a turn.
9 The first child to match all his or her sentences with the correct answers wins the game.

Language Game 4: (Level 3)

Learning Objective: The children will match sentence beginnings with the correct endings.

Picture B: Playing in the Park   **Language Cards**

Why is the pig carrying her skateboard?
Because the path is too bumpy to ride on.
Why is the baby elephant wearing a sunhat?
Because he does not want to get burnt.
What are the birds doing?
The birds are eating the crumbs.
What are the two kangaroos doing?
They are playing with a ball.
Who is on the seesaw?
Two rabbits are playing on it.
Who is cooking the sausages?
Father elephant is cooking them on the barbecue.

Language Cards

How many balls can you see in the picture?
I can see three altogether.
How many birds are swimming on the water?
One swan and three ducks are having a swim.
When will the elephants eat the cake?
After they have eaten the sausages.
When will the elephants have a game of cricket?
After they have finished their picnic.
How will the rabbit get down from the swing?
He will have to jump off.
How high can the kite fly?
As far as the string will stretch.

Picture A
City Roads

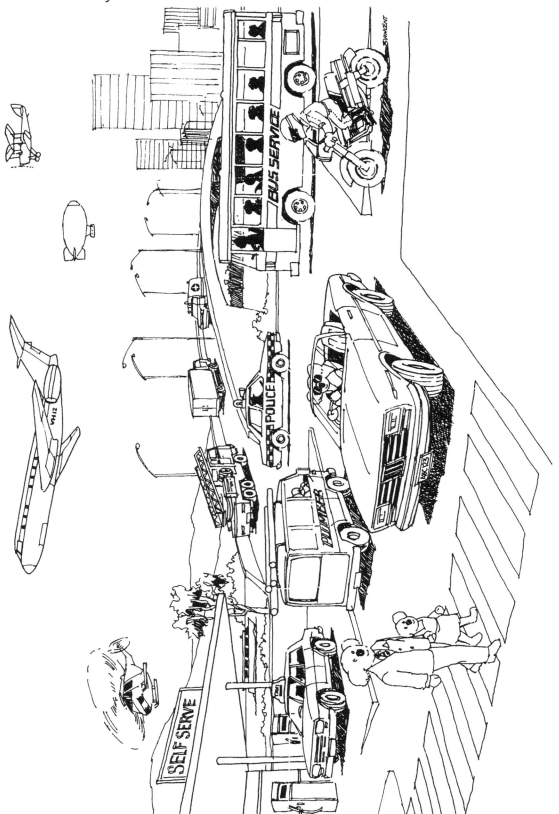

Picture B
Playing in the park

Picture C
The Mouse House

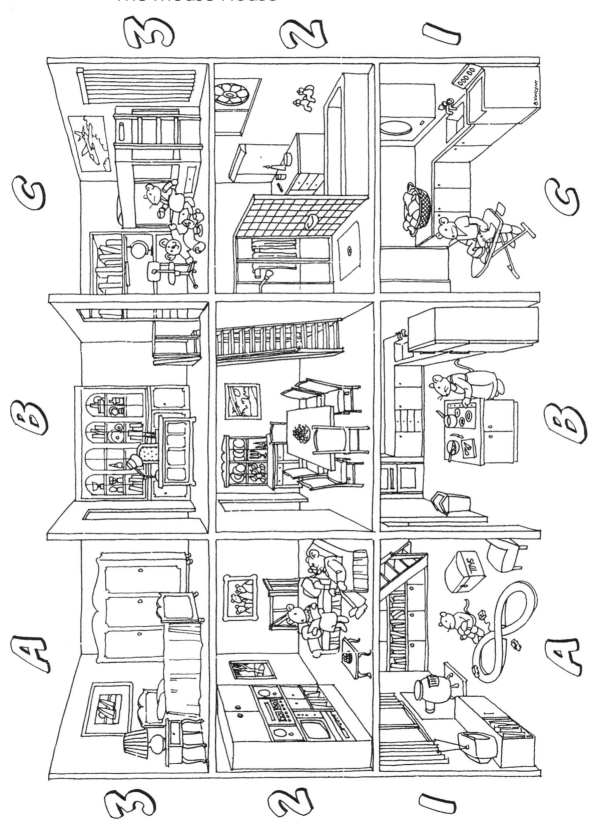

Picture D
Gum Leaf Shopping Village

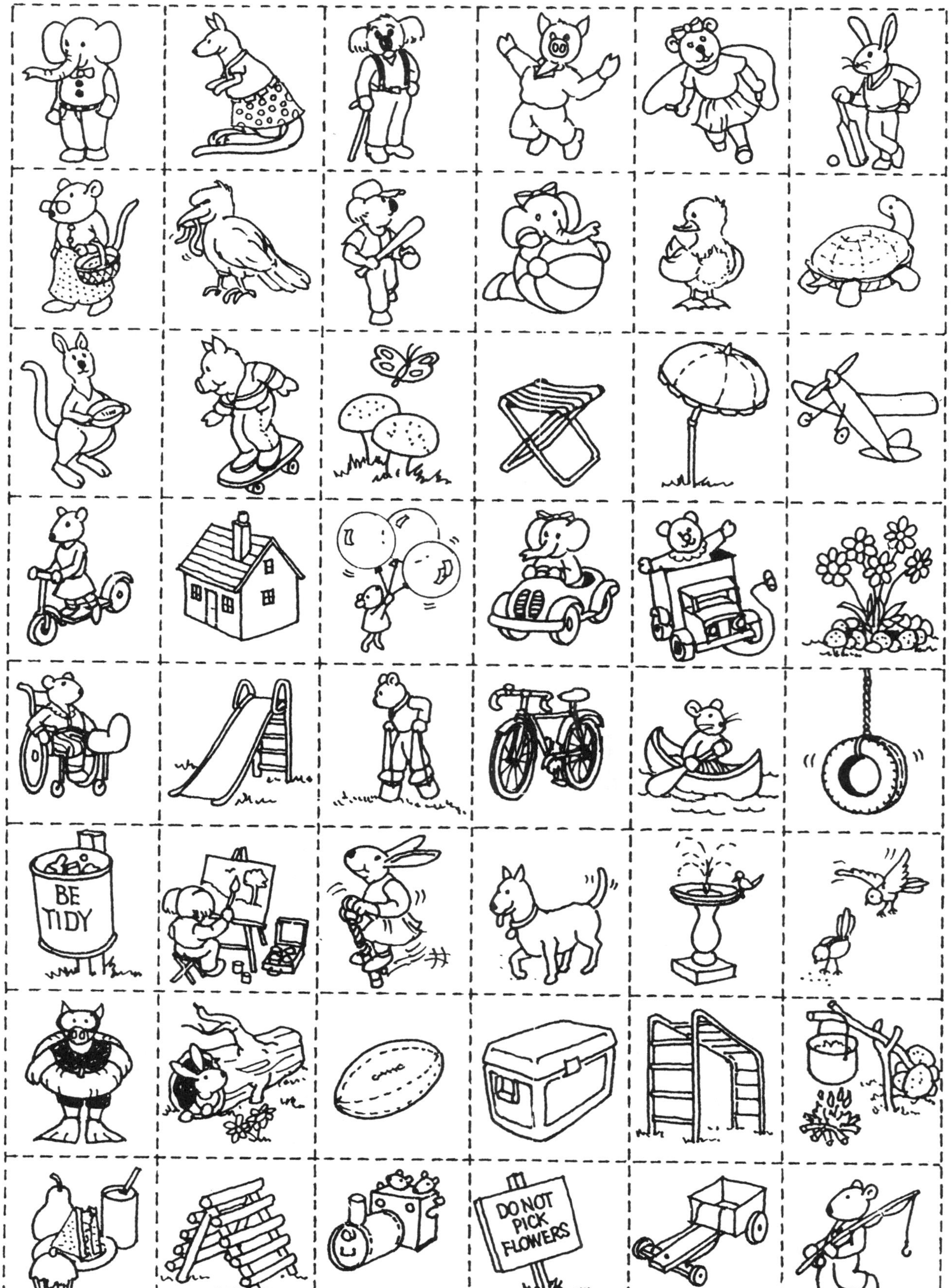
BE TIDY
DO NOT PICK FLOWERS

Acknowledegments

The authors gratefully acknowledge the contributions of the following people to this book:

Mr Peter Short, Senior Curriculum Officer, Ministry of Education, for his advice and permission to use original material in the Informational Texts section of this book, and Kay Kovalevs for her dedication and hard work in the editing and co-ordination of the First Steps books in the early years of the project. She also contributed to and collated the ESL research into children's language learning at Christmas Island District High School.

Alison Dewsbury
Sue Lambert
Judith Rivalland
Kerry Misich
Rebecca Wright
Jennifer Evans
Sheila Johnson

The First Steps Project team would also like to thank the following authors and publishers for their cooperation in granting permission to reproduce material:

Scott Paris, Professor of Psychology and Education at the University of Michigan, for permission to use and adapt posters from *Reading and Thinking Strategy Kits*, published by Collamore Educational Publishing, D.C. Heath and Co., Lexington.

Taffy E. Raphael of Michigan State University, East Lansing, Michigan, U.S.A.

Albert Morris and Nea Steward-Dore, authors of *Learning to Learn from Text. Effective Reading in the Content Area*, published by Addison-Wesley, North Ryde, N.S.W.

Hazel Brown and Brian Cambourne, authors of *Read and Retell*, published by Thomas Nelson, Australia.

Terry Johnson and Daphne Louis, authors of *Literacy Through Literature*, published by Thomas Nelson, Australia.

Finally thanks must be expressed to Sheila Johnson and Greg Taylor for their patience and attention to detail and to Rebecca Vincent for her illustrations.

Bibliography

Belanger, C. 1988, *The T-Shirt Song*, Shortland Publications Limited, Rigby Education, Perth.

Browne, H. and Cambourne, B. 1987, *Read and Retell*, Thomas Nelson Australia, 102 Dodds St South Melbourne 3205.

Browne, H. and Mathie, V. 1990, *Inside Whole Language: A Classroom View*, Primary English Teaching Association, Sydney.

Bruinsma, R. 1990, *Learning to ride a bike and learning to read: Children's Conception of Reading.* The Australian Journal of Reading, Volume 13, No. 2.

Burnes, D. and Page, G. 1985, *Insights and Strategies for Teaching Reading*, Harcourt Brace Jovanovich Group, Sydney.

Cambourne, B. 1988, *The Whole Story – Natural Learning and the Acquisition of Literacy in the Classroom*, Ashton Scholastic, Sydney.

Clay, M. 1987, *Implementing Reading Recovery: Systemic Adaptations to an Education Innovation*, New Zealand Journal of Educational Studies 22(1).

Cowley, J. 1989, *Jim's Trumpet*, Rigby Education, Perth.

Curriculum Branch 1983, *Reading Teachers' Notes*, Education Department of Western Australia, Perth.

Curriculum Branch 1987, *Reading To Learn in the Secondary School*, Education Department of Western Australia, Perth.

Curriculum Development Branch 1991, *Reading Developmental Continuum*, Ministry of Education, Western Australia.

Curriculum Development Branch 1991, *Teacher's Guide for Remote Schools*, Ministry of Education, Western Australia.

Curriculum Development Branch 1991, *Oral Language - Language and Thinking*, Ministry of Education, Western Australia.

Curriculum Development Branch 1991, *Oral Language - Language of Social Interaction*, Ministry of Education, Western Australia.

Davey, B. 1983, *'Think aloud' - Modelling the cognitive processes of reading comprehension.* Journal of Reading, 27(1).

Duffy, G., Roehle, L. and Mason, J. 1984, *Comprehension Instruction: Perspectives and Suggestions*, Longman, New York.

Gilman, P. 1984, *The Balloon Tree*, Scholastic, TAB Publications, Canada.

Holdaway, D. 1972, *Independence in Reading - A handbook on individual procedures*, Ashton Scholastic, Auckland.

Johnson, T.D. and Louis, D.R. 1988, *Literacy Through Literature*, Thomas Nelson Australia, 102 Dodds St South Melbourne 3205.

Manzo, A.V. 1969, *The Re-Quest Procedure,* Journal of Reading, November 1969.

Ministry of Education WA, 1988. *Management and Resources in the Early Years*.

Morris, A. and Stewart-Dore, N. 1984, *Learning to Learn from Text. Effective Reading in the Content Area*, Addison-Wesley, North Ryde, NSW.

Palincsar, A. 1984, *The Quest for Meaning from Expository Text: A Teacher Guided Journey.* 'Comprehension Instruction: Perspectives and Suggestions'. Duffy, G., Roehler, L and Mason, J. Longman, New York.

Paris, S. 1989, *Reading and Thinking Strategy Kits*, Collamore Educational Publishing, D.C. Heath and Company, Raytheon Inc., Lexington.

Pressley, M. and Harris, K.R. 1990, *What we really know about strategy instruction*, Educational Leadership, September 1990, pp.31-34.

Phinney, M.Y. 1988, *Reading with the Troubled Reader*, Ashton Scholastic, NSW.

Publications Branch, 1984, *Early Literacy Inservice Course*, Education Department of South Australia.

Raphael, T. 1982, *Question Answering Strategies for Children*. The Reading Teacher, November 1982, pp. 185–90

Sloane, P. and Latham, R. 1982, *Teaching Reading Is*, Thomas Nelson Australia, 102 Dodds St South Melbourne 3205.

Stewart-Dore, N. (ed.) 1986, *Writing and Reading to Learn*, Primary English Teaching Association (P.E.T.A.), Rozelle, NSW.

Thomson, J. 1987, *Understanding Teenagers' Reading: Reading Processes and the Teaching of Literature*, Australian Association for the Teaching of English INC.

Waters, M. and Montgomery, J. *Children's Writing Proposals,* Reading Around Series, Australian Reading Association, Melbourne.

Weaver, C. 1988, *Reading Process and Practice: from Socio-psycholinguistics to whole language*, Heinemann Books, Portsmouth, New Hampshire USA.

Wong, J. and Au, K. 1985, *The Concept-Text-Application Approach: Helping elementary students comprehend expository text,* The Reading Teacher, 38(7), March 1985.

Index of Strategies and Activities